Fo S. A. N Angwafo III Remembered:

His Leadership, Wisdom and Deeds
As Seen by the People of Mankon,
Cameroon and Beyond

Editors

Ntsewah F. Angwafo
Lumkap B. Angwafo
Francis B. Nyamnjoh

Langaa Research & Publishing CIG
Mankon, Bamenda

Publisher:

Langaa RPCIG
Langaa Research & Publishing Common Initiative Group
P.O. Box 902 Mankon
Bamenda
North West Region
Cameroon
Langaagrp@gmail.com
www.langaa-rpcig.net

Distributed in and outside N. America by African Books Collective
orders@africanbookscollective.com
www.africanbookscollective.com

ISBN-10: 9956-552-93-3

ISBN-13: 978-9956-552-93-1

Notes from the Editors

Putting together tributes to Mbiefo Angwafo III, who bequeathed a rich, multifaceted, and vast legacy to us, is both an arduous challenge and a distinct honour. No matter how profound and inspiring his impact, he meant or shall we say, he means different things to different people at different places and different times. The editors see no holier duty than to convey to you, the reader, the undiluted message of the tributers. The editorial mandate was therefore interpreted to consist in compiling and editing only where there resulted a benefit in clarity. We hope you will find the categories and ordering of the tributes helpful.

The book format precludes audiovisual tributes and their inherent advantages. Further, in the present circumstances, we regret that not everyone who cannot commit a tribute in writing could receive help in recording and transcribing. They, too, have their story.

We find that committing a tribute to Mbiefo is to many a matter of the heart, as quite a few are still crafting and submitting tributes way past the deadline that was necessitated by the imperatives of preparing and publishing a book on time for the Nukwi na Abub. For this labour of love and duty, we hope to emit a sequel or an addendum in the not too distant future. This particularly so because we see this modest contribution as a beginning and hardly the end of the process of recognizing and understanding what Mbiefo Angwafo III represents to all those who knew him.

Mining this for posterity, to advance the cause of humankind would represent fulfilment in our eyes.

We acknowledge with profound gratitude all the efforts that have led to this book. As editors, we would not have achieved much without the active participation and sustained commitment of an editorial team, made up of:

H.R.H Fo Fru-Asah Angwafo IV
Adebang Angwafo
Angu George Che
Angwafor Clement Mankefor
Bih Stella Angwafo
Cheo Nicholas Angwafo
Francis B. Nyamnjoh
Fru Mabel Angwafo

Joseph Awah Fru
Julius Nde Mishimbo
Lumkap B. Angwafo
Matthias Fru Fonteh
Melanie Mankah Ndefru
Nicholas Nde Fofang
Nicodemus Fru Awasom
Ntsewah F. Angwafo, *Tamuhlargh*
Priscilla Lum
Tsi Ghamoti Angwafo

The Editors
Ntsewah F. Angwafo
Lumkap B. Angwafo
Francis B. Nyamnjoh

Table of Contents

Butabatsey (Clan Heads)
Fotibui Hilary (President, Clan Heads)

Ngang Abyien & Butabunipfvu
(Mankon Arbitration Council &
Mankon Traditional Council)
Mankon Arbitration Council
Afuah Samuel Chi (Quarter Head, Alasuatom)
Akenji Zacchaeus Nde (Chairman, Mankon Traditional Council)
Akum Diksons (Quarter Head, Asongkah)
Angu George Che (Fon's Secretary)
Anye Oscar Akumah (Quarter Head, Ndzumambueh)
Bekum Be Mbangye (Female Quarter Councillors of Mankon)
Che Tahnu Nkimbeng George (Quarter Head, Musang II)
Chi Alfred
Chingang John (Quarter Head, Atuakom I)
Fru Alice (Quarter Head Atuakom II)
Fru Asongwe Buzwi
Julius Mishimbo (Assistant Secretary Mankon Traditional Council)
Ntomnifor Richard Fru (Secretary General Mankon Traditional Council)
Ndanga Jonathan Fru (Quarter Head, Atualakom)
Nde Godfred Tumasang (Quarter Head, Bagbanong)
Ndengsa Pius Achu (Quarter Head, Ntankah I)
Ngomanji Nche Emmanuel (Mulang Quarter Secretary)
Nju Spartan Philip Nde Tangyie(Quarter Head, Nitop)
Nsoh Emmanuel Nde (Quarter Head, Alakoro)
Nwabueze Abriham (Quarter Head, Upper Up Atu Azire)
Penn Barnabas T (Azire 'A' Quarter)
Tumasang Hansley (Ntsuabuh Quarter)
Zuah Valentine (Quarter Head, Akohkikang)

Bulyibufo (Fon's Advisers)
Ndi Angwafo IV Tawbargh Fo Angwafo
Muma Angwafo IV Tse Louis Mankefor Angwafo
Nkwenti Angwafo IV Tamitargh

Bumafo (Queen Mothers)
Mafo Ndefru III
Mafo Angwafo III

Bangyebuntaw (Fon's Wives)
Emilia Nanga-Maatsi Angwafo III
Nkwenti Kuko Anna Angwafo III
Tidzang Emilia Angwafo III
Florence Fondoh Angwafo III
Swiri Susana Angwafo III

Government Officials and Diplomats
Abakar Ahamat
Adolphe Lele Lafrique
Anu'a-Gheyle Solomon Azoh-Mbi
Asheri Kilo
Bell Luc René
David Abouem A Tchoyi
Doh Jerome Penbaga
Felix Mbayu
Fuh Calistus Gentry
Philemon Yang
Theresia Nkuo-Akenji
Jonathan Koehler
Michael Hoza
Richard Bale

Assembly, Senate and House of Chiefs, Fons, Council
Achobang Paul Tambeng
Fon Bahmbi III Mathias Njuh'
Benigo Matilda Ngah
Kalak Flavius Boteh
Ntaintain Blasius Kibam
Wendy Lima
Fon FSN Azehfor III of Nkwen
Fon Chafah of Bangolan

Fon Gwan Mbanyam Sid II of Guzang
Fon Ndofoa Zofoa III of Babungo
Fon Nforchesiri III of Bamendankwe
Fon Mbomchom Akotohm III of Ndzah
Fon Teche Njei of Ngyen Muwah
Sa Majesté Tsala Ndzomo Guy

Part 5: Tributes from Religion and Education Authorities & Representatives

Charles Ndikum Ngwa
Festus A. Asana
Fonki Samuel Forba
Kidzem Christopher Chi
Mary Kemjei
Mbaku Henry Ken
Musa Shu'aib Imam
Neba Muangu
Ndidi Anozie (MSHR)
Tangyie Ndoh Neville
Warah Solomon Tse
Wara Stephen Angu

Part 6: Tributes from Trade and Cultural Associations

Bih Angu Mercy (National President Nkah Ni kwi Mankon)
Donald N. Anye and Fru Emmanuel, President MACUDA Limbe
Mankon Development Council UK
Mankon Jurists Association
Ndanga Funjong Eunice Siri (National Vice President, Nkah Nikwi Ni Mankon)
Inspirational 84 Ladies (LESANS)
Nji Felix Ngwamatsom (Vice President, MACUDA Douala)

Part 7: Tributes from The People: Home and Away

Achidi Achu Jennette Akwa
Adebang Angwafo III
Ade Richard Nguti (RICK NGUTI)
Agendia Mrs. Priscilla and Mr. Benedict
Agwara Loveline Angwafo Ndifor
Akere Achiri Ndefru Joseph
Ako-Ngum
Akofo Forba Placid Achiri
Akwa Emelda Angwafo

Aliah Atonji of Bagmande
Aliah Elisabeth Angwafo
Alieh Lizette Angwafo
Aloysius Fru Asaah Angwafo
Amy Banda epouse Youmbi
Angwafo Margaret Sapkah
Angwafo Vivian and grandkids
Angwafor Clement Mankefo
Antoinette Angwafo
Anye Ndiene Gideon
Anye Rawllins, Ngang, Mankah, and Tse Kabba
Anye Taboh Angwafo
Anye-Nkwenti Nyamnjoh
Arkan Akwa Tawbargh I
AsandomZamngang
Asanji Fru Fobuzshi Angwafo III
Asongwe Mathias
Atrouafor Angwafo Francis Azinwi
Atsu Atanga-Tabah Pa Nkumfo
Awah Angwafo Vera
Awondo Fru, Harrison
Azah Jackline Chey
Bei Kelly
Benardine Aghanwi Ngu-Nnoko
Bi Angwafo Epse Nde Fonchingong
Bi-Neh Mishi Awantang
BiAwah Angwafo
Bih Joyce Epouse Kabba
Bih M Akenji
Bihnwi Blair Angwafo
Celestina Neh Fru Tassang
Charmaine P. Angwafo
Che Cletus Awah
Cheo Paul Ndefru
E.N. Ngwafor
Elijah Che Munyong-abieri Tangyie
Elizabeth Manka-Mafo Angwafo
Elvis Fonchingong
Emmanuel Fru Doh
Emmanuella Kiyieih Nyamnjoh
Esther Angwafo Foncham
Evaristus Ntoh-akoh Tsi-Angwafo
Fon Emmanuel Ngang
Fondeh Angwafo
Forngang Alphonsus Ndenge (The Family)

Fru Mabel Angwafo
Fru Venasius Kondze Tabe Tangyie Ndzumabeah-Mankon
Frunwi Fletcher Angwafo
Ghamoti Anye Angwafo
Henrietta Nyamnjoh
Hycent Fru Angwafo
Ivense Fru Tadzong
John Fru Aborugong
John Nji Chi
Jones Nkimbeng
Joseph Mumbari
Jude Fru Nkwah Angwafor
Kien-Ngum Angwafo
Lum Florence Angwafo Ndenge
Lum Kab epse Akosah
Lumnangah Angwafo III
Lumnkap B. Angwafo
Maatsi N. Ndingwan
Mafor Joy, Caleb and Harley Bemnji
Mafor Marie Ebie
Mama Awa Anna (Mama Santa)
Mambo Neh Angwafo
Mangyie Alia Tawbargh
Manka Mafor Angwafo
Manka Swiri Angwafo Ngundam
Mankah Grace
Mankah Keziah Nde and Kien Neriah Nde
Mankah Mafo Doris Angwafo epse Malegho
Mankah Mafo Ndibe
Mankah Ngonguru Ntaralah
Margaret Khien Ndenge
Martin Nche Nde Gashu
Matoyah Cletus Anye
Mbongta Nanga-Afuuanwi Awantang
Michael Nde Asongwe
Miranda Muluh Akumah
Muama'ah Nguti JC
Mujum Helen Nimo Barrister
Muma Anye Nsoh
Nji Mbanga Mbaswa E. Joko
Nanga Angwafo Linda Epse Timah
Nche George Ndiforangwafo II
Nche Zama
Nche-Fortoh Atanga
Nde Ningo Forla

Ndefru Daniel Chi Ndifor Angwafo III
Ndefru Linus Betterman
Ndefru Manka Mafo Melanie
Ndemuafo David
Ndisah Philip Fon
Neh Tabo Angwafo
Ngang Prudence epouse Fuh Wung
Ngum Adela Angwafo
Ngum Angwafo Eps Bemnji
Ngwa-Nkwenti Wangia
Nimae Ngumna'ah Awantang
Njom Tarnu Muaze
Nko'zhum F.M. Mantohbang Tsagineu
Nkumfo'o Ntseh Awa
Nkwenti Angwafor III
Nkwenti Ignatius Ndefru
Nkwenti Wilfred Anye
Ntawmu nwi Angwafo
Ntseh Tangie Angwafo Nfo Mukare
Ntsewah Fobuzshi Angwafo III
Ntsuntaw Ndisah C.F.N
Numfo Beris
Odette Swirri Ade
Oliver C. Fonteh
Peter Schofield Tse Ndefru alias Isahfo Prince
Priscilla Lum
Prudencia Ngum Angwafo
Richard Nde Lajong
Roselyn Muma Mbah
Samuel Azunwi Tsifo Ndingwan
Samuel Fonteh (Makwuswiri clan)
Sanjou-Tadzong Abel Ndeh
Sebiso Switdzu Tamuhlargh Angwafo
Stella Bih Angwafo
Swiri Caroline Fobuzhi
Swiri Ethel Angwafo
Swiri Voilet
Tabehre. Asanji. Tawbargh I
Tabufor Michael Che
Tagei Achiri Nbomnifo Angwafo III
Taku Jobs
Takumbeng
Tambungang
Tanah Arnold
Theresia Ngu

The Sarki's Office (Bamenda)
Tse Fonguh
Tseghama Ndatare Angwafo III
Tseofo Angwafo
Tsi Ghamoti Angwafo
Tsi Julius Ndefru
Tuma Anye Angwafor
Tuma. A. Angwafo
Wankah Wilfred Nde

Part 8: Tributes from Cameroon

Anne Mie Descheemaeker
Ayafor Florence Neba
Bernadette Atanga
Christopher Atang
Ephraim Banda Ghogomu
Francois-Xavier Mpopi-Keou
Gladys Shang Viban Yaah:Mafor
H Sama Nwana
Jato Richard Tonga
Mmamouko et toute la famille de Belgique
Randy Joe Sa'ah

Part 9: Tributes from Historical Perspectives

Tambu Ngang
Wankah Wilfred Nde
Nixon Kahjum Takor
Nicodemus Fru Awasom
Thaddeus A. Achu
Jean-Pierre Warnier (*Sang'toh*)
Ndeh Ntomambang Ningo
Francis B. Nyamnjoh

Part 10: His Royal Majesty
Fo F. A Angwafo IV:

Part 11: Fo S.A.N Angwafo III in Photos:

Editorial

We are thrilled to share with you this collection of tributes on Fo Solomon AnyeGhamoti Angwafo III of the Kingdom of Mankon. The tributes are by people from Mankon, Cameroon and the world at large, who knew him well and who generously responded to our call for tributes to mark the transitioning of King Solomon Angwafo III from *Atsum* in Ntaw Mankon to join his ancestors at *Alankyi*. We heartily thank the tributers who have opted to share with the reader their thoughts and memories on various aspects of who the Fon was and what he meant to them. We hope you find these tributes as inspiring as we the editors have found them.

A tribute offers an opportunity to share the things you appreciate about the departed, to reminisce about their accomplishments, and tell friends, family and humankind as a whole about their unique charms and the indelible defining moments that you shared with that very distinctive person. Such a commemoration, such bearing of witness is good for all. Some cynics would view tributes as illogical and a waste of time, since the departed are assumed not to be able to hear them. In Mankon where kings may disappear or go missing without entirely losing their capacity to act and react, such cynicism is ill-founded. Others contend that tributes by their nature are only full of praises. That is far from being the case with this volume.

As the tributes to *Mbiefo* Angwafo III flooded in from all quarters, it quickly became clear that these tributes are indeed for the living. The content of this book inevitably suggests that these tributes for the most part, say more about the tribute writers themselves than they do of the Missing Fon. The disappearance of a Fon (or anyone else for that matter) offers the living an opportunity for introspection in the manner of someone looking at a mirror.

A common thread in the plethora of tributes in this collection is the irrepressible admiration for the ideas, ideals, values and principles championed and lived by the 20th monarch of the House of Ndemagha. His leadership, wisdom, deeds and sociality are in focus. His effusion of wisdom was constant and effortless. His generosity and kindness knew no bounds. This made of him a container king, holding some of the most exquisite distillate refined and decanted through the processes of previous human experience. The initiated rarely bothered much with its provenance. They knew it to be divine kingship.

In these pages, there is here and there thinly veiled disapprobation that is swiftly followed in the next breath by a contradictory approval of the highest order. We are offered a short motto of the Mbiefo phenomenon: Malice to none, goodwill to all. Yes, though many of the submissions were entitled *"Tribute to Fo S.A.N Angwafo III"*, the material reads more like a call to arms. Part of the godly about Fo Angwafo III was not just his acceptance of the condition of humankind, it was rather his constant and sustained preoccupation with what or who we could become! He demonstrated a lifelong commitment to cultivation. To him, living was not just about tilling the soil for sustenance, it was also about tending the mind and the soul. He valued agriculture and culture in equal measure and in the full senses of the words. In this and other aspects he was a pacesetter all his life. There seems perhaps nothing godlier than educating and fashioning oneself and others, tending and improving for a higher calling. The ultimate public service. As a leader, he distinguished himself most by serving in the manner of a servant. Agriculture and culture are hardly about keeping one's fingers clean or resting on one's laurels!

Inspired by lessons learnt from and conversations with Fo Angwafo III, many a tributer in these pages make pleas for the return of character and courage, for the restoration of the nobility of the human spirit that is endangered whenever social institutions and achievement are denigrated, pleas to strive towards higher values, for more competence and diligence, to unerringly eschew falsehood lest ruin ensue (*le'eh nkob, nkob sa'ah nda nwon*), pleas for the unbridled quest for more knowledge that culminates in better understanding of fellow man. A plaidoyer for true enlightenment.

The master of metaphor par excellence, Fo Angwafo III extolled competence as a virtue famously saying there is a difference between climbing Mt. Everest and getting helicoptered to the summit. On integrity he explained that an individual does not have to steal the sun from the sky in order to qualify as a thief. In like manner Creation must not be devoid of vice for God to be associated with the infinitely good.

Mbiefo Angwafo III was Father of both the beginner and the expert, the pupil and the teacher, the fool and the philosopher. He was the Father of All. The good, the bad and the ugly. We wish you equally an all-encompassing and nuanced state of mind as you leaf through these pages. May you be more Angwafoesque on its completion. For your own good. For the good of all.

Now that the chief-friend of humankind has proceeded onward to the realm of Our ancestors and is in union with God, we cannot have hoped for a better intercessor.

The ineluctable cycle of birth, renewal and growth has given us Fo Angwafo IV.

All hail the King.

May the peace and force of *Alankyi* be with you all.

The Editors:

Ntsewah F. Angwafo
Lumkab B. Angwafo
Francis B. Nyamnjoh

Part 1

His Royal Highness Fo Fru-Asah Angwafo IV

Tribute To My Father Fo S.A.N Angwafo III

Fo Angwafo III, Solomon AnyeGhamoti Ndefru has joined his ancestors in the world beyond. A journey he started on the 21/05/1925 and rested on his birthday, and perhaps at the same time he was delivered. A life he lived at the service of humanity for 97 years, and lived 63 years of his adult life as the spiritual and wise leader of the Mankon people. Sixty-three years of service without a single holiday. Delivered to the Royal family by HRH Fo Ndefru III and Mafor Manka Theresa, he had a lone brother, "Tse Zee" from the same womb who died at the age of twelve. He ascended the throne in April 1959 during the advent of political discussions gearing towards independence, and transited at the time when there are currently violent moves from the two Anglophone regions in their quest for independence. These two incidents, your birth and departure on your date of birth and political events of your enthronement and departure, make you a man of special descent, a man whose enormous wisdom will be sorely missed.

Growing up in a large family with scarce resources, my father had to force his way to attend school since education was not a high priority at the time. There were moments his teacher had to intervene before he went to school. He equally had to sell firewood and fetch water for people at "Ntambag" to generate resources to enable him sponsor his education. While in college in Nigeria, he had to engage in cultivating yams and other crops which assisted in clearing some of his bills.

Unlike in his days, he made sure that every prince and princess obtained some minimal education. Irrespective of his numerous assignments, he would devote time every evening to guide us to do our school assignments. He did not only sponsor his children, but he also equally took full responsibility in supplying the educational needs of some children of Mankon and without. Mankon is the host of most of the best schools in Cameroon thanks to his benevolence which was motivated by the fact that he wanted to avoid Mankon children travelling long distances like he did to study in Nigeria. He provided land and financial assistance for the construction of many

1

of the schools. In the recent past, he led the campaign for the construction of technical schools. We now have four government Technical Schools in Mankon. To him, his people needed an educational system that enhances job creation skills more than a system that graduates jobseekers.

"Teach a child to sow rice and don't give the child rice" my father gave a cutlass to me at the age of nine, and was in the farm with us where he personally demonstrated various farming techniques. He discouraged in strong terms traditional farming methods like the burning of "Ankara". This was met with stiff resistance from his people, who eventually followed his wisdom. Being very pragmatic, he had several demonstration farms which caught the attention of the natives because of the high yields. He introduced the farming of watermelon, guava, tomatoes, pears and other vegetables at Asongkah in the late 70^s through irrigation farming. His people discouraged him and rejected the consumption of watermelon on grounds that it is uncooked pumpkin.

As a dynamic leader, he did not arrogate all powers to himself. He believed very much in power-sharing and empowering people to look after themselves. He organised Mankon into local government areas with quarter heads elected by the people to adjudicate on most matters within the quarter.

I can't conclude this tribute to you without thanking you for the confidence you bestowed on me. This is something I had never thought of in my life, nor had aspiration for such a huge position, but I recall your conversations with me in the recent past were pointing to this huge assignment. Once you rebuked me for not coming close to you and whether I do know your activities. I remained silent and you went further to say, "Do I know that any prince can succeed you?" On one other occasion, you were very angry when I requested farmland and your conclusion to me was that "you are suffering because of me". It's now that I understand exactly what you meant. May you strengthen the wisdom you saw in me for the service of your people. May your spirit continue to inspire and guide me, your successor. Rest in Power, my father.

Part 2

Traditional Guilds

Butabatsey (Clan Heads)

To Fo S.A.N Angwafo III, by Clan Heads of Mankon

It was with sadness, broken hearts, and deep sorrow that the news of your disappearance was announced to us by the Kwifo of Mankon.

You took the reign of Mankon from your predecessor Fo Ndefru in 1959.

When you took over the reign, only 26 quarters were existing in the entire Fondom. You moved them to 76 quarters showing how hardworking you were.

Then there were about 250,000 inhabitants in Mankon, today the population stands at over 800,000 inhabitants. During your reign, You moved the period of death celebrations in Mankon from 4 weeks to 2 days, giving the population enough time to do their work.

You embraced people from all over, who could stay and respect the laws of our Land, Mankon.

You were once asked who a Mankon man is, and you replied that a "Mankon man is anybody living in Mankon." You added that all of them are your children.

Your Majesty, at the time of your disappearance you led the Mankon fondom peacefully, reason why Mankon is the only village as of now without any conflict with neighbouring villages.

You held several meetings with us the Clan Heads in which you gave us useful advice, in the last of such meetings held on the 22nd of April 2022, you frowned at the current crises in the region and advised us the Clan Heads to work in close collaboration with the quarter heads so that peace can return to the fondom of Mankon.

You insisted that people must not kill, kidnap, or behead to solve the crisis.

Not only that, but You prescribed dialogue as the only means to solve the crisis.

Your Royal Majesty, you treated us as a father, frequently schooling us on our functions as Clan Heads.

Being a farmer, you encouraged the Mankon people to embrace farming and today Mankon has become the breadbasket of Bamenda. We will always remember you positively and for the wise choice of Fo Angwafo IV as your successor. For the short time that we have been with him, he is a square peg that has been fitted into a square hole. No wonder you were often referred to as King Solomon.

Your Majesty, forever, we will miss you and you will always remain fresh in our memories.

Adieu your Majesty Fo S.A.N Angwafo III

For the Clan Heads of Mankon
Fotibui Hilary
(President)

Your Majesty, can we say, we are disappointed with death, or with the Almighty who created death. Not at all. We cry and weep, we reflect on your charismatic attitude of administering Mankon. We cry and weep when we remember your forgiving attitude of those who wrong you and later come confessing and the camwood as an instrument of peace. The thought of asking the Almighty " why" is a crime for the pot can never question the potter. All we can do is to say father farewell. May the Almighty forgive whatever sin you might have committed in your reign and send his angels to hold you up with their hands to keep you from hurting your feet on the stones. Ps. 90-12.

Mankon Arbitration Council
Mankon Palace

He was one of the wittiest leaders of his time. Full of knowledge and loved by his subjects.

He was the first traditional ruler to institute democracy in his land. Quarter Councillors are elected, not appointed as it used to prevail in the past.

He loved development, not only of the people but of the mind e.g., during his reign many Primary, Secondary and Higher schools of learning were created, like GS Alankyi, GTHS Alabukam, GHS Ngomgham and you name the rest.

He made sure that parents sent their children to school and he sponsored most of the Mankon children in Secondary and Higher schools. Parents with financial constraints sought financial support from HRM.

He defended Mankon land from infiltrators not by war but by the power of the pen.

In the sphere of agriculture, he thought the Mankon people to own and cultivate farms as he himself was a good example with farms and cattle.

Afuah Samuel Chi
Quarter Head, Alasuatom

On that fateful day the Mankon baobab fell. You passed on. Mankon lost both a pearl and an architect of a leader. It seems as if we will never cease feeling the impact of this loss. Our memories are still very green of who you were and what you mean to us.

In December 1961, you took me to CPC Bali as I had performed brilliantly well at the entrance examination into that school but had not been admitted. The then Swiss Principal, Dr. Rudin threw cold water on us. Right after that, you apportioned part of your hunting ground at Ngomgham for the construction of Sacred Heart College. You next advocated for the proliferation of learning institutions in Mankon, both public and private. Watch a public match past of schools at the Bamenda II grand stand at the Commercial Avenue for your testimony.

As an agricultural expert you taught by example in poultry farming, food crop cultivation - maize, beans, cassava, plantains, oil palms. You produced and sold palm oil, planted medicinal plants and protected water catchments through tree planting.

In community development you insisted on a pit toilet in every home. You instituted Zakob, one day per week for this activity. Existing roads were cleaned and new ones prospected and dug. Bridges were built: at Asongkah: one linking Mbingfibye to Alabukom. All this led to rapid urbanisation of Mankon. Little wonder that a visitor remarked that "You can take your car to wherever you want to go".

You revamped the Mankon Traditional Dance. It became renowned in both the North West and in Cameroon. The song and dance enjoyed new dynamics. Songs were created on local physical features (Nta' a Tabyen, Mezam River), institutions, events and happenings. "Ghenti ma chie" has been translated, sung and danced far beyond the borders of Mankon.

In traditional administration, Kwifo, the Mankon Traditional Council, Bikums, (Notables), Takumbeng, these institutions worked to administer the land. MACUDA (Mankon Cultural and Development Association) saw the light of day; branches of these function both in Cameroon and in the diaspora. Quarter development takes place in the charge of Quarter Councils. You initiated breaking the Ngemba Council into Lower and Upper Councils. The Mankon Area Council evolved from this and eventually into the Bamenda Urban Council. This metamorphosed into the Bamenda II and Bamenda City Councils.

In like manner, you advocated for the creation of the Bamenda Central Subdivision. Today it has been broken into Bamenda I, II and III Subdivision. Your political career started as member of West Cameroon House of Chiefs. Later you entered West Cameroon House of Assembly as an independent candidate. Finally, you became Vice President of the ruling party. The catalogue is long and dense. Let the above spotlights and landmarks suffice to portray who you were, what you stood for and what you mean to us. These footprints in the sands of time will forever be indelible. Great One, ADIEU.

Akenji Zacchaeus Nde
(Chairman, Mankon Traditional Council)

Asongkah quarter is honoured to have a say amongst the seventy-six quarters that make up the Mankon Fondom.

The legend, the wisest, King Solomon Angwafo III of Mankon whose works go beyond Asongkah and Mankon as a whole, stamped an unforgettable print on the hearts of his people. We as a people have been very fortunate to benefit from his love, generosity, and kindness.

We, the Asongkah people will live to remember him for our health care centre popularly known as Alabukam Health Centre (which is precisely located at Ntah-Ngang Asongkah) as a health facility and G.T.H.S Alabukam, G.S.S Alankyi which are educational facilities closest to us.

On behalf of the Asongkah People

Akum Diksons
Quarter Head, Asongkah
Mankon-Bamenda II Subdivision

To My King, Dad, and Boss Fo' S.A.N Angwafo III
If Tears Could Build A Stairway

Oh, my great King! Oh, my Dad! Oh, my Boss!
If tears could build a stairway,
And memories were a lane,
I would walk right up to heaven,
Bring you back again.

Oh, my great King! Oh, my Dad! Oh, my Boss!
I will never forget how often you always told me,
One morning you will come and not see me.
If you do not see me, continue working the same way,
Continue respecting the same way, as though I was here.

Oh, my great King! Oh, my Dad! Oh, my Boss!
I really miss your smile and advice,
My King, I really miss your great sense of humour and love,
My Dad, I really miss your care and understanding,
My Boss, I really miss your words of encouragement and
perseverance.
Amid all adversities that surrounded the atmosphere,
Your tender and gentle voice stood tall, that which I will no longer
hear.

Oh, my great King! Oh, my Dad! Oh, my Boss!
I miss the extraordinary qualities that cannot be measured,
Your uncompromisable principles of truth, honesty, hard work,
Discipline, respect, endurance will never follow the wind.

Oh, my great King! Oh, my Dad! Oh, my Boss!
Never will I ever forget your smiles that gave me courage
Never will I forget how you fondly pampered me,
And the echoes of *"Georgy, King George, chief secretary"* will never end.
Your departure is painful, but I cannot question God.

Oh, my great King! Oh, my Dad! Oh, my Boss!
No farewell words were spoken,
No time to say "Goodbye".
You were gone before I knew it,
And God knows why.

Oh, my great King! Oh, my Dad! Oh, my Boss!
My heart still aches in sadness,
And secret tears still flow.
What it meant to love you –
No one can ever know.

Oh, my great King! Oh, my Dad! Oh, my Boss!
But now you want me,
To mourn for you no more.
To remember all the happy times,
Life still has much in store.

Oh, my great King! Oh, my Dad! Oh, my Boss!
Since you'll never be forgotten,
I pledge to you today
A hallowed place within my heart
Is where you'll always stay.
Adieu my great King, Dad, and Boss.

Angu George Che
Fon's Secretary

The advice of a true father, HRM Fon S. A. N Angwafo III

His Royal Majesty, Fon S.A.N Angwafo III succeeded his father Fon Ndefru III as the paramount Fon of the Mankon people after the passing in 1959 onto glory of the latter.

As the new Fon, he positioned himself as a father to all within the Fondom and never hesitated to give out advice. In fact, he earned the admiration of everybody who listened to him talk, be it at the Palace or during any of his numerous nationwide outings. He meritoriously was known as King Solomon by all his admirers.

His most cherished phrase," Mankon, miikong teh-eh nkara" summarised his main wish vis-à-vis the Mankon Fondom. He preached unity amongst the people in order to ensure and guarantee strength.

As a true father he never hesitated to remind the people that our forefathers fought wars to own our present village location. That is why he always called upon the people to remain strong to defend the very much converted geographical location of our village.

Another saying often heard from him was, "respect" others, thus the famous saying "when man pass you, carry his bag", which in reality was a call to everybody, especially to settlers or "foreigners" to respect the Mankon culture and be law-abiding.

As a true father Fon Angwafo III advised other parents in Mankon not to fail in educating the girl child alongside the boy child. He advised and recommended the exchange of landed property by parents so as to be able to pay school fees for children.

At the level of succession in homes, the advised emphatically that the successor should not own all the family land at the detriment of the rest of the children.

Above all, Fon Angwafo III preached love amongst the people as the true loving father that he is.

He preached by example especially on self-food sufficiency. He had the largest farmlands both for cash crops and subsistence food crops as well as cattle rearing.

Such are the few deeds that Fon Angwafo III could show to the world that he was a true father ready to share his knowledge with all. May the land of our ancestors and forefathers be lenient and receive our beloved father Fon Angwafo III, Fon of Mankon.

From your humble servant

Anye Oscar Akumah
Quarter Head, Ndzumambueh

God saw you were getting tired
and there was going to be no cure.
So he put his arms around you and whispered "come home"
Although we loved you dearly we could not make you stay.

A golden heart stopped beating.
Hard work hands at rest.
Your life touched so many people
Who learned from the advice you gave

Asking us to educate our children,
Not to sell inheritable land,
Live in peace with our husbands and neighbours,
Work farms, keep animals,
And have a source of revenue for the family.
Your love for us was so strong and real.
We miss that little twinkle
That used to light up your eyes.

And we miss the sound of your voice,
Your laughter and your sighs.
No one really wants to say goodbye,
So we'll just wish you eternal peace.

Bekum Be Bangye
Female Quarter Councillors of Mankon

Our Great King! King Solomon A. Angwafo III of the Blessed Mankon Fondom

Aptly named Solomon, you espoused the wisdom and courage of the legendary King Solomon.

When our forebears led the great wave of a multitude of people (the Mah-Nkung) from the hills of the Widikum to settle in this blessed land that is known as Mankon, no one could have imagined that it would become the great Fondom that it is today.

Like those before you - Fomukong, and Angwafo II, you not only continued to lead this mother of waves (the Mah-Nkung) you nurtured and nourished it to an even bigger and longer one. Mankon remains a giant of a Fondom in the grasslands of Cameroon, because of your courage, vision, wisdom, and stewardship. You cultivated it into a land compared to none in the Grassfields and highlands of the North-West Region - a blessing to indigenes and non-indigenes.

Whilst our great land may not have had to fight off any condescending and extractive colonialists like Zintgraff, you gallantly led the modern Mankon warriors against other challenges – seeing our land through many episodes of drought and famine, and always inspiring our people to work towards peace, unity, and prosperity for all who live in this great land.

Now you have passed on the torch, yet we know that whilst you sojourn amongst the ancestors and great Fons before you, you will continue to maintain watch and remain a true warrior of peace and prosperity for this great land - Mankon.

Long will your name live!

Bigger and stronger will this Mah-Nkung become!

Che Tahnu Nkimbeng George
Quarter Head, Musang II

Mbeh, we met whenever I could at your Ntaw/Palace during my trips to Mankon, given that I have stayed, worked and retired with Limbe as base.

Our initial interactions with you, as younger persons/subjects and later to this ripe age, brought to bear your true leadership endowments. You had to contend with tradition and politics. And that you did so meticulously as experienced especially during the country's return to multiparty politics in the early 1990s.

Your legacy is as brave as that left behind by a leader which will be a suitable path for posterity to follow. You have been immense with your showcase of the 'Biblical King Solomon's wisdom' in handling cosmopolitan community affairs as host traditional leader.

The Limbe-MTC had the opportunity to experience your visits with HRH, the late Chief Manga Williams more than once. And each time you were hosted by MTC-Limbe, you would also visit with the S.D.O for Fako. Noteworthy is the fact that the former received you at his residence in the midst of other Chiefs and state dignitaries during one of your visits.

We of MTC-Limbe are proud of you because your initial collaborations with the Fako royalty paved the way for the Mankon Mbaghalum (dance group) to lead the other North West communities during the funeral of the Limbe Paramount Chief. Such brilliance by the Mankon Mbaghalum (dance group) was displayed under the watchful eyes of the then Prime Minister, ambassadors, Ministers and other state officials.

Your historic moments with us on earth made us have a feel of cooperation between leaders hosting populations of diverse extractions and thereby demonstrating your innate reflexes as God-chosen. Your souvenir write-ups were always very appreciative-stating how MTC-Limbe topped the chat in your outings as the Fo/King of Mankon.

Fo/King, your name will shine in the pages of world history and enlighten future generations for living life with dignity and freedom as a venerated traditional leader of Mankon.

Chi Alfred
Head, Mankon Traditional Council, Limbe

To Our Beloved Father Fo Angwafo III
On behalf of the Atuakom I Mankon Traditional Council, all the Institutions inclusive the Churches, Health Centres, Schools, Hotels

and Commercial Centres, we jointly share with deep sorrow and pains in our hearts the disappearance of our beloved Father, His Royal Highness Fo Angwafo III. Our Father was a great, humble, and peace-loving one. He welcomed every one of us to His Fondom and treated each one's matter with justice, sympathy and love. We appreciate his slogan of preaching peace and love all over the Mankon Fondom not only to the sons and daughters of the soil but to everyone who settles on Mankon Land. He treated every one of us as his children. Mbeh you are missing but we shall forever have you in memory and deep in our hearts. We know your journey is a safe one and you are seated by the right hand of our Heavenly Father because He loves you better than us you have left behind. Your works shall live to be a remembrance for us and the entire world for you did not only pass your wisdom and knowledge to the Mankon Fondom but also to the whole world. Adieu Mbeh

Chingang John
Quarter Head, Atuakom I

My loving father, my superhero, my smart handsome and hardworking papa. Writing about you can be an endless novel. Your life story as father of the Mankon people including everyone on the Mankon soil is too rich because of the context. What a wonderful father, despite the number you could identify each one by name. You were my father, my resource person, my mirror and above all my role model.

A Poem to his Royal Highness Fon Angwafo III
God took the strength of a mountain,
The majesty of a tree
The warmth of a summer sun,
The calm of a quiet sea
The generous soul of nature
The comforting arms of night,
The wisdom of the ages,
The power of the eagle's flight,
The joy of mountain spring,
The faith of a mustard seed,
The patience of eternity
The depth of a family need,
Then God combined these qualities,

When there was nothing more to add,
He knew his masterpiece was complete,
And so, he called him "The Fon of Mankon"
Go well, father of all.

Fru Alice
Quarter Head, Atuakom II

Fru Asongwe, born on the 21st of July 1974 and successor of Daniel Asongwe Buzwi.

I gained profound knowledge of the Fon beginning in early 1997 when I was performing a holiday job at the palace to raise money to further my education.

The Fon assisted me wholeheartedly to see that I gain admission into the National Institute of Youth and Sports, Yaoundé. In December 2010, when I lost my father, the Fon actively took part in his burial/celebration and to see to it that all the necessary rites were carried out. Two years later, precisely in August 2012, I was, firmly crowned and presented before the Fon of Mankon as Successor of my father. The Fon performed the various rites in accordance with our tradition. In 2016, I was privileged to perform with the Fon some of the traditional rites at Alah-nkyi prior to the Annual Dance "*Abinghe-fo*". The Fon has stood behind me, guiding me in my charge of handling and leading the entire Buzwi family in the positive direction. In a nutshell, the Fon to me, has been a source of inspiration, an icon, an ideal ruler with an encyclopaedia of traditional, cultural, and moral values.

Fru Asongwe Buzwi (*Nkum* Mankon)

Each life is a journey - a uniquely personal passage through time. You travelled through difficult times but you stood firm at the helm of Mankon for 63 years. I am very grateful for the privilege given me by God Almighty to have served our community with you for years. You were a father, teacher, mentor and life coach to us. There was hardly a dull moment with you as your life experiences as reflected in your conversations are indeed a treasure for those who took part in them. The manner in which you discerned to settle disputes often left those who brought such matters to you in the first place thinking twice why they could not settle such disputes themselves.

'I am installing you all as the transitional Mankon Traditional Council. You should be prepared for it. If there is anything you do not know, ask now. Many people see me as a stone in the valley that would never roll again'. These were your words in December 2017. And the STONE finally rolled in May 2022 and within the five years' mandate of the Mankon Traditional Council. RIP as you watch over the kingdom back here. Adieu.

Julius Mishimbo
Assistant Secretary, Mankon Traditional Council

Your Highness, the witty King Solomon, King of vision, I have been privileged to tap from your fountain of wisdom when you appointed me to serve you and the Mankon people in varied capacities amongst them, the Secretary General of the Mankon Traditional Council, Secretary of the Mankon Museum and Tourism Board and your emissary.

As the shining beacon of our time, Mankon Kingdom in particular and the nation at large will profoundly miss your unwavering service and never-ending work for humanity. We greatly treasure all you did.

May God imbue the royal family with the necessary strength and fortitude to be able to sail through this extremely challenging period of your disappearance. Long live your great legacy.

Son,

Ntomnifor Richard Fru
(Secretary, Mankon Traditional Council)

Your royal majesty Fo Angwafo III of Mankon though missing your footprints will forever remain in our memories your legacy is told all over the world and our children shall tell of you. May Almighty God grant you a safe place as you have joined your ancestors.

Ndanga Jonathan Fru
Quarter Head, Atualakom

Your Highness, on behalf of the people of Bagbanong Quarter, a quarter that shares immediate boundary with the Palace, l wish to express our unprecedented sorrow and pain for your disappearance. I can vividly recall how with broad smiles you always call me the Printer whenever we meet. You always gave me printing jobs and generously paid me. We will forever miss your wise words, great sense of humour and generosity. May the good Lord grant you a very peaceful rest with our ancestors.

Nde Godfred Tumasang
Quarter Head, Bagbanong

Oh, is it not a perfect call you have answered? Indeed, you resisted not, as dreaded the imperishable and imperfect image of the world. Let now your unquenchable thirst for the beatific vision be the fruits of your strivings.

HRH a fallen HERO always smiling.

I remember in 2008 after the death of Solomon Anye Manjong, you assigned me to work as the quarter head of Ntahnkah and the chairman of the Ntahnkah-Mulang area council which I honoured up till 2013.

I remember when I contested the legislative elections in 2013 and won, I came and told you and you asked me to go and make sure that I improve on the roads at Ntahnkah which I did and gave you the report and you were so happy.

I remember when you sent me to Ndop to buy you sheep and goats to improve your paddock and increase your flock which I did and when I returned your face was full of smiles.

I remember when I was doing castration on your farm uphill, you were always by me, passionately sharing many stories in the domain of agriculture and livestock.

I remember we were locked up at the police because of the road we constructed, you came up and has us released together with our community and the whole town was shaken by your appearance just to release us and we came out as heroes. I remember two times you called me for important discussions and when I came, we talked in your library for more than an hour.

I remember when you called me and we went to the governor's office at Up Station for land and boundary issues between Nkwen, Bafut and Mankon which you assigned me with a delegation and instructions only to show them the boundaries from Mulang to Bafut and that I should not attend to any questions which I did and when I came back, I was given two bottles of wine, half a chicken and food.

I remember when I told you of a friend in the ministry of secondary education, a delegate in Yaoundé who told me if I have a site, he can give me a technical school in any community. I remember when I met the Fon with the form already filled out and the Fon had

15

to sign, together with me assuring for the site and it didn't take three months and the school was approved, GTC Ntankah and Ntingkag.

I remember during deliberations with quarter heads, with King Solomon's wisdom, everybody always left very satisfied. There is much that we did that cannot be all said now. Nevertheless, it becomes obvious that when perfection called, you gave up imperfection. May we continue to draw inspiration from your great deeds.

Ndengsa Pius Achu
Quarter Head, Ntankah I

Your Royal Majesty,

We have always been one of those quarters that boast amongst the other quarters for the many developmental projects realized through his Royal Majesty Fo S.A.N. Angwafo III such as our community hall, G.S.S Mulang, Water borehole etc., etc.

News of your disappearance hit hard on us because when told that life is like a candle which can be blown out at any time, the concept is understood in theory but literally hard to believe that you have been blown out too. We miss you and your wise counsel desperately, Mbeh but are blessed for all you have been/done for us.

Even though you have departed, we know your vision as you kept reminding us of each time you invited the quarters in the palace *"to be strong and not to relent in our efforts in developing our quarters"*. Therefore, we will not hesitate to attribute you as *"the old broom that sweeps well and best."*

You have made goodbye sad, but you are not saddened because we know you are just smiling, saying your journey is a great gain because the ancestors lived in you.

For and on behalf of the quarter

Ngomanji Nche Emmanuel
Mulang Quarter Secretary

His Royal Majesty Hon. King Solomon A.N. Angwafo III, became Greater than All the Kings of the Earth in riches, Knowledge and Wisdom which God had put in His Heart as a Blessing from King Ndefru III for Shepherding the Mankon-Bamenda Kingdom. This is like to King Solomon of Israel in the Holy Scripture in 1st Kings. His Royal Majesty Hon. King Solomon A.N. Angwafo III,

Ruled on and 50 years saw His Golden Jubilee and 13 years were still pending to clock 63 years as the 13 Children of Jacob in the Holy Bible. This was the Timing for Him to Complete the Building of the Mankon Palace in the atmosphere of War in the North West and South West Regions of Cameroon where Kings and Fons Fled Their Palaces His Royal Majesty Hon. King Solomon A.N. Angwafo III Remained Focused with the Almighty Lord in the Very Name of Jesus Christ and on 11/05/2022 Witnessed the Vision and Mission of God's Servants in Leadership of Archbishop Andrew Fuanya Nkea, who offered Prayers His Royal Majesty The Hon. King Solomon A.N. Angwafo III and His accomplishments and the Entire Mankon Kingdom. The Blessings were and are a Sweet Aroma to God Himself Who Accepted and Immediately Blessed His Royal Majesty Hon. King Solomon A.N. Angwafo III and The Mankon Kingdom thereby Leading These Blessings for Onward Shepherding of The Kingdom of Mankon by His Royal Majesty King John F.A. Angwafo IV 07/05/2022. His Royal Majesty Hon. King Solomon A.N. Angwafo III's 21/05/1925 and 21/05/2022 Reminds Us All that His Royal Majesty Hon. King Solomon A.N. Angwafo III is One of The Saints sitting with Our Lord and Saviour Jesus Christ, Who was Yesterday, Today and Reigns Forever.

Tangyie Nju Spartan Philip Nde
Quarter Head, Nitob 6

The Light, the Smile of Mankon

You were the lion that tamed other animals instead of feeding on them.

Your wisdom was immeasurable as Mankon and mankind found shelter in you just like the forest shelters it numerous species.

You were a mighty forest that sheltered us all and your departure we thought will expose us to the wild but your wisdom once again gave more than you to us.

The unique smile that was regular on your lips otherwise known as the Mankon smile, inspired and gave your people hope even when there was no sign of light. You were a father to all. Rest well, you will forever live in our hearts and your legacy we will continue to benefit. Adieu

Nsoh Emmanuel Nde
Quarter Head, Alakoro

To The Best Dad Ever

You were a true and loving father, you were a very hardworking and relentless dad. The sky has always been your limit. You laboured day and night to send your children, family members, friend and even stranger to school. You were always willing to forgive. You were always there to settle disputes so that everyone will be happy. Peace and justice had always been the words on your lips. You were so down to earth. Father, I miss you wherever you are, you should please look after us and may your gentle soul rest in peace. l can't write all the good things about you here. But you were a great King. You will always be remembered in my heart. I will always love you.

Your Son

Nwabueze Abriham
Quarter Head, Upper Up Atu Azire

HRH Fo Angwafo III of Mankon Kingdom, was a BAOBAB tree which for the past 63 years has harboured all kinds of birds, white, yellow, red, black, blue, green etc, where they build their nests, large and small,

They lay eggs, their chicken are protected

In the BAOBAB,

No sun heat

No rain to kill their chicks because they're shaded.

HRH Fo Angwafo III of Mankon Kingdom like a great BAOBAB tree shaded all kinds of animals, white, yellow, red, black, blue, green etc big and small.

From his quote, "Everybody living in Mankon Kingdom is a Mankon citizen, l make sure there's no difference."

The great BAOBAB allowed anyone from any part of the world

To buy, sell, build, farm, marry, and get buried in Mankon Kingdom. He was full of wisdom, love tolerance, humility, etc.

HRH Fo Angwafo III, HRH Angwafo the Great of Mankon Kingdom.

The Azire 'A' Quarter will never forget

Adieu Our Fo.

Penn Barnabas T.
Azire 'A' Quarter

On behalf of Ntsuabuh quarter, I, the quarter head, regret the missing of our loving father the paramount ruler of the Mankon Fondom. The entire quarter is in deep grief because they will miss his great wisdom and fatherly love. In fact, the population is so grateful for his generosity for providing lands for PC Ngomgham and the prestigious Sacred Heart College which also serves the Ntsuabuh Community. Your generosity and determination to see into the educational, spiritual and moral development of the population cannot be overemphasized. You were an agent of peace and encouraged us to use our hands to better our lives. The entire Ntsuabuh regrets your absence and prays for your successor to continue from where you have stopped. We miss you so much.

Tumasang Hansley
Ntsuabuh Quarter

His royal Highness Fon Angwafor III, the iconic Fon of Mankon leaves indelible marks on our collective memory. His disappearance leaves us grief-stricken. We, however, take pride and rejoice at the legacy he bequeathed us. He taught us to love without borders. Severally he made us understand that whoever is in Mankon is entitled to fair and just treatment. Our installation as quarter head and councillors by the Fon in person will remain unforgettable. We rejoice that he has given a worthy heir on the throne. We pledge to continue to work for more development. May the Almighty God receive him till we meet to part no more.

Zuah Valentine (Quarter Head, Akohkikang)

Part 3

Tributes from the Palace

Bulyibufo (Fon's Advisers)

Noblesse Oblige: Leergh nko'ob! nko'ob sargh nda nwon

Selflessly, Fo ANGWAFO III of Mankon, transformed thousands of hectares of his most prestigious landed assets within the Bamenda Metropolitan area into citadels of learning. Amongst such is part of his historic hunting ground, Atvurafo, which is today renowned far beyond our homeland for its decades of unabated academic excellence. Time literally stands still during the proclamation of G.C.E. results when it comes to: *Centre N° 031: Sacred Heart College, Mankon. 100% passed had become the norm and anything else was a momentary aberration.*

Akin to the legendary gigantic migratory wave, Ma'kunghe, that his forefathers led to present-day Mankon; he has rallied our palm-wine tapping and farming households to produce an unprecedented and seemingly endless nexus of sons and daughters of the homeland at the cutting-edge of academics, medicine, modern technologies and social innovation. We, and countless more generations to come shall remain inspired by the likes of Tata Dr. Nche Zama, MD, PhD, a son of our homeland of humble beginnings, for his trailblazing journey of excellence and service to Mankon, Philadelphia and mankind as a whole.

The life, works, dreams and aspirations of Fo Angwafo III of Mankon constitute fertile grounds for historians and researchers in quest of hallmarks on the notion of *Noblesse Oblige*. With proverbial selflessness, unassailable integrity and breath-taking service to Man, God and the Universe, you re-shaped and shared nobility; extending it beyond mere entitlement, requiring of those bequeathed such status the duty to protect and defend the sanctity of the common good, Mukong tse'eh a nkara! The pinnacle is your now trademark admonition and call to arms as your son or daughter sets out from Nüschwim into adulthood: *Leergh nko'ob! nko'ob sargh nda nwon.*

No surprise that you ensured our most defining sense of nobility was embedded in throwing the fishing net, rolling up our sleeves and leading by example at the forefront. You would characteristically submit that talk is cheap. Your most adorable and unique attribute

21

though, was your passion to defend the less privileged of society. In your teenage years, your mothers fondly referred to you as *Mu Babvrua, heavenly child* – how telling! The unfailingly bright sky over our homeland even in moments most daring reminds of and reaffirms the intricately woven simultaneity of the trinity of the past, present and future of our being. The ubiquity of the sacred union of the dead, living and the unborn.

We, your children of the great Mankon family and beyond are well aware of the divine burden of *Noblesse Oblige*, though not able to promise to follow suit with a near 100 years of service to man and God on earth, oh dear King Solomon, the Great, – but we do promise to exhaust every gust of breath exemplarily serving the common good to the very best of our abilities. So, help us Tsazui.

Tawbargh Fo Angwafo III
(Ndi Angwafo IV)

Your Royal Highness, I really miss you. You were a real father and friend to me. A mentor in my life particularly as I studied Law (LLB) at the University. Inspired by your sense of good judgement, I equally studied Political Science BSc (Hons) due to our arrangement for a relay in your political career. I even did a master's degree in Public Administration (M.Sc.) as a move to revive your leadership drive in Public Administration and as an axillary to local government. I wish you stayed a little longer for us to have completed the deal regarding my award for a PhD in Public Administration in view this year.

As a repeat of history, I am now a mayor and a Civil Status Registrar just like you were the chairman of the Mankon Area Council between 1968 and 1972 and Mankon Rural Council from 1972 to 1977 respectively. Thus, your legacy lives on.

What I am today is an epitome of your work as a father, friend, and mentor. I assure you that where you ended, I will continue as a catalyst and rallying crucible for the family.

Your Majesty: you were great at keeping the royal family and our village together, a genius, an icon, a great teacher, a highly disciplined father, and a great adviser. As we look back over time, we wonder if we ever thanked you enough as you stood by us to celebrate our successes and accept our defeats.

You taught us by your example to value hard work and carry on with courage, commitment, perseverance, and integrity. If any person came to you our father with a problem, they were sure to return with a solution. Daddy, you were *Selfless,* a decent man. For this and much more you will be remembered for generations to come.

Son

Tse Louis Mankefor Angwafo III
(Muma Angwafo IV)

From the hills of Nta'ah Fo, through the plains of Asongkah , meandering across the valleys of Ala'ah korè, HRH Fo Angwafo III, taught us the meaning of "Green Revolution". Today, Mankon is self-sufficient in food. We can even sell the rest of our produce to cities beyond Mankon. Mankon can call its self the undisputed citadel of learning, all thanks to your foresight, hospitality and generosity. Thank you Mbeh. Your Great Legacy will live on!!

Tamitargh
(Nkwenti Angwafo IV)

Bumafo (Queen Mothers)

Forge on Mankon

My brother crosses over and leaves me behind with a feeling of accomplishment. We discharged our duties harmoniously in accordance with royal protocol. The *completion of his Growth* is in accordance with the rules of Nature. This we shall not unduly bemoan. He has left us with an assignment.

Let us organise ourselves and work for Mankon to flourish and bloom evermore. May Mankon determinedly forge on.

Mafo Ndefru III

My Father, My Sovereign, My Son: Fo S.A.N. Angwafo III

At the dawn of Saturday, May 21, 2022, I turned in thanks and praise to God for it was the birthday of my father, teacher, son, mentor and friend. A portentous day it came to be.

I am filled with infinite gratitude to the Almighty God of my fathers for the rare blessing His Majesty Fon Angwafo III of Mankon was. Born into the Royal House by the Grace of God, Father, your works carry something of an earthly manifestation of a heavenly will.

Tsazui, I have been honoured like no other to go a long way by your side not only as daughter but as a friend and, *yes your mother, Mafo*

Angwafo III. The bond we shared gave me a window to knowing exactly who you were. A man God created from very special clay and endowed with the wisdom of King Solomon of old. You were the chief custodian of the Mankon Tradition and Culture, a leader and an exemplary teacher who matched theory with practice, a passionate historian, an innovative farmer, an astute lawmaker, a strict disciplinarian, an adviser, an indefatigable educator, an original intellectual, a good sportsman and a solemn statesman. Your excellence in all of the above fields of human endeavour has compounded your reputation.

Tsazui, heart-warming memories of me running your errands are still so fresh on my mind. As a child, you assigned me to keep the Palace and its environs clean before going to school, to water the garden and flowers, to cart salt to the herdsman as needed after school. Now as then, your assignments will be carried out with the customary diligence and unstinting devotion.

You sowed and nursed the seed for a well-planned and fulfilled life in me. The agricultural techniques you imbibed in me now seem inborn. This knowledge and way of life is central to my livelihood. You groomed me character wise, taught me the virtues of life and the fear of the Lord. Wherever I went wrong, you corrected me with love. You made life worthy of living. We practised both commercial and subsistence farming. Your Majesty, your life was a light into my path. A father like no other. Your generosity was boundless, your doors were constantly ajar to all who came your way. Your love for humanity and education went beyond the Nation as you assisted anyone in need who came your way. Thanks for mentoring me. I remain most indebted to ALL persons who did inspire or make my Dad's whole life more meaningful in one way or the other.

I seize this opportunity to appreciate the host of caring and competent medics and nurses who worked relentlessly as care providers to His Majesty especially Dr. Angwafor, Dr. Ndo, Dr. Mbuagbaw, Dr. Nsame and his team, Dr. Tanah and associates.

My very special friend and son, You have worked and it is time for a well-deserved rest. You exited on the same day I sang you birthday praises. Strange happening? Let the Holy Will of God be done.

Your Highness, May your works proceed in infinite Power.
Gone, Yet with us forever.

Mafo Angwafo III
Daughter and Titular Mother of Fo Angwafo III

Bangyebuntaw (Fon's Wives)

The Benevolent King: Fo Angwafo III

Our terrestrial journey started in 1951 when you made of me, yours, *Mrs. E. N. Ndefru III.* The life we led initially in Nigeria and later on in the Southern Cameroons had little in common with how we lived upon the disappearance of your venerated father, Fo Ndefru III in 1959.

On ascending the throne of Mankon in 1959 *Prince S. A. Ndefru III,* became Fo S.A.N. Angwafo III and I was entrusted with the sacral responsibilities of Mangyie-Ntaw. With the help of various lodges of the Royal Court and under the tutelage amongst others of our mothers, late Mafo Ndefru III and late Mafo Angwafo III, we were able to adapt to the new circumstances. For this we remain forever indebted. In hindsight, our unwavering devotion and sense of duty coupled with our experiences abroad were of cardinal importance in our transition.

Immediately you set to work as always without sparing any bit of yourself. Male or female, royal or not, Mankon or not, no one was left out in your drive to improve the lot of the people. The results are there for all to see.

The most recent testimony was delivered unequivocally by the mammoth turnout of Mankon people at Samne on June 7, 2022 on the occasion of your *Growth.* Your works are also a clear pointer in what direction further progress is to be made.

You have *heeded the call of the Force Supreme.* Still, we remain in your keep till we too are admitted into the hallowed realm.

The world has not lost a piece of goodness. Instead, we have gained one more advocate with the ancestors.

Bughe bvuru tsi tse'eh a mbo Tsazui. A lehngti ngwoghe. A nwi akwate wughe bo'ghe.

Nimontaw Emilia Nanga-Maatsi Angwafo III

My Great King, My Father, My Husband, My All

It is not easy to say goodbye, after a blissful life together of over half a century. However, I thank God for your life all the same and I take this opportunity to sincerely thank you for being a great Father to me, a loving Husband, a wonderful Father to our children and a Great King of the Mankon Fondom. You are the architect of my life and you nurtured me from a small girl into a queen mother.

I bless the day our paths crossed and thank God. I got to do life with you. I went villages and countries with you that I could never have imagined. Life with you was a discovery!

Thank you for the trust and confidence you bestowed on me. Each time you confided a task to me, you never bothered to come back on that because you were sure I will do it and do it well.

Thank God for giving me the grace to take care of you to the best of my ability. It was with much love that I did it and if I had to do it all over again, it will be you, with you and for you.

God being my helper, I will take care of the family you've entrusted to me, and make sure all your wishes come true.

Go well my King, my All and stay in the bosom of the Lord till we meet to part no more.

Your wife

Nimontaw Nkwenti Kuko Anna Angwafo III

Since the Fon's disappearance, I am still to come to terms with it. I am deeply saddened. I have had to project into the future and at the same time look back at the life we lived together. The work we used to do together; how am I going to do all that now? You have left me alone. We used to prepare the farm for the planting season together, sorting the plantain suckers together. Who will bore the holes for me to plant now that you have gone to the world beyond? Who will transport the farm produce back home when I harvest?

When you were with us, you would always tell us to open our ears and listen attentively when you spoke to us, because there would come a time or day when we would be faced with strange happenings. That time is indeed now. How I wish I made meaning of all these sayings back then. I find it hard to sleep, just having a flashback on the life we spent together; we, your wives and your children. You didn't teach us discrimination because we were equal before you. We even farmed with the ordinary Mankon woman in the same fields. This was because, to you, we were one. You told us to always stick to the truth, no matter the circumstances.

But I have hope, and believe that the new Fon will work just like you did. We, too, are ready to show him what to do when he reaches out to us with questions. Being the farmer that he is, I know he will be up to the task.

One thing that brings tears down my cheeks, is when I remember how you would personally go around the palace very early in the morning, waking everyone out of bed. You would ask: "Have you cleaned the palace?"; "Have you fetched water for the palace?"; "Have you done your own chores in the house?"

Our husband was an educated Fon.

You were always ready to teach us what we did not know. The manner in which you did it too, left us desiring more and more of your knowledge and wisdom. You made sure we played a key role in the education of our children. It was a collective effort. You warned us seriously about the dangers of self-medication and buying medicine from street vendors. Only the pharmacy could sell trusted medication. You didn't take lightly the health needs of the family.

We know our new husband would keep providing for us like you did before him.

Mbiefo! Wherever you are heading now, I pray you arrive well. May our ancestors watch over you.

We will miss you.

Nimontaw Tidzang Emilia Angwafo III

In loving memory of a wonderful husband

We had 47 truly joyful years.

The deepest love and happiest marriage life.

May 21, 2022 will always be in my heart.

Your last words to me still echo in my ears,

You will forever be in my heart, my king and husband.

Your care and love I will never forget. You have been a wonderful husband and father to your children. I have been proud of you, and I know you will keep being there for your children even in death. Keep being their guardian angel. Those we love don't go away; they walk beside us every day. Unseen, unheard but always nearby. Still loved, still missed and very dear.

Your children and I will forever miss you till we meet again.

Rest on! Adieu!

Nimontaw Mangie Florence Fondoh Angwafo III

Hah! my father, where and to whom do I turn? I call you father because that's how you took me in, a perfect father figure. I was brought into the palace as a kid after I lost my parents. You stood the gap, and I grew up knowing you as a father. You handed me over to your mother, late Mafo Manka Therese Angwafo, and you both have been the perfect mould and pillar that shaped and erected me into the person I have become. Due to my submissiveness, humility and hard work, you all saw me fit and graduated me into a queen. There is no better way of describing who you were to me my stronghold. If I am still alive today, it is all thanks to almighty GOD and you for your generosity, love, care and support. My ever-crumbling health has been managed and rebuilt by your empathetic nature. From one jaw breaking health problem to the next, you stood firmly by me. I will forever be grateful to you, my backbone.

I pledge my gratitude once more to you because you ensured that our children received the best education even down to our grandchildren, you eased my farm work, made sure I had a comfortable roof over my head. I feel fulfilled because I stood by you till your very last breath. It was an ordained time your maker needed you home because, I abandoned myself for two whole years, making sure that my own human efforts to sustain your life were not short of. Was it absolute care I didn't give? Was it to the best hospitals I didn't take you? Were they your drugs I didn't serve on time? Was it fervent prayers I didn't offer? Was it a perfect menu for your health I didn't provide and on time? Was it my presence and encouragement I didn't give in? Oh! If money and all effort could buy life, you could still be here today.

Where do I go to from here? I neither have a front nor back, but I am certain you are now my guardian angel and will still lead me through, even from the world beyond. You fought a good fight; you finished the race. You prepared my heart severally for this eventual end but is it never easy to accept. You have created a vast vacuum in my heart, a deep wound, an unending scar that will only take the grace of God to heal. All your pieces of advice and good counsel I received, all your teachings and assignments I have kept jealously. I will continue the race in faith as you have empowered me. May you continue to rest peacefully in the bosom of your maker, till we meet to part no more, you are loved.

Adieu.

Nimontaw Swiri Susana Angwafo III
(Sue as you called me)

Part 4

Administration

Le Fon Angwafor III s'est endormi. Il a reposé sa tête sur l'oreiller (comme on dit des Chefs, dans ma communauté).

Ma douleur est sans égale surtout que je suis dans l'impossibilité d'aller à Mankon pour y célébrer sa vie avec son peuple. Mais je peux, tout de même, adresser mes condoléances, à distance au peuple Mankon, à sa famille nucléaire et à son digne successeur que j'ai connu à distance.

Sans grande prétention, j'ai eu, moi aussi, à partager quelques instants de convivialité avec ce "Baobab" qui vient de nous devancer.

Ma dernière rencontre physique avec lui fut celle au "Dancing Jamboree" du 23 mars 2012 au "Ntamulung Presbyterian Church Hall" lors du Send Off organisé à la veille de mon départ du Nord-Ouest.

Il avait joyeusement et longuement dansé avec nous ; c'était un privilège exclusif !

La meilleure manière, pour moi, de lui rendre hommage, est de me rappeler qu'il m'avait ouvert ses bras et se plaisait à discuter avec moi ... De l'avenir de la Région du Nord-Ouest et de la Chefferie traditionnelle, en général.

Pour rester fidèle à notre serment, je continuerai, pour autant que possible, à défendre cette Région avec les moyens qui sont les miens et la dignité de la chefferie traditionnelle.

May his soul Rest in Eternal and Perfect Peace (RIEPP)!

Governor Abakar Ahmat

In Loving Memory of Late Fon Angwafor III S.A.N.

There are countless manners of honouring or hailing someone who positively impacted one's life during various encounters and mostly in several discussions or tête à têtes.

Primarily, what I could briefly reminisce of late Fon Angwafor III S.A.N, twentieth (20th) Fon of Mankon, former member of parliament and first vice chair of the CPDM party till his demise, is manifold; a mentor, role model, charismatic, dynamic and exemplary traditional Ruler, as well as an iconic politician.

I equally remember him as a steadfast Traditional Ruler and Republican Statesman who served the Nation with abnegation, devotion and commitment, he stood firm to his words, principles and ideologies of the State such as togetherness, maintaining sustainable peace, social cohesion and fought the illusion of separation and a divisible state, instead was for a one and indivisible Cameroon.

As an administrator and present Governor of the North-West Region, I can vividly recall our first encounter in 2012 during my installation, our mutual conversations thereafter from a father to a son, that of republican icon who always cast his votes during elections. The pioneer Regional elections of 2020 meant to establish the first ever Regional Council after the resolutions of the Major National Dialogue granting the Special Status to the two English-speaking Regions. We all bore witness as he chaired the session of right devoted to the election of the Regional Executive Council members of the North West Regional Council.

To all those who came along his path or got acquainted with this epitome, the Mankon community, I quote the Hebrew proverb *"Say Not In Grief, He Is No More, But Live In Thankfulness That He Was"*.

While honouring our acquaintance and hailing our unconditional collaboration either as Administrative Authority and Fon, or father and son, I wish you an eternal rest wherever you are, I pray you ceaselessly keep on watching and guiding the footsteps of your children, descendants and loved ones. Safest trip.

Adolphe Lele L'Afrique
Governor, North-West Region

The King and The Great King on High: Tribute to His Royal Majesty S.A.N. Angwafo III, Fon of Mankon

The "disappearance" of His Royal Majesty Solomon AnyeGhamoti Ndefru Angwafo III, Fon of Mankon, plunges the entire Nation in mourning.

Fon Angwafo III was a towering figure in Cameroonian political and traditional circles. He was Member of Parliament from 1962 to 1988, and from 1990 to his demise in 2022, he was the CPDM First Vice Chairperson.

He was one of Cameroon's most venerated traditional rulers and will be remembered as an iconic custodian of our traditions, and for his somewhat iconoclastic responsibility of driving change and modernity in our nation.

Fon Angwafo III played these apparently conflicting roles with courtly circumspection and charm, avoiding stirring controversy and conflict in his various public roles and responsibilities.

He was regal and rigorous in manner and method, stately and solemn, imposing in stature and integrative in style. He was a moral voice on issues of national unity and was regularly consulted by state authorities on sensitive policy issues.

As one of the pillars of Cameroon, Fon Angwafo III has sadly passed on at a time the nation he contributed so much in building is facing trial and testing over the vision and ideals of its Founding Fathers. Fon Angwafo III who passes on at the venerable age of 97, is known to have remained resolute and firm in his public pronouncements in favour of National Unity, peace, progress, and shared prosperity for all Cameroonians. Like many of his peers gone on before him, Fon Angwafo III has fought the good fight for unity and concord to reign in Cameroon.

As we mourn his passing and remember those other patriots who have similarly dedicated their lives to the cause of unity in our land, let us reflect on these powerful and penetrating words by Abraham Lincoln in his Gettysburg Address: "…It is for us the living… to be dedicated here to the unfinished work which they who fought here have thus far so nobly advanced. It is rather for us to be here dedicated to the great task remaining before us… that from these honoured dead we take increased devotion to that cause for which they gave the last full measure of devotion…".

Hail the King who returns to his Maker and Master, and may the Great King on High look kindly upon His returning vicegerent.

Anu'a-Gheyle Solomon Azoh-Mbi
Cameroon High Commissioner to South Africa

The Setting Sun Raises a Shining Star in the Mankon Fondom

Aza, is what the Fon fondly called me in acknowledgement of my mother, the jewel of Abakwa Town. This made me feel reassured that "our" place in the Fondom was never lost considering the fact that my grand uncle; Papa Michael Chenjo lived in the Palace for decades. Fon Angwafor III always made me feel special especially in public when he would bellow out "AZA" as I shied away in complete reverence for the throne.

Fon Angwafor III was phenomenal; he was big in statue and in deeds. He left nothing undone if he knew it had to be done. He lived for 97 years, and shone brighter as the custodian of the tradition and customs of the Mankon People for about 60 years. He ruled over his dominion with a firm yet peaceful hand. He maintained order and respect. There was calm in Mankon for the most part, but always so in the Palace as we saw it. He carried such a regal aura that hardly anyone had the temerity to challenge his orders or authority. He was a just Fon. He stood firm for the truth. He protected the meek and lowly, providing moral support to the orphaned. Thank you Fo, for standing by Aza and her children. With you, the truth always prevailed. You supported my father, Mr. S.K. Kilo to get him settled as a businessman in Abakwa, you endorsed her union with him and stayed close to the family with Papa Michael Chenjo as the palace liaison with the family.

Yes, the sun has set in Mankon, but this is only to usher in the light of a star. We wish Fo Angwafor IV well. May his reign be peaceful as his father's. May the leopard skin soothe him and grow the fondom in a way that will please his forebears.

You blended tradition and politics in a unique way. As a political bureau member, you served the Cameroon People's Democratic Movement for decades, yet you held your chieftain with great admiration and respect from your subjects as well as all those who encountered you.

Yours is a good stalk, may your legacy live on. May we emulate your sense of decorum and justice. May the rising star shine in Mankon as we celebrate the setting of the sun.

Dr. Asheri Kilo
LESAN
Secretary of State, Ministry of Basic Education

J'ai appris la disparition de SM Angwafor III. Je voudrais présenter à la famille royale, au nom de toute ma famille et au mien propre, nos sincères condoléances. J'ai connu SM Angwafor III pendant mon séjour à Bamenda, d'abord comme préfet de la Mezam, ensuite en qualité de gouverneur de la province du Nord-Ouest. C'était pour moi un père. Chaque fois que j'ai eu à le rencontrer, j'ai appris quelque chose de nouveau. Je garde de lui, le souvenir d'un père aiment, un conseiller bienveillant, en définitive, un meilleur ami. J'ai eu à apprécier sa grandeur de caractère quand des vandales ont brûlé sa résidence en pleine ville de Bamenda. Au moment où le seigneur le reprend à lui, mon vœu est qu'il repose en paix. Selon les saintes écritures, il est compté parmi les plus robustes. Je profite de cet instant pour féliciter le nouveau Fon. Je lui souhaite plein succès dans ses lourdes charges sur la grande chefferie de Mankon. Que l'Éternel lui-même vous guide, vous garde et vous bénisse.

Bell Luc René
Former Governor, North-West Province

Eulogy in loving Memory of our beloved Fon, H.R.H Fon Angwafor III

It started in 1976. Appointed as Governor of the North West Province, I was somewhat apprehensive of the daunting task ahead of me. To make matters worse, many of my colleagues in the Ministry of Territorial Administration and elsewhere kept pitying "that young man thrown into the den of political lions", as the North West Province was then termed in Yaoundé. After all I was only in my early thirties, and had not even served in the field before.

But the unknown turned out to be an honour and a real blessing. An honour to serve the hardworking people of this magnificent part of Cameroon; a blessing to be welcomed everywhere as a beloved and promising son by caring elites of all categories.

Among the Traditional Rulers, H.R.H Fon Angwafor III had a very special place. I had known him through my history books for the role he played during pre- and post-Independence days. I knew that he was one of the most influential Fons in Cameroon.

But I quickly realized that my knowledge of him was very scanty when I came to discover other dimensions of the monument. He was indeed a multi-facetted monument: a living library; a strong defender of the State of Cameroon and its institutions; a clairvoyant and development focused leader; a fountain of wisdom; and much more!

But for me particularly, the best was still to come. By words and by deeds, the Fon proved to be a caring father, an esteemed counsellor, always watching over my professional steps even after I had left the North West Province. He sometimes embarrassed me with surprise visits in Yaounde. That is why, wherever I found myself, I kept consulting him on State matters, political party issues as well as Cameroon history. I greatly benefited from his precious counsels and his own example through the values he lived for.

That is why I will miss him so much! But not totally! Because the values he propounded will definitely outlive him. May all younger generations strive to know them, live them, impart them on the other coming generations! May all of us learn from the lives of our founding fathers, in order to make Cameroon greater, stronger, a country where Justice and Love reign.

My Respects, Father.

David Abouem A Tchoyi
Former Governor, North-West Province

Fon Angwafo III was an eminent political personality, astute and visionary traditional authority, who stood for the truth for his people and country despite dissenting voices and headwinds within the anglophone circles during the last years of his reign. With his demise his Mankon people have lost a legendary father and leader, and our country Cameroon have lost one of the vestiges, pillars and astute defenders of the unity of our fatherland.

We shall forever miss him. May his soul repose forever in the Lord.

Minister Doh Jerome Penbaga
Secretary of State,
Ministry of Justice Yaounde

Truth be told!

By his physical aura, his political and social gravitas as well as his remarkable royal reign, His Majesty Fo Angwafo III was such a presence that it is difficult to imagine his absence or write about him in the past tense.

He was a lambent luminary in nearly every sense so much so that from his pedestal he could see and do what ordinary minds could not.

Prominent amongst his many visionary actions, was his early recognition that education was a social equalizer. He enticed many premium educational institutions (such as my Alma mater Sacred Heart College and sister school Our Lady of Lourdes)to locate in the Mankon Fondom through free land grants and other incentives. This partly explains why per capita, Mankon until date still has one of the most educated populations in the entire country. Even as a scion he went to school when it was common for descendants of the royal family to stay back. This could also explain his avid interest in education.

Notwithstanding his outstanding stature and socio-political engagements, he remained a father and father figure not only to his biological children but also to those like my humble self, whose deceased parents where his acquaintances well before his accession to the royal throne.

That was the bedrock of my personal relationship with our Father Fo Angwafo III.

Having lost my parents before the age of 17, my encounters with him were so special and enriching. He told me untold and unknown stories/facts about my family which he knew like the back of his hand and particularly about my Father Cletus Mbayu, also known as Mr. Money (including why he was called Mr. Money).

During my meetings with him, most often in the company of my childhood brother, friend and classmate, his prime offspring – Professor/President Asanji Fru Angwafo, he mirrored a colossus with in-depth knowledge and wisdom on local, national and international issues.

Having spent nearly 20 years of my diplomatic career out of Cameroon, the audiences he granted me even during his illness, were an invaluable fount of re-acclimatization and wisdom.

I remember him pondering with some level of anguish how some people could think that the only way to solve even legitimate governance problems of the country is through secession, a position which he unequivocally abhorred considering that he had devoted his whole life working for the unity and development of Cameroon in general and the Mankon Fondom in particular. He wondered how some of his Mankon kindred could believe in the pipe dream of secession to the point of engaging in activities that endanger the Unity and Serenity of their own Fondom.

He did not only ponder about it. But determinedly took actions to guarantee in his own words: "Be able to, at least, bequeath to my successor a Fondom as strong and united as that which I received from my Father."

He no doubt succeeded in this endeavour, if the spontaneous outpouring of grief as well as the projection of strength and unity demonstrated at his disappearance and announcement of his successor is an index to go by.

From all objective perspectives and to his credit, His Majesty Fo Angwafo III bequeaths to Fo Angwafo IV a better Mankon than he inherited.

I will fondly miss his fatherly presence;

I will miss his majestic aura and wise counsel;

I will miss his many royal gifts particularly the special kola nuts and bitter cola! Hmmm.

His Legacy Will No Doubt Live On;

Le Roi Est Mort, Vive Le Roi!

In testimony thereof I pledge my unalloyed support and allegiance to his chosen successor Fo Angwafo IV.

Your son

Felix Mbayu
SHESAN,
Minister Delegate to the
Minister of External Relations in charge of Relations with
the Commonwealth

It was with a big sense of loss that I received news of the disappearance of our father, the Fon of Mankon.

Against the backdrop of the mystery of birth and death, we can only but accept that a good name is better than precious ointment and the day of death than the day of one's birth.

His Royal Highness the Fon of Mankon was an astute personality of an exceptional calibre. He has been one of the long-time political pathfinders who played a primordial role in the politics and genesis of our Nation right from the pre, post-independence to the present era. He distinguished himself in the exhibition of a remarkable prowess and consistency making him a role model to many as he scrupulously followed the basic tenets of an emerging democratic society. Until his disappearance he was the 1st National Vice President of our National Party. As a young politician, I was a great beneficiary of his political advice which he did not limit to Mankon sons and daughters but to all the Northwest political students like me who used every opportunity of proximity to tap into this vessel of wisdom.

Noteworthy is the fact that despite his political exploits he remained a seasoned traditional ruler with a particular inherent civility of his own and his 63 years reign has been a landmark achievement serving as a standard to other royal families not only in the Northwest, but the Nation as a whole.

His love for family and mankind cannot be overemphasized. He has been a father to everyone.

I have always seen in him an embodiment of patience, consistency, respect, humility, and leadership especially in the way he handled the current crisis.

Prof Fuh Calistus Gentry,
Secretary of State, Ministry of Mines, Industry and
Technological Development

I had the honour of meeting Fon Angwafo III during a visit to the North-West Region with Yaa Gladys Viban in March 2013. Fon Angwafo came to the throne when John F. Kennedy, Jr. was the U.S. President. He was a leader who unified his people and led them through challenging times. I recall him spending time with me and Yaa Gladys, explaining the history of Mankon, as well as the region's challenges and its unique culture. One of his closest advisors gave us a tour of the Mankon Palace Museum and its unique and historical artifacts, including some from the German colonial period. The Fon was gracious, a man of deep warmth and hospitality, and his longevity and wisdom will remain a tribute to the Mankon people for a long time to come.

Jonathan Koehler
Former Cultural Affairs specialist,
US Embassy Cameroon

We honour His Majesty, Fon Angwafor III, for the eternal legacy he leaves his people. I remember being welcomed by His Majesty at the Mankon Palace during my tenure in Cameroon, and being humbled and impressed by his wisdom as a traditional ruler. His Majesty's deep understanding of traditional values, appreciation of cultural diversity, commitment to his people, and pride in his kinsmen at home and in the United States exemplified the extraordinary uniqueness and cultural treasures of Cameroon's heritage.

Michael Hoza
Former US Ambassador to Cameroon

As High Commissioner for Canada to Cameroon, I had the immense privilege not only to be received by Fo Angwafo III at his Palace in Mankon (on April 24th 2022) but also to be honorifically "adopted" by him with the name "Asah'ndom." This memory will stay with me always once I return to Canada. I was left with a deep impression of the very strong cultural identity of the people of Mankon, embodied by the Fo himself. This is something that I am confident will continue to exist going forward, in conjunction with the modernising forces of the world around us. I will also not forget the personality of the Fo himself, in particular his sense of humour. He was and remains a towering figure for the people of Mankon, and for the whole of Cameroon. And now also for at least one more person in Canada.

Richard Bale
Canadian High Commissioner

I first saw Fon Solomon AnyeGhamoti Ndefru Angwafo III of Mankon, during the school year 1966/1967. I was in my first year of CCAST (Cameroon College of Arts, Science and Technology) Bambili, Mezam. The King, who had come to visit our school was only 42 years old, and had been Fon of Mankon for hardly eight years. His eloquence and fluency in English were remarkable. As the King spoke, his finesse and charisma became apparent. He was a modern, outstanding traditional ruler, who exhibited a royal confidence that was rare in those days.

On 30th June 1975 the Head of State appointed me Vice Minister of Territorial Administration. In that position I received the Fon time and again to discuss issues concerning the Mankon Urban Council. His Majesty was a key player in that Council and Mrs. Bongadu from Kumbo, was the council's Executive Secretary.

Before I met the Fon in 1975, my senior brother, the Honourable Daniel Yang, member of the National Assembly, had developed a marvellous, parliamentary friendship with the Fon of Mankon. That facilitated many things for me. With his Majesty, I gradually developed a professional relationship. The Fon would conveniently see me at my office or at my official residence in Yaoundé. On one of those occasions his Majesty came along with Prince Dr. Fru Angwafo III, who was visiting from the U.S.A.

My professional relationship with his Majesty continued when I was Minister of Mines and Energy (1979-1984). During the presidential campaign in December 1983 and January 1984, the King gave me important ideas, before I drafted campaign speeches for

H.E. John Foncha, our campaign team leader in the North-West Province.

During my diplomatic service at the Embassy in Ottawa, Canada (1984-2004), I met His Majesty in Bamenda in March 1985 at the CPDM congress and in Yaoundé in June 1990 during another congress of the CPDM. After I returned from Canada in 2004, I continued to see from time to time, the Fon, who was also the Vice President of the Cameroon People's Democratic Movement (CPDM). Between 1975 and 2022, I remember having had, time and again, long conversations with his Majesty. I enjoyed listening to his advice. When he spoke, I listened carefully. In a yogic sense, he was sowing and I was harvesting.

The Fon of Mankon evolved with Bamenda, which went from a small town to become one of the biggest cities in Cameroon. The city became an economic colossus in the North-West and in our nation.

The King was a witness to endless transitions as political parties and similar associations evolved in Cameroon. He saw all political parties in Cameroon come together on 1st September, 1966 to create the Cameroon National Union, the one and unified party that existed in Cameroon from 1966 to 1985. The Cameroon National Union disappeared on 24th March 1985, yielding place to the Cameroon People's Democratic Movement (CPDM). Accordingly, the old order changed yielding place to the new.

The Fon watched the Social Democratic Front (SDF) appear, rise, blossom and struggle for its survival in the North–West and in Cameroon. Whatever goes up will one day come down. The truth is stubborn. All creatures such as associations, political parties, or economic organizations, should never forget Charles Darwin's warning. Creatures that do not adapt themselves to changing circumstances will disappear or perish. The King also witnessed the socio-political crisis in the Regions of the North-West and South-West. In heaven he will explain everything to the other late founding fathers of the nation.

The Fon of Mankon governed his people with wisdom and kindness. He came, he saw and ruled his people with foresight. During his 63-year reign he had at different periods to be passionate, persevering, persistent and patient. As a modern ruler the Fon had to develop these invisible qualities, in order to succeed psychologically, physically and materially.

His Majesty at all times was the very embodiment of the spirit of the times (Zeitgeist). He had to think carefully and understand the aspirations, fears and hopes of his people. The Fon had to be tolerant and patient in order to deal with different transitions and manage psychologically colonialism, independence, federalism, centralization, unitary system, decentralization and now the Special Status created by law n° 2019/024 of 24th December, 2019. It takes a genius to deal healthily with so many transitions.

The King leaves behind him, a great Cameroon which was, is and will in the future continue to be a work in progress. His successor will continue the endless « work of art » that the late Fon started in 1959. During his reign (1959-2022) Fon Angwafo III played key roles, which brought changes in Mankon, in the North-West Region and in the whole Cameroon. During his Majesty's long reign, he saw political, economic and cultural changes. It is obvious that, like Italy's Nicolo Machiavelli, the Fon understood that effecting change is always difficult. Carrying out change is always difficult, because both the eventual losers and winners are reluctant to embrace change. Change frightens a lot of people.

The Mankon people celebrated the enthronement of his Majesty in 1959. The same people have unhesitatingly celebrated his departure to be with God Almighty. In his poem "Morte d'Arthur", the English poet, Alfred Lord Tennyson, states clearly:

"The old order changeth, yielding place to new,
And God fulfils Himself in many ways,
Lest one good custom should corrupt the world".

The late Fon of Mankon, came, saw his people, ruled them for 63 years, and died honourably at the age of 97 years. His journey on earth allowed him to be a witness to our history in the 20th century and during the first part of the 21st century. To paraphrase John F. Kennedy, the Fon did not ask what Cameroon could do for him. The Fon instead constantly asked himself what he could do for our nation. His Majesty gave to our beautiful country more than Cameroon gave to him and his service to our country in many fields is invaluable.

The King has left us for paradise. We can confirm that he was truly a man of finesse and a charismatic ruler. He was a man of character. He was inhabited by an impenetrable aura, which makes him continue to be unfathomable.

May his soul rest in perfect peace.

Philemon YANG
Grand Chancellor of National Orders and
Former Prime Minister of Cameroon

The recent transition to the land of our ancestors of Fon Angwafor III of Mankon is a big loss not only to the Mankon people, but also to the North West Region and Cameroon as a whole. The venerated and iconic traditional ruler was equally an astute politician whose immense contribution to nation building transcended ethnic, regional and even political lines. He worked relentlessly for the development of Mankon, the North West Region and the advancement of the socio-economic development of Cameroon.

Coronated Fon of Mankon on April 1, 1959, he was the first university graduate to become chief in the Bamenda Grassland and Southern Cameroons in General. His level of education and hard work contributed immensely to raise Mankon to a first class Fondom. His representation of the Southern Cameroon House of Chiefs at the 1961 Foumban Constitutional Conference, his subsequent election into the West Cameroon House of Assembly in 1962 as well as his five-year mandate as a parliamentarian in the Cameroon National Assembly greatly changed public perception about the participation of traditional rulers in politics. In fact, he successfully blended politics and traditional rulership without compromising any.

A peaceful leader and promoter of peace, Fon Angwafor III will remain indelible in the minds of many for his frequent outings to denounce anti-patriotic acts and violence in favour of peace and a pacific resolution of the differences of the sons and daughters of Cameroon. This same position prevailed in all his discourses in the wake of the current socio-political crisis.

His Royal Highness the Fon was one of the earliest people to see the need for a University in Bamenda and this became a reality when in December 2010 the Head of State, Paul Biya created The University of Bamenda.

Long live the Fon!!!

Prof. Theresia Nkuo-Akenji
LESAN
Vice-Chancellor
The University of Bamenda

Assembly, Senate and House of Chiefs, Fons, Council

Bamenda city in mourning. The "disappearance" of Fon S.A.N Angwafor III of Mankon, has left a huge vacuum in the city of Bamenda. A towering figure, a multi-faceted personally, endowed with so many talents as well as energy and fortitude to use all of them, Fon Angwafor III was different things to different people.

Fon S.A.N Angwafor III, the traditional ruler par excellence, who fought for the preservation of our customs and traditions;

Fon S.A.N Angwafor III, the father to all children irrespective of origin;

Fon S.A.N Angwafor III, the politician of sterling quality;

Fon S.A.N Angwafor III, the farmer who modernized agriculture;

Fon S.A.N Angwafor III, the architect of the Rural Council which today has morphed to the Bamenda City Council.

Here we are mourning the passing of a great man; we are sad, but as we mourn, we take solace in the fact that his highness lived up to 97, bequeathed a prosperous kingdom to his successor, and giant footprints in the sand of Bamenda in particular and Cameroon in general. As City mayor of Bamenda, I take pride that I interacted with his highness at a personal level, drank from his fountain of wisdom and saw first-hand his promptitude in seeking solutions to the myriad of problems and challenges facing the population. A man of powerful and compelling ideas, Fon S.A.N Angwafor III was hard to ignore. He was generally admired and respected even by those who struggled unsuccessfully to hate him. His passing is a huge loss to Mankon, Bamenda and Cameroon. On behalf of the population of Bamenda and in my capacity as City mayor, I hereby extend our deepest condolences to the royal family, the people of Mankon, the House of Chiefs, and the CPDM party for the colossal loss.

Achobang Paul Tambeng,
Bamenda City Mayor

I write with tears. The man HRM FO ANGWAFO III was seen as a father and colleague to me. I knew him from the date of my coronation thirty-one years ago till his missing on 21st May 2022. If I should write all what papa did to me it will take the whole pamphlet. He confided in me and I respected him for his wisdom. He usually called me Bah and I will answer papa. He took me to the innermost part of the palace; he took me to the farm and showed me crops he had planted and the sheep we bought from Nso when we were on NOWEFU meeting. Papa journey well. He will be remembered as the first ever presiding president of the first session as of right of the North West Regional Assembly on 22nd December 2020. As member of the House of Chiefs we were honoured by this great gesture. He was very instrumental in the growth and a pillar of the House of Chiefs. I miss his fatherly advice especially to the House of Chiefs. I miss you papa. I will always remember your fatherly advice to me. Journey well to the land of our ancestors. I loved you, but our ancestors loved you most.

HRM Fon Bahmbi III Mathias Njuh
Secretary, NW Regional Executive Council
Member, House Of Chiefs

Fon Angwafo was a father, a leader and a visionary. He was an inspiration. I have been privileged to have had so many wonderful memories of him. The moments we shared together in his palace were filled with conversations that kept me rushing for a pen and paper, so his insights and wisdom may not be lost to me. He believed in continuities especially of the values and achievements of the various communities to which he belonged. I largely credit him for his teaching and mentoring on various aspects of life and politics. An opportunity to share a chat on politics was infectious and his wisdom dropped a pearl of brilliance on how to handle matters or resolve issues. My family and I were privileged to spend some moments with him in his palace a few weeks before his passing on to Glory. Every moment in his presence was full of memories.

His passing away is not only a great loss to his immediate and extended family but a great loss to the North West Regional Assembly. He will be remembered for the role he played in the institution of the Special Status to the North West and South West Regions. In one of my visits to his palace even before the existence of the Regional Assembly he talked about his vision for this institution. He explained that whenever this institution will be put in place it must put all strategies in place to restore peace, stability and development in the North West Region. Let's hope that his comrades of the North West Regional Assembly that he has left behind would step up to keep his vision alive.

Dr Benigo Matilda Ngah

Your Majesty, I met you in person for the first time on Tuesday the 22nd of December 2020 when you chaired the first session as of right of the North-West Regional Assembly. To me, it was like a dream taking into consideration my knowledge about you as a heavy weight Traditional ruler, Political big figure and a patriarch in the history of Cameroon.

During the 22$^{nd\ of}$ December 2020 session as of right of the North-West Regional Assembly that you chaired, I was elected Secretary of the Regional Executive Council alongside other members of the Regional Executive Council. You may be missing but memories of you linger on. I will not forget your fatherly inspirations and teachings in your speech as chairman of the first session as of right of the North-West Regional Assembly. Most especially your pronouncements of "Today I am asked by the Head of State to speak to you. There cannot be two Cameroons. The Head of State has asked me to inform the public that unity is strength, experience is the best teacher, Cameroon is one and indivisible. That is why God has allowed me to remain and tell you the story".

You have joined our ancestors of our beloved Fatherland. I pray you to watch over us and guide us to continue carrying on the esteemed business of our beloved Country from where you ended.

Kalak Flavius Boteh,
Secretary, North-West Regional Executive Council

His Royal Majesty, you were a Traditional and Political icon of the North West Region. The source of inspiration of this nation. If we believe, dream and work together as your words to us, we shall always live to remember you.

In Bamenda, you crowned the head of State H.E. Paul Biya Fon of Fons. National Vice President of the Cameroon People's Democratic Movement, you exercised your love for our Fatherland.

As the Eldest member of the North West Regional Assembly, we shall continue to remember your soft words of peace and living together. We shall continue to be inspired by your example of a better North West Region for a better Cameroon. Farewell our icon.

Hon. Ntaintain Blasius Kibam
Member of the North West Regional Assembly

For the short time I was by you, you impacted wisdom. I remember you told me, "My daughter, when you get married, respect your husband". Your legacy lives on.

Farewell "the oldest member"

Hon. Wendy Lima
The Youngest Regional Councillor

I worked closely with the late Fon of Mankon immediately I succeeded my father in November 2013. I learned a lot from him. I remembered when I made my first outing to his Palace and the advice he gave me was so amazing. He told me a great task and challenge was ahead of me and that I should remain very strong and face my destiny. He recounted how when he succeeded his father, he was faced with the challenge of managing the education of the large family his father left behind. He said that how he was going to manage the big Royal family and his own family before the Fondom of Mankon remained a big challenge. I took his advice seriously and barely after eight years he joined his forefathers. He was a great icon of the 21st century.

He transformed Mankon village in so many aspects, especially in the field of education and agriculture. The modern Mankon is highly urbanized, thanks to his efforts. I remembered him for merging traditional administration to political leadership especially as he was the then member of parliament immediately after independence. He evolved with the new deal party as the first Vice President of the ruling party and he passed on as a member of the House of Chief and the eldest member.

This was a great King who witnessed the complete transformation of Cameroon since independence. From plebiscite to the Federal Republic, to United Republic and to a single party state up to multiple party politics in the 90s and also one of the pioneers of the decentralized unitary state. He can be termed a library of modern Cameroon. He witnessed the Anglophone crisis before passing on to eternity. He was a true statesman.

He told me that he has blessed me and that I should move on during our last encounter. Little did I know that he was speaking the words of a great man.

It should be noted that Mankon and Nkwen shared one of the longest boundary in the Bamenda Metropolitan city and since I succeeded the throne of my ancestors, we have remained very peaceful and both villages respecting the administrative limit between Nkwen and Mankon unlike the other villages sharing boundaries with Nkwen who have either taken the advantage of their new elites and influence and more to that connections to violate the existing administrative boundaries with complicity with some of the new administration who pretend not to know their predecessors did everything to maintain law and order by genuinely putting all the administrative parameters to made reliable and honest boundaries with the villages sharing boundaries with Nkwen. I respect him a lot for that.

May he continue to bless Mankon and also ask God to bring back peace in North West, for he witnessed all what we are going through in this region.

I strongly believe he will intercede on our behalf to the great God. May he rest in perfect peace.

HRM Fon FSN Azehfor III of Nkwen

In 1982 when I ascended to the throne of Bangolan after losing my father I thought my world had come to an end until God almighty connected me to late Fon Angwafo of Mankon. In fact, I felt the warmth of a father the very moment we met each other. Ever since he remained my mentor both Traditionally and politically. I tapped a lot from his world of experience. He was a man of his words. His sense of patriotism was unquestionable. He fought and stood for the unity of this country till the last minute. In all, he lived a fulfilled life. His departure was a very big shock to me.

Rest in perfect peace, as your legacy shall live forever. A baobab has fallen. Long live the king.

His Highness Senator Fon Chafah of Bangolan

To The Legendary, Astute, Warm, Welcoming, Traditional cum Politician King S.A.N Angwafo III, Fon of Mankon

Back in the early 70s, Empire day used to be celebrated in Ntoh Mankon. It was such a great joy for us to trek from Small Mankon for this event. So much joy especially as we were to March pass the revered Fon with a broad smile always on his face. I finally came very close to him in 1992 thirty years ago when after succeeding my father my people presented me to him. Though he took me with very warm attraction and narrated stories about my grandfather in the days of the Widikum Council and my father whom he settled at Small Mankon, I saw in him a father and always called him PAPA. Our ties became even closer when I spent eight years as Principal of GBHS Mankon.

Believer in African Religion. He who talks of Traditional rule, talks of Nature and Fo Angwafo has the biggest Royal Forest in the Region and Traditional rites in Mankon are respected to the letter in spite of its cosmopolitan nature. At his ripe age as Patron of CAMTRACC, Cameroon Traditional Rulers Against Climate Change, we travelled to Nkambe on rugged roads in the rainy season to talk on ways of mitigating Climate Change.

One thing remains indelible in my mind, as Principal. There was the phenomenon of rampant collapsing of students in schools. Despite pressure on me to bring in a Man of God to pray, I was reluctant and instead consulted with Pa. In the meantime, students who called me Mbehman and even some colleagues suspected me to be behind the spell. The day Pa sent the traditional people to cleanse the school, there was perfect tranquillity in school. The day after, I mounted the rostrum and addressed the whole school sternly and told them as parents, we want the best for them and any student who will collapse again will be outright dismissal. From that day till date, collapsing stopped.

Fo Angwafo for the Youths. As leaders of tomorrow, he believed in a healthy you so when I drew a project on AIDS sensitization and sponsored by The US Embassy, I informed Pa of the visit of the US Embassy to the school and why not the Palace. Pa was the first to be tested and I followed. People were in awe since there was the erroneous belief that AIDS was brewed in the palaces because of polygamy. Pa later took Ambassador Neils Marquardt to the Palace and Knighted him.

Fo Angwafo a great mind. In the late seventies, most of the top shots in Bamenda came from Guzang. Here, I think of Bah J A Ngwa with his Geography For West Cameroon, who was Education Officer, Pa D T Mbah BICIC Bank Manager, Bah Takere Mishack of Kingfisher Poetry in Local Government and the only one alive today Pa Munji Marcus who bagged two Masters Degrees from the US in Agricultural genetics. Pa made sure they were all by him to advice on issues relating to their various fields of operation. There can be no doubt that the reason for the so many educational institutions in Mankon today, the many financial institutions and the well-structured local administration of Mankon came because he had a great mind to give his community the best.

Loving, Caring and Humble Father. These are all ingredients that made Pa a magnetic force to his peers reason why each time there was an occasion in the Mankon Palace, you could find a plethora of traditional Rulers from all over in attendance.

As a traditionalist to the core, doing everything to maintain Mankon tradition, there is no second or third class Fon in Mankon.

When I asked PA, he laughed and asked me are there two ,three hearts in any human being?

Fo Angwafo governed with his class and got women in MTC Mankon Traditional Council and towards the end of his reign and to hand over, he replaced the old guards with young talented and devoted Mankon men to then work with his Successor to take Mankon to another level. We will miss him dearly and people will now understand his actions. Regrettable that what he fought for was not well managed reason why the country is where it is today. The king has joined the ancestors.

Long live The King.

Good Luck to The Mankon People.

HRH Fon Gwan Mbanyam Sid II,
SHESAN, Fon of Guzang

Fo S.A.N Angwafo III Lives Forever

On May 21, 2022, we saw smoke, thick smoke which engulfed the clouds hovering over the Babungo Market Square.

It frowned upon us angrily from the sky and then vanished into thin air

Our Chief Priest was precise, Darkness in Mankon Fondom

In Babungo we tore our dresses and went by with arched bodies.

It's been Fo S.A.N. Angwafo III whose Kingdom communes with ours for centuries

But we could not be downcast for long because the Fon was merely changing his cloths. Yes! Changing his cloths

Fo Solomon AnyeGhamoti Ndefru Angwafo III remains Fon forever.

After crying and mourning for weeks

Mankon natives were in their "Adzaahgi" and bare body, Babungo sons and daughters joined.

We commune with you because Fo Angwafo III was our father too

Then on June 7, 2022, HRH Fru Asaah Angwafo IV emerged from the "secret forest."

He is the new Monarch of Mankon

Long live the Fo of Mankon

Mankon-Babungo perfect union will continue

Babungo people salute the choice of Fo Asaah Angwafo IV

Our gods proclaim with absolute certainty that it will be a beautiful era

In which Mankon and Babungo communion will continue,

Our age long relation is assured, our offspring will follow the same path

All hail Fo Angwafo III

The Fo is alive. He lives forever.

Fo S.A.N. Angwafo III's contribution for nation building is immeasurable

Under his reign, Babungo blacksmith tools and carvings were hot cake in Mankon.

The Mankons and Babungos are in-laws

Fon Angwafo III levelled grounds for our children to study in his land.

We were so grief-ridden that there was smoke in Mankon Palace

But we are happy the fire is blazing again.

For Fo Fru Asaah Angwafo IV is Fo S.A.N. Angwafo III

Fo Angwafo III lives forever.

HRH Ndofoa Zofoa III
Fon of Babungo

The Fon of Mankon was an exemplar and custodian of the North West culture. His role in bringing traditional rulers together in order to resolve boundary issues especially within Bamenda Central cannot be underestimated.

Over the years, our people have continuously lived as brothers as we share a common boundary, customs and traditions. Fon Angwafor III played an active role in cementing this foundation.

As a young traditional ruler my wish was for HIM to live longer, so I benefit from his wealth of experience in traditional Administration.

The Fon has embarked on a faraway journey into the land of the ancestors and will return stronger and younger.

HRH Fon Nforchesiri III
Fon of Bamendankwe, Bamenda I Sub – Division

An Eternal Memory Until We Meet Again Great King 👑 (Grandpa)

These special memories of yours will always make me smile. If only I could have you back for just a little while.

Then we could sit and talk again just like we used to. You always meant so much to me and always will do. The fact that you are no longer here will always cause me pain. A thousand years wouldn't be long enough to learn all the lessons and wisdom my grandpa had to share. As I say goodbye to his physical presence, I am comforted knowing my grandpa's spirit will always be a part of me. But you're forever in my heart until we meet again. (Father, Grandpa, King, Legend).

HRH Fon Mbomchom Akotohm III
Fon of Ndzah

The Beacon of Tradition Sleeps Finally?

It is true that, "Leaders are Born," while others are made. This may probably be a fitting compliment of fact, per se.

However, His Royal Highness, Fon Solomon AnyeGhamoti Ndefru Angwafo III was naturally born to be a great Leader. Indeed, he was the King of Mankon; a Kingdom of warriors known and revered for military exploits in defence of Paternal Inheritance bequeathed.

The Royal Long reign of His Majesty, spanning more than five decades was not only eventful but punctuated by multifarious challenges which he used wisdom, tact, and charisma to contain from spill over. Can we forget so soon the controversial post Presidential Elections violence of 1992 which ushered in the phenomenon of Ghost Towns? This was a new way of Life by which the grassroots could express their feelings and thinking, as it were.

What of the ongoing Anglophone Conflict, whereby he Advised Government to Call the Children for Lunch and their problems shall have become a thing of the past?

His Royal Highness remained the unique Beacon and Epitome of North West Tradition and Values; the Peacemaker; Promoter of the philosophy of Self-reliance Development. In this, he de-emphasised dependence on the White-collar jobs that are hard to come by these days.

Moreover, I can't ever forget his invaluable inputs to me as 1st Adviser to the North West Fons' Union (NOWEFU) from 2011-2018, and again elected to the Presidency of the General Assembly of NW Fons.

Finally, the passing into glory of our Father, Fon Angwafor III Solomon AnyeGhamoti Ndefru is indeed, a huge loss, not only to the NW but to Cameroon as a nation.

His Life was unique in a couple of ways namely:

- He was empathetic and generous to his peers, regardless of their individual social standings.
- He stood tall for the total Unity of all NW Fons as an Institution because he believed that a House divided against itself can't stand.
- Above all, he was approachable; a good listener and problem-solver.

Indeed, he lived his Life to the fullest and deserved his rest. I can't resist invoking the timeless words of the venerated Longfellow who once declared, "the lives of great men all remind us, if we would make our lives sublime, and departing, leave behind us footprints on the sands of time."

RIP with our Ancestors and also intercede for us all!!!

Sen-Fon Teche Njei 2
Ngyen Muwah Village (Batibo Sub Division)
Former President General of NOWEFU/
General Assembly of NW Fons

C'est en l'an 2000 que j'ai eu l'occasion de rencontrer Fon Angwafor III pour la première fois lors de l'un de ses séjours à Yaoundé. Une fois les présentations faites par votre fils le Professeur Angwafor qui avait suivi médicalement, mon feu père, Sa Majesté Ndzomo Nkomo Christophe, nous sommes restés tous les deux pendant de longues heures dans la suite qu'il occupait à l'hôtel. Je ne m'attendais pas à passer autant de temps avec lui lors de cette première rencontre !

Après m'avoir écouté répondre à ses questions relatives à la chefferie d'Endinding, aux traditions locales et à mes projets, la suite de notre entretien a été des conseils d'un père à son fils, que l'on prépare à de nouvelles et importantes responsabilités qu'il doit désormais assumer. Il y avait beaucoup d'affection dans sa voix. J'avais alors au fond de moi, à cet instant, senti sa disponibilité à m'encadrer en tant que Chef traditionnel. Mon émotion était à son comble d'avoir été ainsi accepté et adopté dès la première rencontre.

Il m'avait parlé de la chefferie traditionnelle au Cameroun en général, de son rôle important dans notre société, relevant au passage des espoirs déçus et des espaces que cette importante institution devra conquérir sans oublier les défis. Au passage, il avait fait une comparaison entre les chefferies traditionnelles du Nigéria voisin et celles du Cameroun. Nous nous sommes séparés tard dans la nuit après m'avoir exprimé sa satisfaction et le plaisir de m'avoir rencontré. J'étais particulièrement et heureux d'avoir été si bien reçu.

Quelques mois plus tard, il m'a fait l'honneur d'être présent à la cérémonie officielle de mon intronisation à Endinding en 2001, les mains remplies de présents. Il fut le dernier hôte à quitter le palais au terme de la cérémonie !

Plus tard en janvier 2010, Il était à nouveau à Endinding, m'assister à l'occasion de l'enterrement de mon épouse.

J'ai été reçu dans son palais à Mankon plusieurs fois. Mes visites quasi annuelles étaient l'occasion de retrouvailles, de rencontrer certains de vos proches collaborateurs, des notables et surtout certains membres de la famille. Son affection à mon endroit était toujours perceptible et les échanges très enrichissants. La dégradation de la situation sécuritaire ne m'a pas permis de lui rendre visite ces dernières années hélas! Comme je le regrette profondément !

Maintenant que je ne peux plus vous voir physiquement, je voudrais vous dire que ce fut un grand honneur pour moi, d'avoir bénéficié de votre présence, des conseils avisés d'un ainé, un père et de de votre affection. Je mesure davantage la dimension qui était la vôtre et le privilège de vous côtoyer qui aura été le mien. Je vous exprime solennellement ma reconnaissance et vous dire simplement Merci Beaucoup Majesté.

Thank You So Much Your Royal Highness.

Chef Traditionnel de premier plan totalement encré dans sa culture, épris de paix et acteur important de l'histoire de notre pays le Cameroun, homme politique, je me joins aux autres pour présenter mes sincères condoléances à votre famille éplurée, au peuple de Mankon et, pour rendre un dernier hommage solennel à Sa Majesté Fon Angwafor III de Mankon qui va retrouver ses ancêtres dans l'au-delà.

Que L'Éternel Vous Accueille Dans Sa Céleste Demeure Et Vous Accorde La Récompense Pour Votre Œuvre Abattue Dans L'intérêt Du Peuple De Mankon Et Celui Du Cameroun Tout Entier.

Rest In Peace Your Royal Highness !

Sa Majesté Tsala Ndzomo Guy
Chef De Premier Degré D'Endinding,
Département De La Lekie, Région Du Centre

Part 5

Religion and Education

On Ethnic Lineages and National Leadership Achievements of HRH Solomon AnyeGhamoti Ndefru Angwafo III of Mankon Dynasty

Leadership in question is the capacity to influence through inspiration generated by passion motivated by vision birthed by conviction that produces a driven purpose. To render a worthwhile service to a people or nation, one must add to it three things which cannot be bought, sold or measured with money but the fear of God. These involve love, integrity and accountability. His Royal Highness Solomon AnyeGhamoti Ndefru Angwafo III of Mankon dynasty who ruled from 1959 to 2022 after taking the throne from his late father HRH Fon Ndefru II who ruled also for a very long period of time stands out outstanding, proactive and reactive in matters of leadership qualities, that has and is facing the test of time from a very talented, great and natural ruler HRH Angwafo III who has inspired other traditional rulers from the North West Region Cameroon to emulate.

"When a traditional leader works to keep others down the person has to go down too!" great leaders gain authority by giving it away and it takes a leader to raise other leaders. The Chomba, Mbatu, Alatening, Akum, Njong Santa, and Nsongwa villages that intrinsically emanated from Mankon Dynasty and have their common history linked up with the patriotism of Fo Angwafo III. These villages that exist today as indigenous villages have a common ancestry and immigrations to the Mankon. Their migration occurred at some point in time in the 11th century (1197 and 1252).

Once you understand the culture of your people you understand the people! Everything that makes an ethnic group or village is wrapped up in their cultural and political admixture. Prior to the 1992 elections, the SDF had won the hearts and minds of people in the North West Province, Mankon and sub villages inclusive. While most kings in the North West Province were allied with the ruling political party, their subjects all at odds lined up with the opposition. The kings were all at odds with their subjects. HRH Fo Angwafo was the only bravest King who worked out collaborations and was vetoed.

He worked out for the entire North West Region to invite and crowned the President Paul Biya as "Fon of Fons".

Integrity is major bedrock of authority! Praise is like sunlight to the human spirit. No matter how hard life in the jungle is, lions will never eat grass as the people of Mankon believe, because their soils are slippery only at the heart of the dry season they claim and never the rainy seasons! For the Mankon man has indeed, already made a name for himself as a successful warrior and is feared by his surrounding village neighbours. HRH Fo Angwafo and the Mankon people own the Zintgraff's warrior title in the whole of Western grass fields of Africa where the Germans settled during the first and second world wars. The King Angwafo II of Mankon was awarded an armoury by Dr. Eugen Zintgraff and his eight pioneering explorers as the bravest people of the Grass Fields.

Associate with successful people and success will follow you! To be upright is to end right up! You cannot stand out until some life's standards are maintained. Success starts with believing you can because you know you can't. Success is not the key to happiness, but happiness is the key to blooming success. Farewell to you, and you and you Fo Angwafo! Thou have been all these and now asleep! Farewell my King! To thee and your countrymen my heart yearns for new horizon that yet I all my life I look forward! My compatriots and I look again for another Octavio to solidify our unbeatable patrimony. By this vile conquest of leadership, talents, development and mutual achievements shall be sang on every lip from one end to another.

Adieu Fo Angwafo III!

Fly, fly, my lord!

There is no tarrying here!

Reverend Charles Ndikum Ngwa

God blessed Fon Angwafor III with long life and a peaceful reign. In the year of his coronation, 1959, I was a young standard two pupil in Nseh, Nsoh. At that time, with the none existence of the current modern communication systems, and as a child, I knew very little of what was happening.

As the years went by, I began to understand from the media and oral information. From the radio, newspapers, television, and school lessons, I came to understand that the Fon of Mankon is one of the outstanding great Fons of the grasslands of Cameroon.

Knowing someone from information is one thing and encountering that person face to face is quite another experience. During his lifetime I did not meet with Fon Angwafor III many times but when I began to relate with him face to face, he came across to me as a calm and wise ruler who was not unfamiliar with his vast kingdom.

In my years at the helm of the Presbyterian Church in Cameroon, as Synod Clerk and later as Moderator, I came closer to knowing Fon Angwafor III, mainly on an official basis. During this time, I visited his palace twice. At the laying of the foundation stone of the church in Ntingkag, the Fon decorated my wife and I with beautiful grassland regalia. On the day of same exercise at the Presbyterian congregation in Ntuhmbong II the Fon was actively present. Very touching to me was the fact that he came to the church service twice, having come the first time too early. What a show of humanity from such a great monarch!

I will remember him for his calm humility, great hospitality, calculated wisdom, and humanitarian tolerance. One of my curiosities of knowing the Fon better is because my maternal grandmother came from Mankon. I was also fascinated by the museum at his palace since I have an affinity for preserving our African culture and history through meaningful artefacts. Long live the King!

The Very Rev. Dr. Festus A. Asana
Moderator Emeritus PCC

The King – Godman

The Moderator of the Presbyterian Church in Cameroon, the Rt Rev. Fonki Samuel Forba and the entire Christian Community of the Presbyterian Church in Cameroon received with regret the passing on (disappearing) into eternity of the Paramount Fon of the Mankon Kingdom, His Royal Majesty Fon Angwafo III S.A.N. His Royal Majesty was not only a devoured Christian of the Presbyterian Church in Cameroon including a large portion of the Royal Family, but one who promoted the course of Christianity in His kingdom. This is glaring in the way you handed and promoted Christianity in your kingdom. Paul in Philippians 1:21 says "For you to live is Christ and to die is gain" "You have fought the good fight, you have finished the race and you have kept the faith. The crown of righteousness now awaits you" (2 Tim 4:7) "The souls of the righteous are in the hands of God and no torment will ever touch them. In the eyes of the foolish they seem to have died and their departure was thought to be an affliction and their going from us to be their destruction but they are at peace".

The entire Christian community of the Presbyterian Church in Cameroon fondly remembers you for your relentless efforts in providing land for the development and growth of the church.

Death, you are inevitable and no respecter of Persons. Kings and Commoners are reduced by you to the same level and denomination.

His Royal Majesty Fon Angwafo III S.A.N as King Solomon of old, you epitomized wisdom, love, unity and peace. You united not only the Mankon Kingdom but also the Kingdom of God Almighty within the Mankon Kingdom. To the Presbyterian Community in particular and to all the other denominations and churches you were a loving and caring Landlord. As you now depart this earthly kingdom to live in eternity with the King of Kings in the greatest of Kingdoms, May your soul find perfect rest in the bosom of the Almighty God.

Rt. Rev. Fonki Samuel Forba,
Moderator PCC

Our Father, our Father, the wisdom of Mankon Kingdom, other kingdoms, our nation and of many other nations is gone never to return again !!!

Your majesty news of your disappearance is one of the shocking news I've ever had. I wish I was there to pray with you as usual for god to add 15 more years to you as he did to king Hezekiah in (Isaiah 38:1-5).

We all knew you will one day go the way of all the earth but not too soon your majesty.

If one could oppose god's will, then I think the whole world would have done so because you, Fo Angwafo III, were the Solomon of our time, an encyclopaedia to many generations. However, we, the Mankon people are proud you propagated Mankon. Though you're gone, your works are still very much alive. Good night and see you in the morning, your majesty. I pray that your wisdom be passed to your successor, Fo Angwafo IV of Mankon Kingdom.

Your son and pastor,

Rev. Kidzem Christopher Chi

To HRH Fo S.A.N Angwafo III of Mankon: On behalf of all the staff and students of Our Lady of Lourdes College Mankon-Bamenda

Our dear father, the great ruler of our time, the great leader of our land. Your journey beyond to the maker of us all is just a transition because great ones like you never die. You have made a journey which to many may be a journey of no return but since you are alive in God, you live on among us.

It is on your land which through your generosity, a home of formation to thousands of young Cameroonian women was built; **Our Lady Of Lourdes College Mankon-Bamenda**, a name synonymous to success, standard and value. We will remain very grateful to you for eternity.

We promise you that we will always do our best to give the young minds the formation that can only be got here and that you were proud of. God surely has rewarded you with eternal life because you deserve it. Mbeh, your fatherly presence and words of encouragement gave us courage to keep going despite all the challenging times we are living through now. It is through this that our college even after 50 years and soon to be 60, has remained the best in the country and why not in the world. We wish you were physically here to celebrate this Diamond Jubilee with us come 2023, but we know that in spirit, you will still be with us and pray for a very beautiful celebration of this mile stone. We are convinced that your prayers will touch the heart of our merciful God to heal our land of the wounds and pain of war and trauma caused by the crisis in our region.

Rest on great one after a life fruitfully lived. The world will remain grateful that you once walked the earth because of the great impact your life has had on all who knew you or even just read about you.

Adieu, Adieu, Adieu!

Sr. Mary Kemjei (Principal)

From PSS Mankon to His Royal Highness S. A. N. Angwafo III of Mankon following his disappearance from the throne

It is with shock and disbelief that the PSS Mankon community learned of your transition to the land of our ancestors. At a very early stage of your 63-year rule, you demonstrated your love for knowledge and moral education by surrendering vast portions of land in your "fondom" for the development of educational infrastructure. We are grateful to you and your "fondom" because PSS Mankon is a success story of that dream. Your regular participation and contributions to our yearly board of governors meetings enabled us to put in place policies for the sustainable growth and development of the quality educational institution which we now incarnate. We admire the wisdom and tact with which you handled issues of common interest and the moral support you have always given us in our challenging moments. We remain indebted to you and your "fondom". May your great legacy live on.

Dr. Mbaku Henry Ken
(Principal, PSS Mankon)
For the community

Condolence Message

May the peace and blessing of Allah be upon you.

To Allah we belong, and to Him shall we return.

I was deeply saddened to learn of the disappearance of Fon Angwafo III of Mankon. The Nation has lost a powerful force for peace, unity, democracy and human rights.

From early on, the Fon was a tireless advocate for the environment, for education, agriculture and for all those in Bamenda and out who are unable to realize their potential. He founded the plantation agriculture that has planted thousands of trees and helped the population throughout the country improve their lives and the futures of their families and their communities. He understood the deep connection between local and global problems, and he helped give ordinary citizens a voice. His death has left a gaping hole in the nation, but I believe he leaves behind a solid foundation for others to build upon.

May Allah give us Sabr (patience), on the disappearance of our beloved Fon and reward you with guidance and sincere repentance. Amen.

Imam Musa Shu'aib
The Central Imam of Bamenda

Tribute To Fo Angwafo III: "The Big Iroko"

You lived your time and you kept your mark. To many at home and abroad you were "Cameroon's 'King Solomon' Fon Angwafor III. For others you were simply "The Big Iroko" that stood tallest, one of the most influential, and greatly respected traditional rulers in the Mankon land and indeed in Cameroon.

For 63 years we lived and enjoyed peace, unity, stability and development at all levels. You journey on as a great leader, not only for my homeland Mankon, but for Cameroon as a whole. You were indeed the Big Iroko, a great architect in shaping the life of the Mankon people and Cameroon as a whole. The history of this great nation will be incomplete without you "Cameroon's King Solomon".

May your journey to meet your ancestors be smooth as you abducted yourself to be with them. Let your spirit live on, intercede for your children you have left behind and grant to us the peace and unity that we so desire in our land.

The 'Wise King Solomon' lives on.

Reverend Neba Muangu

To The Illustrious Father, Fon Angwafor III

A great light has gone out in Mankon with the departure of Fon Angwafor III, who was a towering figure in our time; a legend in life and a true hero. The entire Mankon and beyond mourn a man who was the embodiment of grace and wisdom. He never missed any function he was invited to and when he came, he would honour you with his presence.

Mbe was one of the most influential, courageous, and profoundly good human beings that anyone would want to share time with on this Earth. He made generous donations of land to the Church including the present site of Our Lady of Lourdes College, Mankon.

I am one of the countless millions who drew inspiration from his life through the many encounters and interactions I had with him. Mbe was a symbol of unity and peace. Meeting him was one of the greatest honours of my life. The climax of my ministry in Cameroon was the Golden Jubilee Celebration of Our Lady of Lourdes College, Mankon when Mbe decorated me as a 'Mafor'. What other honour could be more than that!

His departure constitutes a huge loss for us because over many decades, he served both as a guide and a father who inspired millions of people across the globe. Mbe walked a long walk and made enormous sacrifice to secure peace for Mankon. Fon Angwafor III was convinced that a peaceful coexistence and a peaceful change are what make the world a better place and he set out to do that for both Mankon and Cameroon in general.

Mbe was wise, warm-hearted and humorous and had a very clear memory. I had the pleasure of experiencing these traits personally each time I encountered him. He remembered many past events including names of all the past Principals of Our Lady of Lourdes College, Mankon.

The support from Fon Angwafor especially in challenging times was one of the most prized memories of my missionary work in Bamenda, Cameroon as Principal of Our Lady of Lourdes College.

Mbe, you were a giant of history, a statesman with a message resonating all over Cameroon and for all times. Your passing signals the end of an historic era represented by the heroic deeds of your generation.

May God bless your memory and keep you in peace, Amen.

Sr. Ndidi Anozie (MSHR) (Mafor),
Principal OLLC, Mankon, (2003-2014)

TSÁ ZÌ Fɔ Angwafo III

You were an embodiment of Wisdom.

God indeed gave you the wisdom of King Solomon which went along with your name.

It reminds me of my students days when you sat on the throne at the inaugural meetings of Mankon Students' Association (MASA) back in 2006 when I was the National Publicity Secretary of MASA.

You encouraged us to speak and master the Mankon language.

You advised us not to make choices in marriage not without getting the advice of our parents.

It was your desire to have the Bible Translated into Mankon language. You challenged all the churches in Mankon saying: "Mà lô ŋgə Ndá Ɖwi tsing tsum à ishe Máŋkon wenə ŋgə bì ntɔŋə Aŋwa'anə Ɖwi wu à nye nìgham nì Máŋkûŋə..."

You even wrote to the Synod Clerk of the PCC proposing that I be transferred from Ndian Presbytery to somewhere around Mezam, so that I could assist in the work of the Translation of the New Testament into Mankon with CABTAL.

The Translation of the New Testament into Mankon is still on course and the lights have gone off.

As the lights have been turned on again we will see that we read a portion of the New Testament translated into Mankon as we celebrate your legacy.

You offered land for the Mankon Bible Translation and Literacy project which we are yet to have complete control over the land.

Tsá Zɨ advised me after my ordination when I was presented to the palace that I should be a good example of a Pastor.

Back on the 17th of March 2022 when we visited the palace to present to Tsá Zɨ the Presbyterial Secretary for the newly created Mezam South Presbytery, your wisdom was still flowing to us to carry on with the Work and Word of God.

I believe that the gift God blessed Tsá Zɨ with it was a sharp brain that could identify almost everyone by name, family and clan. We have wholeheartedly accepted the "new you" that you placed on the throne. We pledge our unconditional allegiance to him just as we did to you.

You were available, approachable, administrative and accommodating to accomplish an advanced state and stage for Mankon.

Your precious memories linger.

Reverend Tangyie Ndoh Neville
Presbyterial Treasurer Bali Presbytery
Parish Pastor Pc Njenka Parish
Member- Mankon Bible Translation and Literacy Project

Fon Angwafo III, King Solomon the wise

Once upon a time, came a man sent from God by name Solomon AnyeGhamoti Angwafo III, to the land of Mankon.

I'm privileged to be a partaker of that same name(Solomon), which means the king of peace.

From my childhood days rotating from Ndzong, Ngulung and Alamatu, I grew up experiencing that atmosphere of peace under your reign.

By 2006 while serving as a Presbyterian pastor in lower Fungom Wum, a place where you had previously served as an agricultural technician, I greatly benefited from your wisdom table. My close interaction with you made me bring boys from Fungom who have not only lived and served you but have been adopted and firmly rooted in the palace of Mankon.

Your passing away to eternity is a well-deserved rest. May your legacy of peace continue to reign in the land of Mankon, Bamenda, Cameroon.

Legends don't die, their wisdom and inspiration will forever live with us.

Reverend Pastor Warah Solomon Tse

Your spirit and your legacy lives on forever!!!

In everything, you excelled in natural practical wisdom. And that made you who you were and are – a reputed and inspirational father and leader of your great Mankon people.

When news of your being "missing" was first roaming the air, nobody would hear of it, let alone believe it! But at the end of the day, it goes as God Almighty Father had decided it to be - that you are indeed "missing", in this world, but never again to happen in the next. Your spirit and your legacy lives on forever!!! So very quickly, and with great faith and thankfulness we say: RIP!

Long live!!

In continuity be your long inspirational leadership!;

Long live the Mankon Fondom!!

Reverend Fr. Wara Stephen Angu (Monk)

Part 6

Trade and Cultural Associations

Nkah Ni Kwi is a philanthropic group created by the elite women in Mankon in 1986 with a vision of empowering the Mankon woman and girl child. We have today executed projects including training young girls in basic life skills, granting scholarships to underprivileged girls, giving grants to orphans and other vulnerable young children. We have branches in Mankon, Buea, Limbe, Kumba, Douala, Yaounde, Bafoussam, DMV USA, DC Metro USA, Minnesota USA and Nkah UK coming up.

Today we celebrate the legacy of Fon Angwafor III. He was the leader and father we looked up to every day for inspiration because of his endless support and advice to Nkah in diverse areas. His departure is a great loss to us and memories of his earthly life will linger forever.

Our hero with rich qualities, leadership styles and knowledge. The Fon knew everyone by his or her name, with lots of love and commitment to serve his people. The Fon did remarkable works including empowering the girl child in Mankon, by changing the myth of sending girl children to school, and having a girl child take up leadership role in their families after the demise of parents or family member.

The Fon believed in Nkah and supported the vision of the Nkah woman and demonstrated this in many ways, some of which included offering land to Nkah where its multipurpose hall is constructed. The Fon showed interest and encouraged Nkah in its activities.

To consolidate the legacy of our king, and following the current socio-political environment, we, the ladies of Nkah included the boy child as part of our vision as they have also become very vulnerable. The Nkah centre will design projects to train young boys on carpentry, building and customized projects as the need arises. The memory and legacy of the Fon will live with us forever.

For and on behalf of Nkah ni Kwi ni Mankon
Bih Angu Mercy
National President

Mankon Cultural and Development Association (MA.CU.DA)-Limbe branch had a peculiar relationship with you our 'missing' King, Fo S.A.N Angwafor III of Mankon.

You were without a doubt one of the most observant, attentive and knowledgeable men we had. You were compassionate and represented the royal man we would wish to have. We would like to believe that all MA.CU.DA-Limbe members reading this know exactly who has been presented here and we are fairly certain that most of our previous tribute contributors as Mankonians, friends and well-wishers know too…

As Fo (king) you did not only interact with us through your notables to run the community's cultural and development affairs, but made it a point of duty to visit MA.CU.DA-Limbe to commune with your subjects.

We as an association will want to acknowledge the legacy you as a brave leader left for us a people, which will guide the future generations like a lighthouse when looking for guidance in any troubled society. You showed courage to us during the inception and the peak of the boil up with the anglophone crisis.

Noteworthy are the visits with the Limbe Chiefs at the Isokolo Royal palace with HRH Chief ALAMIN (host), HRH Chief Ekum Dikolo of Bimbia among others. Your actions during that visit were yoked as you had fruitful discussions with the Chiefs. You also found time to have a word with the Senior Divisional Officer for Fako Division which turned out to be phenomenal according to observers with your wisdom during the conversations on the same day (April 6th 2013).

It should be noted that in all your actions in Limbe, you were flanked by Pa Chi Alfred, Chairman of the Mankon Traditional Council (MTC), Pa Tumasang Mathieu the Secretary of MTC and Pa Peter Azinwi the Nkum (Notable) all of MA.CU.DA-Limbe.

Fo S.A.N Angwafor III as referred to in all the MA.CU.DA-Limbe meetings was noted for the tact in which he resolved disputes among his kith and kin.

We want to note your approach in sorting out the differences which arose in the management of a previous plot allocated for MA.CU.DA-Limbe. Also, to acknowledge the contribution to development back in Mankon by the association in Limbe with some appointed and one of them, Pa Peter Azinwi honoured with a red feather.

Your name will shine forever and ever on this planet as you found time to balance the equation of being hurt and hurting your subjects as members of the MA.CU.DA-Limbe branch.

Donald N. Anye and Fru Emmanuel
for MA.CU.DA Limbe

We, the members of the Mankon Development Council in the United Kingdom are deeply saddened by the news of the disappearance of our beloved Fon, HRH Fo S.A.N Angwafo III.

The people of Mankon have lost an extraordinary leader in HRH Fo Angwafo III. One who devoted his life to bringing prosperity and peace to the Mankon land and beyond. His great leadership went beyond the grass fields of the Ngemba land, to the nation as a whole. We, the Mankon people both in grief and gratitude, mourn the disappearance of a great leader.

We will live to remember his legacy "Mukong tse'eh a nkare".

Mankon Development Council
United Kingdom

The venerated Fon of Mankon. Unique in statue and wonderfully created by God Almighty. We pay special homage to the previous departed great kings/ancestors holding brief on behalf of His Royal Highness Fon Solomon AnyeGhamoti Angwafo III, namely, transited Royal Highnesses Ndemagha, I, II, III…VIII, Tako Matsi I & II, Ndefru, I, II, III, Fomukong and Angwafo, I, & II. We say life is eternal, Love is immortal and death is only a horizon. The life of one we love is never lost because your great legacy politically, socially, culturally, traditionally and educationally will continue to impact our lives and the community at large.

His Royal Highness Fon Solomon AnyeGhamoti Angwafo III, you were a symbol of fatherhood, head of the Fondom, the pillar, fountain and epitome of our customs, culture and tradition. The true symbol of our roots, identity and heritage in all aspects. Your strengths and positive values are remarkable and have impacted lives.

In Education

Your Highness, you taught us that education is very vital and it is the key to success. You built or brought many schools to our Fondom, promoted and projected the girl child by advocating for gender parity and upholding the sound doctrine of Non-Discrimination and Equality for all. You gave an opportunity for both genders to exploit their full potentials. Evidence is the fact that

Women are councillors in traditional Administration participating in decision-making of the Fondom. Women in Mankon now are Magistrates, Lawyers, Teachers, Business Women, Accountants, Politicians, etc. His Royal Highness, you successfully rescued the girl child from the relegated position of being purely a housewife, giving birth to children and having a place in the kitchen. You stood for women Empowerment in the Fondom and the community at large. As Mankon jurists, we say a big thank you and equally pledge to uphold your values and via our objectives continue to promote and educate our Fondom and especially the girl child for the empowerment of posterity. We equally pledge emphatically that we will support any underprivileged girl child.

We acknowledge your recognition of this Association and the fact that you constantly concerted with us over burning issues touching on the integrity of the Fondom that warranted legal redress. You taught us that Man can never be above the Law. So, you were a respecter of the Laws of the Nation.

In Agriculture

Your Highness, as an Agronomist, your contribution in agriculture will never be forgotten. You taught by example, your eucalyptus, Palm, Banana/plantain farms are worth emulating. You taught your subjects that the soil can never disappoint them and that agriculture is good.

Administratively

Your Royal Highness, you demonstrated the pivot of your education in the manner in which you structured the Fondom, from the Mankon Traditional Council to the creation and division of the various quarters, their quarter heads and councillors' women inclusive, and the naming of streets. The production of the Mankon booklets containing the alphabet, language and other vital information, booklets guiding the functioning of the Mankon Traditional Administration has eased the smooth running of the Fondom. This aspect has been emulated by many neighbouring ethnic groups with deep admiration.

In Socials

Your Highness, whenever the need arose organized cultural festivities (*Abinefo*) which brought our young boys and girls from all nooks and crannies of the country and the results are unimaginable.

Our Culture and Customs

You proved to us that you were the true custodian. Our beautiful Museum speaks for itself. Visitors and tourists from around the world come to our Fondom because you preserved our cultural values despite the civilization.

His Royal Highness as a Disciplinarian and a Man of Humility

You were hard and wanted the best for your people. You condemned what was wrong without any fear or favour. With your abundance of wealth, you never lived an extravagant life. You remained hospitable and welcoming to those who came visiting nationally and internationally. Your Highness, Your Legacy of Peaceful Co-Existence cannot be undermined. You taught us how to live in unity despite our diversity. You promoted solidarity amongst families, and neighbouring ethnic groups. You held the banner of Peace and not War till your disappearance.

You Live Forever In Our Hearts, Your Royal Highness.

Long Live The Fon

Long Live The Mankon Fondom

Mankon Jurists Association
The President: Bih Che Anye Abegley

As a former president of Nkah Nikwi Ni Mankon branch from August 11th 2013 to September 10th 2017, I had a lot of interactions with our late father; Mbiefo Angwafo III.

He was such a loving father who showed so much love to his daughters of Nkah Nikwi Ni Mankon. He held the Nkah Nikwi women in very high esteem. He presented them as women whose examples are to be emulated by all the Mankon women and even the men of his fondom. He gave the Nkah Nikwi ladies his total support. He supported their main objective centred on empowering the Mankon woman and the girl child economically, socially and culturally.

Concerning our quest for economic development, Mbiefo Angwafo III offered us a piece of land where we constructed a beautiful and magnificent multipurpose hall. On completion, this building was again inaugurated by our father in 2012 accompanied by some dignitaries of the North West and some Fons who were his friends. He expressed his pride in having daughters of substance in his Fondom who are creative and purposeful. His friends who were around him, saw him as a very successful father who has not only brought up his daughters well but has empowered them economically.

67

Today, this multipurpose hall stands tall and rendering services to the population of Mankon and Bamenda as a whole. The financial benefits received from this beautiful edifice are used for empowering our girl children and women in Mankon.

Socially, Mbiefo Angwafo III supported Christianity in his Fondom. Even though a king, he honoured God who is the king of kings and Lord of lords. He opened the doors of his palace on the 20th of April 2015 for a fund-raising that was organized, meant to translate the bible into Mankon. This programme was supported and directed by the Nkah Nikwi women, and it was very successful and still continues to be.

Mbiefo Angwafo III was an Educationalist. He cared so much for the education and moral upbringing of the children in his fondom. He gave land to the government and to the missions on which schools are built for the education of our children. An example is the Baptist High School in Mankon, where he gave land to the Cameroon Baptist Convention to construct this school which has been functioning very well before the crisis set in.

Culturally, Mbiefo Angwafo III did a lot for the Mankon woman and the girl child. These women are allowed to buy and own land in their names.

They also enjoy the rights of inheritance like the male children. They can inherit their fathers land and property.

The women and girl children in Mankon also enjoy the right to succession. They can succeed their parents just like the male children.

Mbiefo Angwafo III did not hesitate to honour some Nkah-Nikwi women who had worked very hard to serve the fondom, with a traditional award. This was in December 2016 during the "Abeng Fo".

Nkah Nikwi Ni Mankon ladies will live to remember Mbiefo Angwafo III as a father who loved all his children both male and female, knowing that all children are given by God.

"Mbe" we will live to remember you in our hearts forever. Though we are very sad now because of your disappearance, we are comforted because you impacted a lot in our lives as your daughters to make us what we are today.

RIP Our Father

Mrs. Ndanga Funjong Eunice Siri
(President of Nkah Nikwi Ni Mankon Branch 2013-2017;
currently Nkah Nikwi Ni Mankon National Vice
President)

Inspirational 84 Ladies Remember His Royal Majesty, Fon Angwafor III of Mankon.

As lord of the land on which our Alma Mater, Our Lady of Lourdes College, Mankon stands, we sang His Majesty's name while we were still in college: *"Angwafor songo mba"* [Angwafor is speaking]; *Songne Ngwafor eee* [It's Angwafor speaking]. Over four decades those little girls that sang His Majesty's name and danced with dexterity to the rhythm of the drums and whistle are now women in all walks of life. We are scattered around the world from Cameroon to Nigeria, and Ethiopia; from Germany to England, and Canada; and the United States of America where most of us work and live.

In January of 2017, a handful of us visited His Royal Majesty, Fon Angwafor III in the Mankon Palace. We bubbled and fizzled with a mixture excitement and anxiety to experience first-hand the palace culture of the Grassfields of Cameroon. Some of us failed the test of palace protocol, and learnt that we could only meet the Fon bare-headed and bare-footed while some of us had already passed the Miyeh rite. So, we had an audience with the Fon in our bare heads and bare feet state. His royal majesty was equally glad to receive us, and was elated to listen to us sing for him a few songs, and especially our ace song:

> Oh, healing river, send down your waters ...
> This land is thirsty, this land is thirsty...
> Oh, seed of wisdom, awake and flourish...
> Oh, branch of peace, spread out and hold firm...
> Oh, healing river, send down your waters. Send down your waters upon this land.

We shared in the palace hospitality, blessings and recognition, as we took turns to kneel before His Majesty, the Fon. In this state he called each one by her father's name, gave her his own fatherly blessing, pouring palm wine from his rhyton into her scooped hands wherein she drank. The miyeh rite granted us the privilege of direct exchange with the Fon and the right to tread on the sacred grounds with shoes on. We thank our sister, Maureen Mafo Angwafo III who facilitated access to this memorable meeting and cultural experience.

When we learnt that the flames of Mankon were smothered, that there was sunset in Mankon land, we all gathered around our sister, Maureen Mafo Angwafo III, onsite and online to say "sister, take heart, our father has rested". And to His Royal Majesty, Fon

Angwafo III of Mankon, we say "ndomnji borna Mbeh, Rest in Peace, Adieu"

Inspirational 84 Ladies (LESANS)
(The Sisterhood of Maureen Mafo Angwafo III)

Our Missing Fon Fo Angwafo III was born in Mankon in 1925, Got Formal Education in Mankon and beyond, got his own profession as an agriculturalist acceded to the throne of Mankon Fondom in 1959, and reigned for more than 63 years.

Fo Angwafo III was the cornerstone and the main architect of the modern Mankon Fondom that stands out as one of the stars on the cartography of North West Fondoms in terms of cultural identity and contemporary civilization.

Fo Angwafo III, when on his farm, was a successful farmer, in the Royal Palace, he was the custodian of the Mankon culture/tradition, and nationwide, he was an outstanding statesman. These different backgrounds and experiences made Fo Angwafo III an all-around personality. Nothing will you ask Fo and lack an immediate and appropriate response and solution.

Fon Angwafo III was a seasoned and charismatic leader, a traditional library who seemed to know of everything around him and every Mankon man by name or at least family name. Each and every Mankon person living in Mankon or Douala and beyond has his/her own account of encounters with the missing Fon. He never asked your name but called you by name or family name.

Fon Angwafo III welcomed all those who came to live in his Fondom and even said "any person living in Mankon was a Mankon man". He loved and empowered his people living in Douala by meeting and making some of the chiefs of Douala to be aware of the presence of his subjects in their chiefdoms. That is why he sometimes paid visits to some of these chiefs during some of his courtesy visits to his subjects living in Douala.

As custodian of the Mankon culture and tradition, he never failed to extend the tradition and culture from the Mankon homeland to his subjects living in other towns like Douala where he set up a traditional council and named notables (beukum) to ensure that the tradition and culture continue until when they will finally retire and return home.

The missing Fo was a leader who was always at the front line amongst other Fons and expected and encouraged all citizens of

Mankon origin not to be different. He never sympathized with discouragement, laziness, pessimism, bigotry, and disrespect. He was a no-nonsense leader. A manifestation of any of these unpleasant attitudes in his presence received immediate and prompt rebuke and correction without fear or favour.

Fon Angwafo III was a tough-minded optimist and saw only possibilities for success where many will see problems and failure. The Fon himself was a symbol of success, never wanted failure in anything that he was involved in. He was a law-abiding personality and never failed to remind anyone assigned by him (Traditional councillors and Beukum) to be law-abiding and always cautioned them to report back to him if they met obstacles and resistance in realizing their traditional assignment, for a way forward, and never take the law into your hands.

A leader who puts people to task, was keen to see those that were engaged in the task and doing it well, no matter how big or small you may be, and will never fail to openly recognize those doing the right thing for the Mankon Community publicly. During his recognition ceremonies, he will always advise that the recognized shouldn't consider their recognition (Red feather award) as compensation for their service to the community. He always said that recognition means your good work has been seen by Kwifo and is just an encouragement to do more.

As we all know different people will have a different experience with the missing Fo and may see things differently but we all know that no one made of flesh and blood is perfect. God alone is perfect.

As the Fo joins the ancestors at Alankyi after a fully accomplished and successful life, as human beings, we are saddened, yet confident that he lives on through the legacy and the cultural heritage he left behind for the Mankon Fondom. As Fo Angwafo III takes his Rightful place amongst the ancestors in the spiritual realm, our hope is that he continues shaping and protecting Mankon. Long Live The Fon.

Nji Felix Ngwamatsom
Vice President of MACUDA Douala

Part 7

From the People:
Home and Away

His Royal Majesty Fo Angwafo III, after the sojourn of everyone on earth, the finality is the pilgrimage back to the creator. This you have undertaken after engraving your strong footprints in the sands of time. To anyone who happened to enjoy the limelight, you can never be compared to any path of fame and fortune.

The proverbs you used to address the Mankon students during their cultural week (MASA), the Mankon people during the cultural dance (*Abinghefo*)and during Nkah nikwi visits to the Palace have left me with indelible memories. Some of these proverbs I must paraphrase, "girls laugh out your lungs for your breasts are still bouncing while your mothers' are flat". To the boys, "laugh like the girls because your fathers are putting on torn trousers and you can see what is in-between their legs".

Mbeh, though heartbroken, I am proud to be your daughter. Father may the journey on the other side be as smooth as your reign my king.

Achidi Achu Jennette Akwa (City Wife)

The Legend is missing but found, in many of us

Daddy, His Royal Majesty Fo Angwafo III, S.A.N. has physically disappeared from this earth but he is found, in many of us. I thought it would be utterly impossible to make sense of a world that exists without my mother and now my father, but he assured me that it shall be well. He is a legend who has left indelible memories that will forever serve us for good, so long as we practice and improve upon what he preached and cultivated. Daddy, I am so blessed to have organized your four months stay and tour of the numerous United States of America cities in 2007-2008. I am so blessed to have learned so many good lessons from you over the decades, even from a distance, and blessed to have had an intimate chat with you at the end of the month of April 2022, the month of your 1959 enthronement, just a couple of weeks before your disappearance on your birthdate.

In the final analysis, even though you were more of a King than my daddy, you hold a special place in my heart that can never be matched. At my infancy, I remember the deep knowledge you generously impacted on me, instilling discipline, and work ethic, during our early morning walks listening to your transistor radio around the Mankon Palace orchard. For me, in my teenage years, I could not get enough of you, I could not spend enough time with you because of my educational pursuits, but you still represent the ultimate role model in cleanliness, organizational skills and time management, a great listening, and a comforter. You were very strict on discipline and time management that my siblings keep reminding today that they could not carelessly watch TV, especially Cameroon Television, if I was not available to turn on the TV. I learned to enjoy your best jokes, as you had a wise pun for any occasion and always reminded us to never let any situation, including a crisis, go to waste. I remember as kids we would practice imitating your voice and laughter while you would sit and watch us without intruding.

Looking over my lifetime of being separated from you because of education and work, I see that certain themes have always fascinated me, and you gave me the grounding and trusting me to carry on, even in your absence. Early on in life, I felt attracted to pursuing banking administration or engineering, but you said I could do both, that I will need both in my life. You also emphasized the need for accountability, candour and transparency in our dealings which landed me in trouble with those who refuse it. It is interesting that there has been a frequent cry for candour and transparency, and accountability, from those who had previously refused such a practice, because they've now seen how warped organizations and nations become without them. You made it clear to me, throughout your life, that the process of becoming a leader and the process of becoming an integrated human being are one and the same, both grounded in self-discovery. You emphasized discipline in all that we do. You were so worried about the many land issues in the Kingdom, and the fact that I elected to stay away from helping you tackle the myriad of such problems. You joked that I was pursuing a European dream and not the African dream. I remember our deep discussions about the difference between the European dream and the African dream, something you fought for with every sinew to make a reality for Mankon and Africans at large.

You spoke regularly about the uneasy encounter your father, and you as his successor, had with the Europeans and land tenure, especially with the various religious institutions that were spreading European values in Africa against African values. You spoke extensively about the differences in each civilization, which I will try to recapture for the sake of posterity. You knew that the European and African dreams, or way of life are, at their core, about two diametrically opposed ideas of freedom and security. Europeans hold a negative definition of what it means to be free and, thus, secure. For a European, freedom has long been associated with individualism or autonomy. If one is individualistic, he or she is not dependent on others nor vulnerable to circumstances outside of his or her control. To be individualistic, one needs to be propertied. The more wealth one amasses, the more independent one is in the world. It does not matter the number of people one has to murder or enslave on the way to becoming a billionaire and accumulating wealth. One is free by becoming individualistic and an island unto oneself, seeking to enslave or control other nations. With wealth comes exclusivity, and with exclusivity comes security. This approach, as we see, is continually leading nations to wars within and without.

The African Dream or way of life, despite being colonized by Europe and mostly assimilated by France, however, is based on a different set of assumptions about what constitutes freedom and security. For Africans, freedom is not found in autonomy but in ubuntu, what Professor Francis Nyamnjoh has written about in "C'est l'homme qui fait l'homme" (2015). Ubuntu is cultural and developmental embeddedness, the role of shared collective understandings in shaping economic strategies and goals. To be free is to have access to a myriad of interdependent relationships with others within the community. The more communities one has access to build cooperatives with, the more options and choices one has for living a full and meaningful life. With relationships comes inclusivity, and with inclusivity comes security. The European Dream puts an emphasis on economic growth, personal wealth, and independent isolation. The old African Dream focuses more on sustainable development, quality of life, and interdependence. African villages and communities participated in the market days of the neighbouring villages, as we in Mankon know the corresponding markets of the neighbouring villages in relation to the Mankon weekdays

The European Dream pays homage to a work ethic that infringes on the rights of others, paying lower than minimum wages. The African Dream is more attuned to leisure and deep play. The European Dream is inseparable from the country's religious heritage and deep spiritual faith. The African Dream is secular to the core. The European Dream is assimilationist. They associate success with shedding our former cultural ties and becoming free agents in the great European melting pot. The African Dream, by contrast, is based on preserving one's cultural identity and living in a multicultural world. The European Dream is wedded to love of country and patriotism. The African Dream is more cosmopolitan and less territorial.

Europeans are more willing to employ military force in the world, even where it is unnecessary, as we are currently witnessing in Ukraine, the Africa's Sub Sahara and Sahel region, to protect what they perceive to be their vital self-interests. Africans are more reluctant to use military force and, instead, favour diplomacy, economic assistance, and aid to avert conflict and prefer peacekeeping operations to maintain order. Europeans tend to think locally, while the loyalties of Africans are more divided and stretch from the local to the global. The European Dream is deeply personal or individualistic and little concerned with the growth and health of the rest of humanity. The African Dream is more expansive and systemic in nature and, therefore, more bound to the welfare of the planet. His Royal Majesty Fo Angwafo III, this is the African dream you laboured to make a reality for your kingdom and the nation of Cameroon to no avail. Can we and future generations bring it to reality?

You are a king who brought joy in farming to the Mankon Kingdom – a man who has lived well, educated many, laughed often and loved much, who has gained the respect of many and has the love of children, who has filled his niche and accomplished his task. You are a man who leaves the world better than he found it, even if we are still in another crisis. A legend who has never lacked appreciation of earth's beauty or failed to express it, who looked for the best in others and gave the best he had. You instilled in us a sense of discipline that has given me a sense of accountability. My appreciation for your greatness as a father cannot be measured. Rest in Power Daddy as we continue with Royalty and Politics.

Your son,

Adebang Angwafo III

His Royal Highness Fo Angwafor III,

We will continue to feel your presence amongst us because your disappearance which is a natural phenomenon is just a transformation of your spirit for a new Mankon.

Being the custodian of our Mankon customs and tradition, your love for music, especially our Bottle Dance, inspired me to take Bottle Dance as my profession.

Your Majesty,

Throughout your reign, I have concentrated on promoting Bottle Dance within and beyond Mankon, thanks to the collaboration and support you have been giving to me.

As we will live to enjoy your legacy in Mankon, my legacy in Bottle Dance will also live to be appreciated through my numerous songs, as I also commend the efforts and handing over the Bottle Dance batten to my younger ones for sustainability: Wara Festus, my wife Ngwe Emmaculate, Jahsandoh and Tse Louis and many others.

Your Majesty,

You did a marvellous job to put our beloved Mankon the way it is today, but since the ancestors decided that you should have a rest, may your gentle soul rest in perfect peace, as we move on with your spirit, to continue building Mankon from where you ended.

God being our Helper.

Ade Richard Nguti (RICK NGUTI)

To My Daddy Fo S.A.N. Angwafo III

I write this tribute with feelings of great sadness but a heart full of joyful memories. My father I hail you, I want to thank God for giving such a blessing of a dad to me and to the royal Fondom of Mankon. You called me "Nimo" as first daughter and sister to my mother, you called me second mother, how do I take care of my followers without your constant advice? Thank you for always being there for me. You will always be the first man I ever loved, the first hand that held me through life, and my one and only daddy! You have been amazing, and I am so lucky to have you as my father, I love you.

I can remember growing up in the palace, how your love for your children (sons and daughters of Mankon and beyond) and people in general trumped. You taught me how to become the hard-working woman I have become. Oh! Father, I can remember how you used to take us to the farm in the Mitsubishi and will work with us, teaching us how to properly plant plantain suckers, mould ridges, take out the bad weed, put fertilizer, harvest coffee, etc., most often singing songs to encourage us to work and you had an endless basket of jokes and riddles, it was all fun and loving family togetherness.

You visited me in school often, making sure that I was comfortable and doing my work especially when it was time for board of directors meeting. These memories are so vivid, chai death! You made me know different places to enrich and embed the culture especially palaces in the North-West Region, showing me the traditions and customs of our land. You did all to educate both the boy and the girl child bringing an end to gender inequality.

We did a lot, I ran errands for you and the family at large, being the time book leader and guiding my younger ones, gave me the leadership skills I have today, but more importantly taught me how to keep account of everything and this bookkeeping has helped me a lot in managing resources and keeping track. You were a great father, always teaching by example. You gave me all the advice and best education any daughter could ask for.

My hero, my angel, I will not disappoint you, you always told me that I am a strong woman and that I should take good care of your grandchildren and make sure they get the best education. You told me that my first husband was my job and that I should not relent. One of the sweet memories as a child growing up was watching movies together especially "Ator the invisible" which made you laugh extensively, I still picture that today and whenever I feel sad, that bright laughter lightens the weight on my heart. Daddy, I promise to continue with your teachings, wise counsel, and encouragement especially to your grandchildren. You were my best friend and gave the best listening ear, we shared many things together such that even my mother got most things concerning me but from you, you were the best girl dad ever. Who shall I call Pana, old man, repe, grand frere and all the best names we fondly called you? Legend lives on!

I cry and mourn with a broken heart because I will never hear your beautiful voice and advice, but it echoes in me daily.

I will miss you, but I know you are with the angels in heaven.

My first love, my adviser and comforter, oh! death, why! why!

God will come to my rescue. Oh! my heart bleeds, my body aches for the lion is down.

My body is sick, my tongue is tight because the great IROKO tree has fallen, a tree that all animals in the jungle come to for food and shelter!

Oh, the world feels empty without you, I am sad because a great hero has fallen. The sun set and has refused to rise, the moon and stars have refused to come out because the baobab is no more.

The world griefs and Mankon mourns as a hero, icon, an asset, and a great historian of his time has marched on to the land of no return.

The longest ever serving king in his time, fondom and country at large.

The 2nd ever served 1st vice chair of our ruling CPDM party since its creation till death.

The royal household is in smoke, queen mothers, princes and princesses mourn because the light on the mountain has refused to shine.

Your grandchildren are wailing, Mankon fondom is in darkness but we know u will not let darkness to roam for long.

Your Majesty, king Solomon of our time, your great works we will emulate, your basket of advice we will keep jealously and your unconditional love we shall implement. Rest on my love, my father, my best friend, my mentor, and adviser. The man who gave me courage to carry on, a man who loves everyone especially his enemies, the one who gives comfort to the deserted and wonderers. Be our guardian angel Papa, for the pain we can't handle, may we be consoled knowing you are resting. Our mothers are so weak, but I know God loves you more and will protect and comfort the royal family and Mankon fondom at large. I love you Daddy and will forever miss you, but your legacy will live with us forever.

Your daughter,

Agwara Loveline Angwafo Ndifor (Nimo)

Since I understood as a youth, I've been enamoured by my grandfather. Even when I knew nothing of him, his majesty preceded my understanding. With limited knowledge of Mankon, I had always been acknowledged as a 'prince' by my American family. Paired with a distant relationship with my father, I thought that my family was being kind, in a way to help support me emotionally. It wasn't until I matured that I realized who I am; an identity for which I owe extreme gratitude to Fon Angwafo III.

Beloved son, brother, father, grandfather, agriculturalist, statesman, and king; he has meant everything to so many. Beyond the daunting obligation of leading our people for over a half a century, he has preserved our culture enduring many changes in our time. Without this steadfast leadership, I myself may not have been able to speak on such an incredible legacy. He lived in service to us. Royalty is truly in deed. I am saddened that we never met in person yet hope that my work was pleasing to his majesty. May he be greeted by our ancestors with joy. Long live Fon Angwafo III. Forever Be Royal.

Akere Achiri Ndefru Joseph

I find it difficult to write a tribute to the great man that you were. The Mankon community in general and my family in particular have lost a great leader - one of its finest ever.

I vividly recollect my first encounter with you many years ago. I was about 10 years old when you crowned me as successor of my deceased father, your great-grandnephew Ako-Ngum. At the time, I did not have the slightest clue as to what was happening or what the ceremony was all about, but I came to realize it with time. Fast forward to nearly a decade later, I came to inform you that I had passed the competitive medical school (CUSS) entrance examinations in Yaoundé. I still remember how delighted you were when you learned about the news and how at that moment of ecstasy you showered blessings on me, those blessings which you showered on me continue to abound to this very day.

I later met you on several occasions thereafter. On some occasions I met you when I came to visit you at the palace, in others it was when we brought up family disagreements for you to settle or during events and ceremonies like the inauguration of the Nkah Ni Kwi hall. In any event, whenever we met you showed great concern for me and enquired about the wellbeing of my family. I can proudly say that our relationship was very warm and cordial.

I often found it difficult to know when you were serious or not because whenever we spoke it was full of pleasantries. I don't know if it was only with me. For example, I remember one time when I came to see you one morning, and I was told you were at the water catchment point. I went there and I met you working and clearing up the place with some people. I told you about what brought me to the palace early that morning and you advised me on what to do concerning the matter then I left without giving a helping hand in clearing the palace. When I later visited you subsequently, you reminded me of the incident of me leaving the palace without clearing and laughed about it. I was later made to understand that despite the lightness with which you took it, in Mankon customs an ordinary Mankon man would have been fined by the palace for that or that the Fon would have asked the ordinary Mankon man or woman to stand there until the Fon finished working. I was baffled and felt special.

I also vividly remember another time when I came to see you for a family issue when my elder brother was killed and complained (quite naïvely) about how Kwifo was handling the matter. You told me that that matter could only be solved by Kwifo because you were also concerned. You fondly called my first daughter Mankah Neh. Even during times when you had gone to rest when you were informed that I had come to the palace, you would come back to see me.

Then later you started having health challenges. The last time I came to visit you, I was led to see you but this time in the inner palace. There we talked and talked.

I remember you came one time to Fumju where the old palace was. You were visiting and inspecting your plots of land there. You were said to be allocating plots of land to princes and when you came to one plot which was adjacent to yours you asked who owned that piece of land and when you were told that it belonged to Ako-Ngum, you said you cannot touch my land and you cautioned that no one should trespass on my land.

Your Royal Highness, your disappearance leaves my family and I in deep dismay, but I am comforted by the exemplary leadership you demonstrated. I deeply admired how you blended tradition rulership with Christianity. You have gone to where you will continue to watch over us and you have joined our ancestors to intercede for us. Go well your Royal Highness.

Ako-Ngum (successor of your great-grandnephew)

You were so great a father. You cherished values and promoted them in individuals who possessed them. The peaceful co-existence of all despite all odds was your prime motive on earth. Thus, the good, the bad and the ugly had to live together and happily. Your lessons taught the good to know that no matter what, they must live happily in the midst of the bad and the ugly for life is incomplete without them. They made the bad see no value in the good and the ugly and thus protecting them from the bad. They left the ugly with their ugliness.

In this inherent character of yours, training and follow-up was one but assistance and advice were individual and based on ability and character. Your life taught me that hard work, resilience and resistance to negativity and prudence in financial management are important virtues to uphold.

Akofo Forba Placid Achiri

My dear Father, I am saddened by your demise. You were and will always be the best father anyone would wish for. You taught me good virtues of human existence, both verbal and behavioural. You gave me the courage to face every challenge ahead of me. I call you a WARRIOR because you fought and won your battles peacefully till the end. I will never forget your powerful and enriching words of advice as you never failed to dish out. I applaud your wisdom, hard work and love; all legacies of yours will live on into the next generations. In my next world you will still be my father. I only cry because I miss you but I'll always be grateful to you for being the architect behind my evolution and what I am today. Thank you father. Rest on peacefully.

Akwa Emelda Angwafor

Unforgettable Memories of Fo Angwafo III

A great farmer: How will l forget that each time we were going to the farm in the morning, you were already returning from your palm farms of Asongkah? Each time l saw you, l saw the hard work that you preached all the time.

A great Dancer: How can l forget the annual dance *'abigne Fo'* when all sons and daughters of the soil will gather. Then came the moment when you will rise very stylishly with a disarming smile to join the dance. Your dancing style is still to be seen elsewhere because it is compared to none.

The Man with a great memory: It sufficed for you to see a grandchild of any family in Mankon. That was enough for you to determine the compound where he/she hails from and call the family name. (Father or Grandfather).

I cannot forget your counsel and advocacy for the Mankon girl child to be educated. You personally gave me your word on this when l headed the Mankon Students Association in 1995/96 and l quote

"Tell the girls that they will be the ones to bring light to Mankon so let them go to school more. It's no longer a boys thing".

Thank you Mbeh for your wisdom and great counsel. You were a Solomon indeed. Your Legacy lives on Mbeh.

Aliah Atonji
Daughter of the Soil (Bagmande Quarter)

Your Royal Highness Fo S.A.N. Angwafo III of Mankon. Fon of Fons, King Solomon the Wisest king, the Iroko tree, baobab tree, my Super Hero, my mentor. The one our grandfather Fo Ndefru III chose in 1959 to lead the Mankon Fondom. I knew a day like this will come but did not expect it to be so soon. The Mankon Community sees you as their King, Fo, Ruler but I see you as my father who was never chosen by chance to lead Mankon and Cameroon as a whole.

I remember while growing up, you narrated how you had to fend for yourself at a very tender age. This is seen in your autobiography *"Royalty And Politics. The Story Of My Life."* You had to fetch firewood to sell at 'Ntambag' now known as Bamenda Town, grow tomatoes and cabbages to sell to buy school needs. This has inspired me so much. Although I live and work in Belgium in the white man's land, I haven't forgotten where I'm coming from. The roots you planted in me are firm, I have my own poultry farm, a garden and corn farm where I use natural products for fertilizer like compost manure. All which I have learnt from you.

Your Highness you taught me that hard work is the key to success. That I do not have to fold my arms because I am a princess, I should not sit and say after all my father is a king and I am a Princess who does not need to work, I have to work hard to make a name for myself to uphold the family legacy. These words have so much inspired me to be where I am today. All praise to you, Dad.

I remember back in 2018 when the kids and I visited you in the Palace, you said "My daughter you are a 'MAN', I'm so proud of you for what you have done at Nchuabu and also bringing my grandchildren to visit me". You said you have seen your hard work in me that I should pass it on to your grandchildren.(Njom, Tarnu and Muaze). You said Education is the key to success that they should study hard to make you proud. I have been singing this like a song to them. Mbeh, you have been so supportive, giving words of encouragement, advice to us and we are so proud of you. The entire Mankon Fondom and I believe that you are only missing and will soon be found.

Your popular quote to me 'Mukong t'se Nkare" which means togetherness is what we shall live and die for. You also taught me to love one another, keep trusting in God and while following your footsteps, we will grow from strength to strength.

Your Highness, you have done so much for your children, the Mankon Fondom and Cameroon as a whole.

Long live Our King, our super Hero the Iroko Tree, long live Mankon and Cameroon at large. Your legacy remains forever.

Daughter,

Aliah Elizabeth Angwafo

A thousand words won't bring you back, I know because I have tried. A daughter's biggest nightmare is that of losing her father, her greatest inspiration. Hello, my first love you hurt me so bad leaving just like that. It's hard because you gave me so much to remember. The brightness in your smile and kindness in your heart made you wonderful always. Thank you for teaching, encouraging, and supporting me all the way. I am grateful for your love and counsel which I couldn't afford if I had to pay.

Daddy, you were the epitome of humanity, diligence, hard work and nation building. You were a brigade between the older and younger generation. You were committed to saving lives and were a personal doctor to all humanity you came across because nobody came to you and went back the same or empty-handed, even strangers! Death leaves a heartache no one can heal; love leaves a memory no one can steal. Your love for family, humanity was undeniable. I think it's fair to say that we have lost a loving father, highly intelligent, vibrant, an individual with a rare friendliness and charm of personality. I wish we could bring you down from heaven.

Everyday your grandchildren are asking to come see grandpa to receive words of wisdom and prizes for excellent performances at school. What will I tell them? Oh! Dead, where is thy stink? Oh! Grave where is thy victory? I now understand the saying that "it's not the years in life that count but it's the life in the years." There exists none of your sort in this country of ours nor the world at large. It's about the quality of life gloved and not the lifespan. Forever you remain my role model and hero, Dad! Your legacy lives.

Safe journey, it is well with your soul. We love you; we miss you and till we meet again, Adieu.

Daughter,

Alieh Lizette Angwafo

A father is a man who expects his son to be as good as he's meant to be. That's who my dad was.

A person who can explain colours to a blind man, can explain everything in life. That's how wise he was.

"Chef man", as we grew up to call him.

Dignity, Discipline, Duty, Loving, Respect, Resilience and a great sense of humour, just to name a few are the qualities that my father not only held in high esteem, but practised every day during his stay on Earth. He was the pure definition of "a man of timber and calibre".

I never got the chance to be with you in your last days though you've always been watching over me. My heart aches to know that my wish of celebrating a century of your life wasn't granted but so goes the saying if wishes were horses the poor won't go hungry. You fought a good fight.

From my name, FRU meaning "Follow". You are someone I've followed, someone I'm following and someone I'll continue to follow. Growing up, I've always tried to impress you and been rebellious against you based on little or less of your actions and inactions towards me.

A story that sums up our relationship can be recalled from that one time you told me to pack in lots of firewood into the warehouse in hopes that I miss my football game. But the thrill of knowing that I outsmarted you with the help of my friends and brothers in finishing the job just in time for my football match was so overwhelming and worth it.

Your passion for farming was inspiring which over the course of time has led me into many entrepreneurial adventures like poultry farming, piggery, cattle rearing, plant nurseries and I'm planning on pisciculture too.

The most valuable lesson I've learned from you is that "there is no greater inequality than the equal treatment of unequals" a quote from Aristotle which sums up to fair Judgement.

To say you'll be missed is an understatement and to say our memories of you will be gone is an even further understatement. No tears and no verse can ever say how much I, will Miss you every day.

Son,

Fru Asa'a Alloysius:
It's Mr Aloysius Fru Asaah Angwafor III

If you visit the Nda Mankon Facebook handle, you will read a publication posing a rhetorical question: "Can a girl child be a successor (chop chair) in Mankon?"

Like the post suggests, succession is only a thing traditionally reserved for the boy child in most cultures, but the missing Fon whose leadership prowess is engraved in our hearts forever, gave meaning to the saying "to every rule, there's an exception."

Nimoh Abine Florence raised the issue of cultural bias and discrimination against the girl child in the domain of succession, saying it's a good thing for the culture to be gender inclusive giving the possibility for the girl child to be a family successor or "chop chair" as we commonly call it. Thanking Mankon for taking a bold and rare step, she attested that children are a gift from the most high, so daughters like sons should inherit from their fathers and carry their fathers' legacies beyond human imagination and belief.

A picture on that post illustrates how Fon Angwafo III (missing king) of Mankon anointed a young lady as the ndzɨ ndâ (chop chair) of Late tɔ̀ Mboh Zachariah.

The Fon of Mankon did something that most people thought was unacceptable. But then he was flexible enough to try something new and Mboh Akwen was anointed as a successor to the Mboh's family because the late man was only blessed with girls (able girls for that matter). She's still the chop chair as we speak and she's doing well.

Why am I bringing this story ?

Talking about Fon Angwafo III is difficult but emulating lessons drawn from his leadership prowess and successful reign, keeps his legacy alive.

It takes a brave Fon to do what is right and just in the face of a multitude expecting him to go by the norm.

It takes a visionary leader and a father like Fon Angwafo III to lead change with such a bold step allowing justice to prevail and preventing the rights of children to be abused.

I have lived in IRD (now IRAD), Ntsuabuh and Alakuma, schooled in GHS Mankon, BHS Mankon, PCHS Mankon and GBHS Bamenda but I have met the Fon only once (March 8th 2015) the day I conducted an interview with him from the palace.

Talking with such a great Fon who unleashed interesting details about the history of my Country, all history books do not provide, was a privilege.

He unveiled hidden facts about the Foumban Conference with ease you could tell he regretted it ever held.

Learning of his demise days before my 37th birthday broke my heart, for the first time in my whole life, I didn't celebrate my birthday on May 26, 2022.

Like myself, many hearts are broken over the missing Fon's disappearance.

As a princess from the Mbaw Yakum fondom, Bambalang village, in the Ndop subdivision of the Ngoketunjia division; daughter of an impact-driven and successful journalist (now on retirement) who inspired so many into the noble profession, I call the "Arch Journalist",

I must admit we will shed hot tears a million times because we haven't only lost a potential rock and foundation of peace, unity, truth, justice...we have also lost a father.

If love alone could save Fon Angwafo III, he won't be gone missing.

We will do little things from our corner to project the peaceful Mankon he built, thus attract daughters and sons of Mankon abroad, to return and develop Mankon. That was his wish.

As much as the Fon loved Mankon, we will make it a hallowed place so others can discover and tap from its wisdom to better their own villages.

Ever heard of the #Alakumapickin concept by Nde Donald we are branding big time online and onsite?

It's a well-defined strategy to share the values of the Mankon people and their culture with the world. I have answered questions from Zimbabwe, South Africa, US and even the UK about #Alakumapickin

Yes the Fon's legacy will be kept alive.

His life was a blessing, His memory is a treasure,

He is so loved beyond belief and missed beyond words.

Long live the Fon.

Amy Banda epouse Youmbi
Journalist & Founder of Target Peace

The king Solomon of Mankon, a man of integrity, dignity and substance who has lived well, laughed often and loved much. Growing up as your daughter and learning from your life style as a revered traditional ruler, political guru and agricultural technician has been a booster in my life. Your prominent role in helping me start up a business and your constant support and advise has been immeasurable. It is difficult to imagine life without the tender moments and joy that characterises your presence, Mbeh. You looked for the best in others and gave the best you had in making the

World a better place to live in. Dad, your guiding hand on my shoulder will remain with me forever. Safe journey, my Hero.

Daughter,

Mrs. Margaret Sapkah Angwafo

An architect of the Mankon culture, a symbol of national unity, an epitome of peace, the pride of our forefathers, a lover of development are some attributes that can be used to qualify a noble ruler of your calibre. The news of your disappearance came to us as a shock considering the fact that we were celebrating your 97th anniversary the same day. Mbeh, you taught us that the key to success is hard work in your usual jovial way, you often said that there is no food for a lazy man. This catching phrase coupled with your constant advice and diverse support has been of great motivation catapulting us to successful lives. Thanks for all you did for us and the indigenes of Mankon and Cameroon at large. Long live the King!!

Grandchildren,

**Anye Samedi, Nde Eransome,
Bih Cynthia and Lum Quinivette**

Words can never explain the void you have created in us. Your reign will forever stay vivid in our memories as we live to testify your ferocious work in the family, the Mankon community and Cameroon at large.

You were such an extraordinary man in every aspect. The way you handled issues both internally and externally (family and community), is proof of your mighty wisdom. You know what to say and how to act in various affairs during your regime. Your teachings will forever remain in us.

Unfortunately, we all did not have enough time to spend with and learn from your intelligence due to the crisis. We will miss you so much, but we are happy that you are now having an eternal rest in the Lord. Love.

Angwafo Vivian and your grandkids

Mbeh,

God gives and God takes.

You taught me to invest in Educating People so that they will be enlightened and serve God better through humanity. You emphasized on the spirit of unity hence the expression *"mukong tse'eh a nkare"*.

I was to be by you to assist you during the ***Turning Point Of Your Life***. Oh!! My ongoing poor health situation could not permit me.

Thank God those who were close to you gave the deserved assistance.

Thank God, I was present when you disappeared on the 21-05-2022. I will continue to pray for you while begging God to pardon you for the errors that you might have made while serving God through humanity on earth. Journey on my king and father.

Angwafor Clement Mankefo

A father, mentor, adviser and so much more....
Your absence still seems to be a rumour and not a reality to me.
My few years of being close to you were so wonderful.
A true father to all. You will always be remembered.
Continue to rest in the hands of the Lord.
Our Hero.

Antoinette Angwafo

Miliŋnə Mbiʔə Tsázɨ (ɨ)fɔ̀ Máŋkûŋə: Mbyiɛ Fɔ̀ Aŋgwaʔfɔ̀ III S.A.N.

Má kɨtsí mbé "Nkûm ɨfɔ̀" zɨmɔʔɔ ŋkɨ mbé Tánɨkfú Tsiŋdeʔ ŋdɔʔɔnə á (nyé) ŋé (ɨ)lôm taʔɨ ŋtsûʔu nɨ ŋyɨ tsinɨbvûʔə nɨ mɨwúm minɨbvûʔə nɨ ŋtsɔbɨ tsi nifə̰, ɨ kɔʔɔ kûʔu á nye ɨlôm ŋtsûʔu tsiba nɨ nɨwûm ŋtsɔ́bɨba ɣé.

Mbyiɛ́ ɨfɔ̀ á zḛ aɣan má fáʔa ʦɛʔɛ nə ádaʔa, má lá, wɛrə á tíʔi ŋkwíʔtɨ tuə ɨfaʔa ʦɨmɔʔɔ a mbo mè ɣé ndzɔ́ŋ fɔ́tə áfaʔa tánɨkfúə.

Mɔʔɔ 1.) Ntsiɛ nɨ kûm werɛ á mǔ ŋgôtə ʦɨmɔʔɔ ʦɛʔɛ ʦo "Ngaŋ ŋkyantə ʦɨwi" á Ndáŋwaʔnɨ zɨŋgwi á mbo mbə̀ Brɛsbitɛriya Máŋko̰(PSS) za (ɨ)tsíná ʦɛʔɛ átùə à lôm átùə àlôm là.

ba.2) Ndə́ŋtə ŋkǎ ŋteginə bilən bɨ fɔ̀ á mû Máŋkǔŋə, bá bɨ kɨnə ŋto̰ ̌ iko̰ ̌ Fɔ̀ ʦá tsi ʦinə a Nkfúrə, á I.R.Z., á Alaʔmaŋdǒm, á Asoŋnkaʔa, nɨ (ɨdiʔi tsi mɔʔɔ ɣé.

Tarə.3) NwaʔAnɨ (ɨ)tuənu á ŋpfú wà bɨ Tabɨnɨkfú ɣénə á ŋtɔʔɔ ánuə ŋgôtə ɣé ŋkɨ ndzɔŋ fɔ́tɨ ŋpfúza bɨ mɨ naŋə ándzan tiʔnə ŋdǒ ŋkuŋə á nɨkfú nɨ Nkfurə lá.

Nɨkwa.4) Ndənti (ɨ)ʃóm ɨfɔ̀ á fo̰ á Nkfurə á Nɨkǒmə ŋkǎ fuʔə mɨdzɨ wú ŋkwḛ nɨ mɛrə á Ntɔ́ʔɔ á ŋpfú ifṵʔɨ mɨdziə. Mà ɣɨ ŋkɨ ŋkiʔi ŋdənɨ tsizɔ́bɨnɨ fɔ́tɨ (ɨ)tɨ ŋkwɛ̰ nɨ tsɛrɛ á Ntɔʔɔ bɨ faʔɨ nɨtsɛrə á mû Tsá ndən ɨtsûm ɨ mbɔ́malaʔa tsá ɨwúə.

Mbɨʔɨ (ɨ)faʔə tsenə, bɨ ɣɨ tɨʔɨ ŋkyaŋnə aɣan á ŋdʒwi ábinəfɔ á mû álômə ntsuʔu tsi-bá nɨ tsi-ŋtûgə nɨ nɨfùnɨŋguə átú ŋkabɨ mé ɣé.

Má lá, mé, ɨfɔ́tɨ ŋgwɛgɨə zan bɨgɨ bo lanə ŋkɔ̌ mɨlɨŋnɨ tsɛʔɛ ŋkə̌ ntɨʔɛ soŋnə ŋgə́, bɨ Máŋtɔʔɔ, bɨ Máŋtɔʔɔ bə́ŋgye, fɔtɨ bɨ nɨmo Ntɔʔɔ á bɨ kwarɨ ámɨlɨŋnɨ mɨtəm mɨgɨ átúəmbəm bo ŋtɨʔɨ ŋkɨ ŋdzɔŋə fɔtɨ Máŋko̰ bɨtsûmə.

Á má kwiʔi ŋkwiʔtɨ ŋgə́ ma zɛ̰ á mbyie (ɨ)fɔ́ Ndeʔɨfru III, tsɔ̌ máŋkɨə á ndánwaʔnɨ zɨ ʃiʔtɨnə́, ŋkɨ mbvúrɨ mbé tsɛʔɛ maŋkɨə ŋkɨ ŋdzen adzaŋza bɨ ɣɨnɨ nɨkwi nɨ Fɔ́ Ndə́ʔfru III mbontiʔi kɨ zɔʔɔ nə ámbyiefɔ̀ Aŋgwaʔfɔ III ɣə́.

Má tsi kiʔi mɛtɨ nɨɣam nɨ mɨlɨŋnɨ wen tɨɣa má kwemntɨ (ɨ)tunu tsɨ (á)wi-áwi tsá mbyiefɔ̀ áfaʔnə á mbo Máŋkǔŋə.

mɔʔɔ.1) ndoŋkə́ áfaʔa ɨ mbomɨnɔ̀, nɨvuə, ndiʔi mɨʃômə, ntaŋə mɨtan á mû Máŋkûŋə.

Bá.2) Ndʒie Awaʔnə: Má wíʔtə ŋgə́ mboŋə Mbyiefɔ̀ áŋkɔʔɔ nɨfɔ̀n lá, Ndánwaʔnə ɨɣɨ mbe tsɛʔɛ tsinɨkwa ɣé.A bé Ndánwanɨ Roma Catoro Mison Atuə Azɨrə(RCM. Big Mankon)fɔtɨ á zɨ Ntaʔmbəŋə. Ntɨʔi ŋkɨ mbə́ bé Ndánwaʔnɨ bə̀ Basərə Mison Azɨrə ɨ fɔtɨ Ntingŋkaʔa. Tɨʔi lɔgɨnə́ á nɨfo̰ werɛ ɨkɔʔɔ kûʔu á mbyie werɛ. Ndánwaʔnɨ tsɨ kiʔɨnɨ (ɨ) bé tsɔ̌ nɨwum nɨ ŋtsɔbɨ tsi nɨfə̰ (18) ɣé,.

Ndánwaʔnɨ tsɨ ləbɨtɨnɨ bé tsɔ̌ nɨwûm ŋtsɔbɨ tsi nɨkwa - (14)(Secondary Grammar, Commercial &;Technical High Schools). Ndánwaʔnɨ tsɨ wi tsi-ba(Cooperative College Bda and Advanced School of Sports - Ntaturu 11 and Nkura).

Tarə.3) Tsɛʔɛ ŋkə̌nù, ŋdoŋkɨ Máŋko̰ ŋgə́ bɨ yɛʔi ŋgamə,nwaʔnə fɔtɨ ŋtɔŋnə à nwaʔnɨ nɨ nɨɣam nɨ Máŋkûŋə. Werɛ a kɔŋnə́ á ziŋə ànu tsɛʔɛ ɨʃiʔnə.

Nɨkwa.4.) Werə á wɛm ŋkɨ ŋkɔn ndiʔi mbɔmə alaʔaə. Tan.5)Werə á bvurɨ tsɛʔɛ á mǔ ɨkɔbɨ nɨfɔ̀n lá, ŋɣɨ ŋkuŋə á Abəgərə á Nda-alaʔa Kamaloŋə ŋɣɨ ntɨʔi ŋgen á Ndá Mɨtɨgə á Yamaŋde, ŋɣɨ ntsi wû tsɔ̌ mɨwaŋnə mɨ mɨntarə ɣé.

Ntûgə.6) Werə á kwiʔi npfvú ntɔʔɔ Máŋko̰ tsɛʔɛ ɨʃiʔnə, ntoŋ mɨŋdǒmɨŋdʒie á mû Máŋkûŋə.

Samba.7.)Werə á kɨə ŋgaʔa ndzən ŋgə́ á "Abinəfɔ" á tsíɛ, bɨkɨ mbɨŋə.

Ti?i lwíginə, nyɔ̂m á sa?ə ŋkiə mbiŋə ŋtsɔ̌. Má ti?iε ntsá?tə á Nwiŋɔn Tari ŋgə́ á líginə ifənu wεrəʒ tsǒ nwɔ misɔŋatsu wəmɔ?ɔ atuəʃé, ŋdɔ?ɔ á ɣari werə ŋdən á di?i zə` iʃí?nə.

i nyɔ̂m wadan á mi bə̀ sa?a mû Máŋkûŋə.

Mbamba ɣɔ átiε ŋdʒɔn-ŋdʒɔn, Ta wigi mbyie fɔ́ Máŋkɔ, Aŋgwa?fɔIII S.A.N.

Á ni mè ANYE Mû NDIENE GIDEON, ala?a Aɣamə tizû?uə./-

(*See translation from Mankon into English below*)

To His Missing Royal Majesty, The Fon of Mankon - Angwa?Fo S.A.N.

I was one of his Royal Majesty's "Nkûm" and also quarter head of Tsindeh Mankon from 1998 to 2012.

He recognized my hard work so much so that I was assigned additional tasks such as:

1.) Representing him in some important meetings, e.g., Board of Governors of P.S.S. Mankon annually;

2.) Supervising the 'Fon's" Palm-wine Tappers spaced out in Nkvura raffia virgin bush, I.R.Z., Ala?mandom, Asongnka? etc.

3.) Secretary to important meetings of quarter heads and at one moment during the encroachment into the Nkvura quarter land by our South Eastern neighbours;

4)Supervising of his farmland at "**ŋi**" "kǒmə" in Nkvura quarter;

5. Coordinating the farming, harvesting and transporting of crops to the palace in due time and season;

6.) Had during work in the internal area of the Museum brought from Nkura bush, good dry bamboos and sticks from the virgin bush to the palace.

For my activities, l was recognized during the 2006 Mankon annual dance "Abiŋəfɔ" with a 'Red Feather' on my cap.

Which is why l share my divine hearty Condolences with all of the Palace Royal Family for the great loss of their father, brother, grand and great-grandfather in particular and the Mankon Fondom in general.

I witnessed the Nukwi na Abub of Fo Ndefru III as a child and primary school pupil.

l cannot end my Tribute without mentioning just some of his achievements as the Ruler of the Mankon Fondom.

- He encouraged economic activities, farming, trading, construction and building, etc. among his people;
- Built farm to market roads;
- Promoted community work in quarters of Mankon;
- He discouraged the rampant and selfish sale of land;
- Education: This was his priority, inheriting only four primary schools viz. RCM. Big Mankon now Atuazire quarter and RCM. Ntaʔmbəŋ for Catholics and BMS. Azire and Ntiŋgnkaʔ for the now Presbyterian. During his rulership, there are now about eighteen(18) primary and 15 Secondary/high Schools in Mankon fondom not forgetting Commercial/Technical Schools, a Cooperative College and a Higher School of Youth n Sports(CENAJES Bamenda).
- Very particularly, he encouraged the Mankon citizens to learn how to Speak, Write and Read in the Mankon Language. (see the trial translation of this Tribute into Mankon by this Tributer)
- He himself was a great Cultural educator/Preserver;
- He embraced politics at his embryo enthronement as an Independent candidate and won with the support of the Mankon people and participated in Parliamentary affairs of Kamerun for more than two sessions.
- He modernized or renovated the Palace.
- He was very conscious at the due time and season, in organizing the most cherished Mankon annual dance called "Abiŋəfɔ."

As the Sun rises and sets at its proper time, I pray the Almighty God to repose his soul in peace and same among his ancestors, forgiving him where he humanly erred while in this life.

Again, The Sun shall rise for Mankon Fondom in due time, season and place.

Bye bye our missing Royal Majesty - ANGWAʔFO S.A.N.

Qtr. Head Emeritus, Tsindeh qtr.

Anye Ndiene Gideon Esq.

Fare thee well Fo Angwafo

There are not enough encomiums to describe the greatness, and achievements, of Fo Angwafo. I will focus on three things.

He was one of the most detribalized Cameroonians. He welcomed everyone regardless of race, ethnicity or religion that came into Mankon with goodwill and who was interested in improving the lot of the people of his Kingdom. This hospitality permeated the community – case in point; Mankon citizens comfortably intermarry with other ethnic groups without censure or resistance. Just as Abraham (in the bible) was blessed because of his hospitality, so too has Mankon and Fo Angwafo been blessed because of the monarch's hospitality.

He was a strong believer in education and assigned land, especially to various churches to build schools. The best schools in the country – e.g., Sacred Heart College Mankon; Our Lady of Lourdes College Mankon are on land donated by Fo Angwafo. One of the largest industries in the North-West Region, and in particular the capital of the region, is the education sector. He invested heavily in his children's education – and led the way in ensuring the girl-child(ren) were given same opportunities to pursue their education as far as they could go. That his children (biological and adopted) are prominent men and women in the WORLD today, is not an accident of history, but a mindful and intentional objective achieved.

He encouraged foreign and local direct investment into the Kingdom. Every time I met him, he reminded me that "home is home" and that I must make sure I build a house in my homeland. He charged me to play the role of a roving Ambassador and encourage others -citizens and foreigners to come invest in the land, not just to build homes, but create industries. He pushed for an airport to be stationed in Mankon so that such investors can easily travel in.

These three things may seem innocuous, but when you look at the history and foundation of great economic cities and mega-cities like London, New York, Lima, Sao Paolo, Jakarta, Hyderabad, Johannesburg, Cairo, etc. – they were kick started by great cosmopolitan minds like Fo Angwafo. He sowed the seed of education and cosmopolitanism. We must continue that journey with industrialization – starting with agribusiness – agriculture being one of his great passions.

So long Fo Angwafo III – you sowed good seeds, we will nurture them to grow into the fruits you dreamed of for the cosmopolitan people of Mankon, Cameroon and Africa at large. Till we meet again.

Sincerely,

Anye NGU (muh-Ntofor)

Grandpa, just when I wrote my common entrance waiting to bring you results and get your blessings, Alieh and I are so sad. We didn't get to enjoy our grandfather as we wish, but for all the times we spent the holidays with him, he was ever so loving, ever so caring and a great teacher. He was very engaging and encouraged us to always work, to read a lot of books and to always keep focus on our tasks.

We pray our grandma to be strong and that God will heal her heart. We love you, grandpa, for the times spent with you, you gave us all drinks, fruits from your huge orchard, food and plenty of books and school supplies every time. Even when we would sweep the palace in the mornings, you will gather us later, tell us stories and ask about school, and we always left your presence with gifts.

Grandpa, we will make you proud even in heaven. We admire your great wisdom and knowledge and will never forget how nice you were and your sweet stories and gifts to us. Grandfather, Rest well.

Your grandchildren,

Ndefru Noel Ndifor
Alieh Joline Madison Ndifor

Grandpa, why now? We used to enjoy your presence, whenever we came home. You would tell us stories and would always tell us to be good children, give us books, drinks and promise to support us in school. Where are you, who will teach us your nice stories in Mankon and where shall we hurry to show our report cards? We love you grand pa, we miss you so much and forever you remain in our hearts. We promise we will not fail you.

May your soul rest in peace.

Grand Children,

Anye Rawllins, Ngang, Mankah, and Tse Kabba

William Shakespeare once wrote "what's in a name?" The naming of a child is one of the first traditional human rights that every person goes through. To many, it is believed that a person's name can shape their destiny. As it pertains to my grandfather, that belief could not be more appropriate. The name Solomon is derived from the Hebrew word "shalom," which means peace. The name itself means "Man of Peace." As the Hebrew Bible tells us, Solomon was the son of David, and succeeded his father as King of Israel. When we look back and read scripture, we see that what defined Solomon was his wisdom. It was that wisdom that became his hallmark, and in the thousands of years since, his name has become synonymous with acute prudence, acumen, and judgement.

As we look back at 97 years of life and more than 60 years of rulership, it is through his illustrious history that we can begin to peel back the golden veneer and appreciate the life of a man who lived through some of the most seminal moments of the 20th and 21st centuries. Born in May of 1925, the Fon was brought forth into a world struggling to repair itself in the aftermath of the First World War. In 1929, he was merely a toddler when the world began its descent into the most harrowing economic crisis it had seen up to that point, the Great Depression. As the years went on, he watched as the flames of fascism began to rise, ultimately leading to the Second World War. During his youth, a dependent Cameroon was still under the colonial thumb of France and the United Kingdom. By 1959, when he was just thirty-four, he assumed his role as Fon of Mankon following the disappearance of his father, Ndefru III. Just a year after he began his reign, Cameroon gained independence. As we sit here now, in 2022, we look back on a reign older than the Republic of Cameroon itself.

My grandfather did not expect his crown, but when the time came for him to assume it, he rose to the occasion. As I reminisce on his life and legacy, I see that he truly lived up to the reputation of his namesake, King Solomon. As with Solomon, the Fon shall always be remembered for his poise, his eloquence, and his wisdom. Just by hearing his name, it only made sense that he became who he did. With a statuesque figure and a commanding voice, he did not need to say much. His presence demanded the attention, respect, and admiration of any who encountered him. Some rulers are made, some are born. He was the latter. It was only destiny that he was King.

As the years passed, and his contemporaries joined the other side, he remained: a mountainous paradigm and cherished relic of the Greatest Generation. While our hearts are heavy, we can find solace in his legacy. While the body may be gone, the soul, the lessons and the memories live on for eternity.

Grandchild,

Anye Taboh Angwafo

In many symbolic ways, HRH has always offered an important sense of cultural pride and rootedness. Growing up, no trip to Bamenda was ever complete without a visit to the Mankon palace.

As children, there was a lot to be excited about. My sisters and I often anticipated eating achu on the banana leaves (which we considered more authentic) and always hoped we'd persuade our parents to give us a sip of their palm wine. Nervously, I would also brush up on my Mankon, practicing with my mother the standard responses to various greetings and small talk. At some point, as the conversation progressed, I would get found and would stare blankly at HRH (much to his amusement) in the hope that my confusion would give cause to have pity on me and continue in English. The most enduring impact on my relationship with HRH is the importance he placed on education. He always took great interest in our educational progress and every visit was an audit on educational achievement. I am sad that I've been unable to share with him fully my journey of education and self-cultivation. I am sad that my grandfather only ever got to meet my wife and her family through pictures. And, given the importance he placed on education, I regret that I won't be able to show him my Ph.D. degree certificate. While I know education is a life-long journey, this achievement, feels in many ways the culmination of the values he instilled in me.

Grandson,

Anye-Nkwenti Nyamnjoh

Looking back, I had several fond memories with the Fon (my grandfather). But what stood out to me the most, on my last encounter with him, was his wise and courageous presence, as he sat on his throne. He leaves behind an extraordinary legacy.

Arkan. Akwa. Tawbargh I

Njuilane! Ngwa Mankon, Mukong tse'eh ankara! Tribute to Fo Angwafo III of Mankon

Present, alongside my father, Bernard Ngwa Zamngang, at the ceremonial "shooting" of Fo Angwafo III at the Mankon Palace, and again at his first public appearance at Ntahbag (current site of Mankon Market), I had the singular good fortune to be an eyewitness of Fo Angwafo's ascension to the throne in 1959.

In my various personal interactions, as a loyal subject, with His Royal Highness Fo Angwafo III, I found in him a visionary personality with a ripened sense of humour, a sage imbued with wisdom. Calm and majestically poised among his people, Fo

Angwafo III, leader of the Mankon Kingdom, always listened, weighed and considered, before proffering a way forward. He welcomed nationals from other parts of the country and encouraged a peaceful and a harmonious coexistence with the indigenes.

As an agriculturalist and a traditional leader, he embraced modernity while safeguarding and preserving the positive values of heritage, culture and tradition of the Mankon Kingdom. With competent dexterity, and a discerning statesmanship, Fo Angwafo III managed the dynamics of change spanning over six decades. From a colonial to a post-colonial era, combining chieftaincy and democracy, navigating through the deep and tumultuous waters of a one-party system to multi-party, Fo Angwafo III stood tall and unequivocally demonstrated a statesmanship unrivalled by his peers.

Indeed, with Fo Angwafo III at the helm, from 1959-2022, the times, events and the personality had coincided and he worked tirelessly to serve and has bequeathed a testimonial legacy of the Fondom of Mankon to posterity - his people, Cameroon, and the world.

His "disappearance" marks the end of an era and the enthronement of the new Fon, the start of a new dawn. Undoubtedly, we will sorely miss Fo Angwafo III. "Ngwah Mankon, Mukong tse'eh ankara".

AsandomZamngang
Nitop - Mankon

King Angwafo III, Solomon AnyeGhamoti Ndefru III, Fo Mankung

Born on tiger skin the twenty-first of May,
You bid bye same twenty-first of May,
In the cherry blossoms' aroma of May,
Your love and compassion left to us this day,
You call one and sundry to celebrate today,
The rebirth, rebrand of society this day.

Blue-blooded, although blood and mood were never blue,
Affable, jovial, often clad in royal blue,
Children, women and men stuck to you like glue,
Your generation say you were born to rule,
A glorious sixty-three year dynasty so true,
You worked your farms with the mule,

Through challenges and changes you will pull,
So, the harvest was almost always full.

Nurtured unlike the prince in the school of life.
Your dynasty began as it ended in strife,
In the struggle for identity, for freedom,
Man of exception, man of every season,
On your ninety-seventh you made your transition.

Never a moment, time or space for boredom.
 You catered for all, the sick, infirm or in prison,
Shared solace, moral or physical to all citizens,
Ruled with heart, mind and reason.
Great patriot you abhorred treason.
Faulted for unconditional loyalty,
You remained true to pristine royalty,
Respected for independence of mind,
Loved for devotion to kind.
Disciplined, you honoured man and time
Or rather you were honoured by time
Fought against decline and crime,
With all your might until the last dime.

You blended the hidden past and the present,
Brought harmony to the cross and crescent,
Stood for right and principle,
Notwithstanding the diversity of decibel,
In the humanity of our great Nation,
Towering in the concert of nations.

The curious uninitiated come to peep
At NUSHUIM you reign so deep
Your assignment as stiff as steel
The promise in perpetuity we keep
Your union with our forebears we feel
Our past, present and future we feed
In union we will conquer need.

Fare thee well loving father of fathers
Sail to the abode of our forefathers
With God protect us and our new father

Together we will nurse our mothers
Nurture and sustain our sisters
And keep the fraternal oath of brothers.

King ASAN fare thee well until we meet to part no more!

Asanji Fru Fobuzshi Angwafo III
The Duke

MANKON, it is with nostalgia that I write but full of gratitude to have witnessed and learnt the lesson of punctuality from Fo Angwafo III. I vividly write as if it were just yesterday, memory of someone whose first encounter was thirty-five years ago as president of MASA (Mankon Students Association) Yaoundé chapter in 1988.

Fo Angwafo III and MASA, various bodies of students, was a perfect symbiosis, I talk vividly about Fo Angwafo III and MASA, Yaoundé branch especially. It sounds like just yesterday, but this is 35 years ago. His active and effective support towards the Mankon student's body cannot be overemphasized, I testify as president then of MASA Yaoundé chapter particularly 1987-1988 in Yaounde when the great leader Fo Angwafo III personally attended MASA activities that culminated with a gala at inside Ngoa Kelle, the University Campus hall.

Prior to the gala, it was organized a session that afternoon where Fo Angwafo III gave mie to a host of students and even some Mankon residents of Yaoundé gracefully. At these two important events in the life of MASA Yaoundé chapter, it was punctuality to the letter. And Fo Angwafo III communed with his in a full-to-capacity hall of students and some elites of Mankon in Yaoundé at the time. He was very punctual for the event leaving me embarrassed, as the students instead were late comers.

Thank You Mbeh, You Will be remembered forever.

Dr. Asongwe Mathias
(Then Yaoundé MASA president)

My name is Atrouafor Angwafo Francis Azinwi. 'Time and tart wait for no man'. These words will last forever in my mind. What of you? What of us? His Majesty Fo S.A.N. Angwafo III said this quote to me on November 7th, 2007, at the Baltimore International Airport, U. S.A. There are many occasions he had said words of inspiration , empowerment and most of these words, sayings have inspired me to get to higher heights in life, since childhood. I am a physical and sports education professor, now a U. S. A. Citizen, performing protective security services at the Department of Education in downtown Washington D.C. in the United States of America. I visit Mankon palace my birthplace every end of year since 2012. On December 17th 2012, I landed at Alankyi with my son Anye Reagan Angwafo Atrouafor only to be surprised by a jubilant and smiling Fo Angwafo III say 'Obama, (*yeng sheena*) come good. He then turned to Anye and said 'm' akiante zerna l'mbo bien ge'. (I am preparing all these for you). On August 23rd , 2018 that we paid another visit to the palace he told me from nowhere that " the child is the old man's walking stick'. "You've been caring for your mothers, thank you" Continue "I had always remembered what we were taught in Teacher Training College" "The Child Is The Father Of Man" That is why my mind and soul, HE is still around until and after.

In Mankon Palace none of my mothers, siblings both male and females Will Ever Live In Lack. I shall do all in my entire life to prove this message. The spirits of my ancestors are what I personally pledge allegiance.

Atrouafor Angwafo Francis Azinwi

When a great king who has left his mark on his people and on his nation disappears, there is hardly any tribute any one can write that will sufficiently give him the honour he rightly deserves. However, I will attempt to do just the little bit that I can in a way that I personally perceive in his actions.

HRH, the Fon of Mankon was a wise ruler and a very savvy politician whose actions were directed towards the progress of his people, and he had a knack for bringing his subjects together. From his days as Parliamentarian in the then West Cameroon, his actions and focus were always to protect the interest of his people and the West Cameroon Nation. His political idioms were such that one had to think hard to understand what they meant, and he did that on purpose. His approach to any situation was never a one-sided approach regardless of the events and situations of the time. He was in the loop of everything and understood the consequences of one-sided leanings. I have over the years had several close conversations with him and each time I came out with an understanding that indicated his wisdom.

As a young man growing up, I was made to understand that the Fon never attended funerals, but I must say that I was and still to date, very grateful that HRH graced the celebrations of my late Dad with his presence and our entire family will ever remain indebted to him. He did it not once, but twice when he joined us in the celebrations of our late brother, Nicholas Nji Asongwe and for that there are no words to express our gratitude. And to crown it all, we are extremely honoured that he made my home in Chicago, his Palace away from home during his tour of the United States in 2008 and we look forward for an opportunity to continue to play that role for the future King. May HRH rest peacefully in perpetuity among his ancestors.

Michael Nde Asongwe

On building a fence: to princes and myself at the Fon's farm at Fumdvu in the early 1970s currently occupied by the Airport.

"You do not ask another person to sharpen a pole for you to insert in the ground, you must do both because in the classroom you don't ask someone to write for you." *Fo Angwafo III, 1973.*

At the end of a full day's work.

"Isn't today's work completed? We now await tomorrow's." *Fo Angwafo III, 2002.*

On borrowing or asking for help, money matters.

"When you ask someone for help, money matters, and you received it, understand that person did not save that money for you, he merely foregoes the current use of that money." *Fo Angwafo III, 2007.*

On expecting future help from someone.

"When someone promises you a favour, keep on moving ahead as you explore other options, you don't sit and wait." *Fo Angwafo III, 2007.*

The above tribute highlights my respect and gratitude for Fo Angwafo III. A manifestation of my interaction with him over the years and particularly during the HRM double visits to the United States of America.

May His Soul Rest in Heaven.

Pa Nkumfo Atsu Atanga-Tabah, PhD
Resident in the United States

Happy birthday to my father, king, mentor, preacher, Teacher, supervisor, legend, Agricultural Engineer, Nation builder, the monument of Cameroon history, my day and night watchman, Fo of the Mankon people; your legacy lives on.

Daddy, I couldn't have asked God for a better father than you. You nurtured, raised, and empowered me to be what I am. Upbringing without you for a day will mean I have no life. Daddy, you raised us not as princes and princesses, but as your sons and daughters. You took royalty away from us and I applaud you for that, for it has made us what we are today. The bible says, "happy is the man whose barn is full of children for he can never be defiled at war." My legend you have raised soldiers who will defend your legacy.

Upon graduation with a Vocational qualification Diploma in Hotellerie; I intended setting up a restaurant, you insisted I further my education abroad to become the best chef to handle your class of guests. I fulfilled all admission requirements in five different schools and gained admission in four. But at the time of departure daddy, you changed your mind and asked me to manage your animal farm. I cried for a couple of days and later obeyed. That is how you brought me into livestock. I managed your piggery and poultry farm for five years and with your mentorship I became an expert and have trained so many graduates who have passed through me on internship. I have emerged the best broiler producer for the region for three consecutive years. Daddy, I want to assure you that your cry of no one taking over agriculture from you ended the day I accepted to join you in farming because I shall never relent.

Daddy, I watched you and my mothers struggle to cater for your millions of guests daily and being a professional cook brought relief to you all as I catered for all your guests. Thank God I was able to put a smile on your face in this aspect. In my journey as a musician, my daddy my source of inspiration. I watched you counsel your cabinet, the Mankon people stressing on and emphasizing that *"unity is strength."* I thought I could contribute by spreading your message far and wide and I came up with the album titled "mukong tse'eh a nkare" during your fiftieth anniversary and daddy you embraced this vision and became the key dancer in this album. Daddy you are a charismatic dancer, your moves have always been peculiar.

Not leaving out health, you have always ensured I have the best health attention. Daddy in all your care and love, you never spared the rod to spoil the child. Daddy, you have always referenced God first in all you do and have been my inspiration in Serving God and

I promise never to look back. I miss you king Solomon the wise of Mankon asking me the message of the day after service every Sunday. Rest on.

Daddy if there is anything that makes me celebrate your life in thanksgiving is God for fulfilling one of your many wishes. You have always wanted to get a tractor to help our mothers with farm work as they are growing weaker and by the grace of God, I, through your farming group Akongne ndwii Mezam common initiative group; I wrote a project in 2018 through ACEFA and it was realized in 2021; which brought a Tractor and it's accessory and a dry house for maize. Daddy, I am glad you received this Equipment and blessed it, even though you didn't watch my mothers and myself till with it, I assure you we will work hand in glove to mechanize farming in the Mankon Fondom.

My Hero, your last words to me in April 2022 are keeping me awake. *"Oh, my daughter I would have loved for you to come from your home to celebrate my life, but God kept you here for a purpose, to take care of me; I am grateful. I'm ready to join my ancestors! Ensure that anyone who steps foot here should eat and drink; cook and hire more cooks to add to yourself for the whole world will be here. Slaughter animals and feed people. And above all God has called me to serve him don't relent."*

Daddy, I learned from your life the joy of raising your children well and catering for the family. Your children did their best, the doctor's offered the best care, our mothers burned the midnight candle to ensure you had the best care, but it was the almighty God's appointed time to call you to rest. My bestie: I celebrate your life in thanksgiving and will do my best despite all odds to ensure that your last wish is fulfilled. You have taught me tolerance, calmness and to be focused. That I shall maintain. Daddy may your journey be smooth. For your legacy lives in me.

Your daughter,

Awah Angwafo Vera (Alias Petite Angwa)

The Gigantic Legend

On an afternoon in 1967 a Volkswagen stopped and hooted by the roadside of our Ntarinkon residence. I ran up and a "man mountain" in traditional regalia stepped out. I thought he was going to engulf me, so I took to my heels.

Surprisingly, he asked his guard to call for me. I came back petrified and trembling and he called out in a soft angelic voice

"Ndefru, are you afraid of your son"? I was born when my father was teaching at Ntingkag, so, the Mankon Palace calls me" Fo Ndefru" - his father . That was my first encounter with the Fon of Mankon. He owned the only corn mill in rural Mankon and my father had left corn there for milling. The Fon in his majestic humility came to deliver the flour in person.

Years later, I became his personal physician and entered places in the Palace uncommon for ordinary folks like me. I therefore had the opportunity to imbibe his wisdom on several occasions. In addition, I had the rare honour and privilege to be a Master of Ceremony at the 50th Anniversary of his enthronement and also host the "Palace" in our home during a granddaughter's wedding.

Legends and Fons never bow out, they only transition. His smiling, charming, broad, fatherly face may be away physically, but is engraved in our hearts forever. His frame was directly proportional to his charisma, wisdom, intelligence, memory, vision, experience, magnanimity, dynamism, wit and statesmanship.

Long Live Fo Solomon AnyeGhamot Angwafor III of Mankon!

Long live Fo Angwafor the III, who towers over the Wise King Solomon in the Holy Book.

Dr. Awasom Charles Nde

A true leader is born, not made. His Royal Highness Fon Angwafo III was a great leader, a charismatic one for that, a leader who treated everyone equally, male or female, man or woman. My mother is a good example, she had the opportunity as a Mankon woman to participate in the development of the Mankon Kingdom as Councillor. His Royal Highness Fon Angwafo III was a role model of a king.

Awondo Fru, Harrison

1. Fon Solomon III

He depicts greatness at first sight:
 He is a great figure in structure,
His nature commands reverence,
His personality sends waves to the spinal,
Many tremble before he would speak,
He is honourable at creation!

He is a king to a people called "Ngemba";
He is king of a people called Mankon,
He is one of the kings in a town called Bamenda,
He is one of the Famous in a country called Cameroon,
He was King at conception!

Often called Angwafor the III;
He is a Royal Majesty
A Royal Majesty in words and deeds
He is all rounded Royal
Likened to the Biblical Solomon
He speaks wisdom to his people often
He is Royal and Majestic per se.

The Fon is a king who loves justice/
He passes fine sound judgments on his subjects.
He has no law enforcement officers yet.
His judgments are enforced straight away.
They thrive because they are clever,
The Fon is attuned to rare wisdom,
His judgments are equitable,
He is a King of justice.

What a Fon you are my King!
Being an only son,
Yet you emerged a father of multitudes,
Husband to a fleet of wives.
Yet he is up to the tedious task,
He is therefore father to many nations,
He was groomed King from start.

He is a King that thrills his subjects:
Angwafor dances amidst his people,
During his famous yearly traditional dance festival,
He entertains and inspires his people gracefully.
He shakes up to every admiration,
This he, does his majestic figure notwithstanding
He is king for his people.

Azah Jackline Chey

2. On The Phone With The Fon

On the phone with the Fon
Is it honour or fun?
Tradition shakes hands with innovation
Yet tradition is not offended
My Mum still spoke in all reverence
Hands on the mouth
Bowing down from the waist
And the chorus remains "Mbeh".

On the phone with the Fon
With no supervision from home
As far apart as Yaounde and Bamenda
Intact is the mode of talking to the Fon
Tradition refuses to succumb to modernity
The Fon of Mankon is Fon indeed
His Euphoria knows no boundaries
As the chorus remain "Mbeh".

Azah Jackline Chey

Words have failed me, Daddy!
It's like a dream that you have gone to meet your ancestors.
Father, with tears in my eyes, you were my last hope, as all the others had long gone to the journey of no return, (my mother and father). I never felt the vacuum because you made sure of it. I am now like a house without a roof.

Grandpa, who I am today is thanks to your unconditional love and care. With your presence in my life, Grandpa, I have never really felt like an orphan, because you gave me everything any father will give a child for them to be successful. I can't forget how you used to discipline us, teach us how to farm, especially during the holidays. My education has always been one of your priorities, not to talk of my health. I will never forget your words, "Bih, take care of your siblings". I promise, Papa, I am doing so with all my heart.

I really wish you could stay a little longer to enjoy the fruits of your labour. You were my guide, you provided me with all the tools necessary and I was just beginning to prove myself. It really hurts me, because I am almost there.

My siblings and I will miss you so much, Daddy. Our hearts bleed.

May you find rest in the bosom of the Lord, father.
May your spirit never depart from us.
In Jesus' name, Amen.
Adieu, Papa.
Granddaughter,

Bei Kelly

HRH Fon Angwafo III was a man I respected and admired most especially on account of his achievement in ensuring that the Mankon people obtained good and solid education at all levels. Looking at the number of schools in Mankon village and city at large, speak for themselves. He made Mankon a force to reckon with when it comes to prestigious schools in Cameroon as a whole.

Coming from a family that has ties with the palace, I have had a few personal encounters with him. The following two encounters with him were outstanding:

In June 2007 during my father's funeral, he was there in two capacities: as the Fon and as an in-law. As the Fon, he would have spent less than an hour, but he did not use his position as the Fon to shorten his stay. He considered the fact that he was an in-law and spent about 3 hours at the funeral to the amazement and admiration of everyone. He danced several times and even went as far as performing the "Mii" ceremony which benefitted some of us who had not had the opportunity of participating in it at the palace. This showed me another side of him that I could never have imagined: his simplicity, humility and consideration.

In January 2014, my siblings and I visited Cameroon for a family get-together and went to seek for his advice on a family matter. The wisdom he exerted and fatherly advice he gave us is cherished till this day. He actually saved my family from a calamity that could have befallen us, had we gone ahead with our naïve plans without seeking his advice. He was patient with us and helped us to understand his viewpoint with historical facts.

Go ye well, great king! The legacy you left behind will be cherished and remembered forever. You were indeed a great HERO who had the best interest of your people at heart.

Benardine Aghanwi Ngu-Nnoko

To the world you are a father but to me you are the world.

Not how you died but how you lived. Not what you gained but what you gave. These are the units to measure the worth of a man like you daddy.

So rare was a dad like you, your loving smile, and gentle laugh made all the difference in my day. Your endless wisdom and timeless advice always helped me find my way. Your sense of discipline led to my sense of accountability, integrity and responsibility. It's an honour to have shared stories and dreams. A father to the entire nation. Your love and kindness put a smile on many faces both home and abroad. I remember how generous and kind you were, my friends who were doing well in school but didn't have the means will always come to you and you will give them scholarship. You made sure they had what they needed to succeed. Everyone is proud to have had a dad in you "Mbeh"!

If I could write a story, it would be the greatest ever told. I could write a million pages but still be unable to say just how much I love and miss you.

In life I love you dearly
In death I love you still
In my heart you hold a place that no one could ever fill
Your wise counselling will help me sail through the ladder of life.
REST WELL MY HERO.... Adieu "Mbeh"'
Daughter,

Bi Angwafo Epse Nde Fonchingong

Tsazui Fo Mankon

My earliest memories of my father go back to him sharing mangoes from the garden with us. That was part of his princely life that took an abrupt end in April 1959. There were many of such idyllic days.

On becoming Fo Mankon, he set about with devotion and heft, tackling a broad range of challenges such as the acuity of housing in the palace, school enrolment, health and sanitation. This was not limited to the palace and its vicinity.

Fo Angwafo III spearheaded a vast Fondom-wide school enrolment campaign with a particular focus on the girl child. In this vein, the abolition of the Ashebbe was motivated by the prospect of better planning and the potential use of the increased income that families could generate by selling their produce.

Fo Angwafo III introduced a wide range of novel agricultural practices. For instance, he established paddocks of Guatemala grass that went a long way in solving the problem of fodder scarcity and dehydration of livestock during the dry season. He offered gainful employment to many on various demonstration and mass production farming projects. Holidaymakers who were engaged on his numerous projects had the opportunity to pick up skills and also earn money for their school needs.

Through the cooperation of the Mankon Area Council and the community the Mankon Health Centre was constructed. Its main focus was primary health care package notably mother and child care.

Fo S.A.N. Angwafo III has a profound impact on the socio-economic development of his people. He was a father to all. For this I am both thankful and proud. I miss you but am comforted in knowing that you are in the company of the rest of our ancestors watching and guiding us always.

Biawah Angwafo III

"Unto dust was man made and unto dust shall man return" Genesis 3:19. HRH Fo Angwafo III my hero was a force to reckon with. A million times I've needed you, a million times you have been there. A million times I've cried to you, a million times you've listened. You were a father to me and the Mankon people like no other. You nurtured us, showed unconditional love, instilled in us peace, Hard work, tolerance, endurance, truth, justice and above all thanks for educating the Mankon man. Your works will never die, you're so wonderful to think of but too hard to be without. My heart is broken. Now I know why you always asked me to be strong because the work of a princess is not easy when you will not be there. Beautiful memories of you will remain alive in my mind, heart and keep me going.

Adieu Papa
Your daughter,

Bih Joyce Epouse Kabba

A Poem in Honour of Fon Angwafo III

I remember,
Knowing that no one up until May 21st 2022 ever gave more meaning to the title of a king!

I remember,

In my days of MA.S.A that our gatherings and fun activities not only sparked meaningful conversations but also gave us, the Mankon students, a unique chance to reflect on our dreams!

I remember,

Not only were you a father to your biological children but a father to all!

All those privileged moments we shared together were open forums to continue to make ready the curious young men and women of communities in Mankon.

I remember,

Those regular nights in my family tradition when we made your name an intentional topic of discussion; we marvelled at your wisdom and greatness and the impact that your life embodied!

I remember,

I have been reminding myself that it's taken your kingly courage, your kingly strength and your kingly wisdom to keep the Mankon light shining!

Now, I feel reassured that it takes even greater courage to do things that no one else has done in your season!

So, I am not afraid of this next chapter because the good thoughts about your reign will always abound!

Love was the very essence of your majestic being and the same love will continue to be the very essence of the Mankon people!

Long live the King of Mankon!

May our Almighty Father continue to bless the Mankon People!

Bih M. Akenji

Dear Grandpa,

I didn't get to know you and see you that much, but I heard amazing stories about you. I even remember when I came to Cameroon and visited the palace, I remember fearing your dog. After I grew up, I was not afraid because I had learned to face my fears and when I heard that your dog passed away, I was sad because I faced my fears with the dog. I was so pumped to play with him when we came back to Cameroon, but he was gone.

When we were at the palace, you would always talk to us. (Btw I don't remember anything he said because I was 2 at the time) Mimi (aunty Lum) told me that when I was little, I will always put my hands in my mouth, and you will say "take your hands out of your mouth because it has germs and could make you sick". You were so sweet and generous to me as I now watch the videos daddy took.

You always carried me and Frunwi on your laps and told us stories, showed us around the palace and even gave each of us our own pet chicken. We left your presence every day with lots of presents. I am so blessed to look back at these videos and pictures that I have such a caring, kind, and loving grandpa. I'm so happy that I got to meet you when I was two years old for the few months, we spent in Cameroon with you.

Grandpa guess what, in 2023, daddy's apartment complex will be finished and there will be a grand opening. I'm going to be sad that you are going to miss it but at least you will see it in heaven!

Bye grandpa,
Love from your Granddaughter Bihnwi:
Forever be missed.
Granddaughter,

Bihnwi Blair Angwafo

My great-grandfather was an educator, a farmer, a politician, the Fon of Mankon, but most important of all, he was a great person. Even though I only have a few memories of him I will hold them close to my heart. Our visits to the palace were the most memorable aspect of my visits to Cameroon. I remember to get to the palace, we had to ride on a bumpy dirt road, which sometimes made me car sick. There was dust in the air as we drove and a weird gas smell that made my tummy uneasy.

When we got there, I remember sitting on his lap as a young child. While he talked to me, I couldn't help but smell the nice rich earthy smell he had which smelled much better than the smell on the road. I also remember his dog, which I loved playing with. Sometimes he gave us soft drinks that were very refreshing, my favourite being "Djino", a grapefruit soda I have only had in Cameroon. I wish I was able to see him more and spend more time with him because when I look back at all the pictures, we look so happy and cheerful. I just wish that I could relive those moments where I can be happy and cheerful with my great-grandfather.

Sadly, I can't do that anymore, for he has disappeared. Nonetheless, I will always remember him and keep him and his memory close in my heart.

Your great-granddaughter,

Bi-Neh Mishi Awantang

111

A Humble Fon, A Rare Fon

It gives me great pleasure to speak on this motion on behalf of late papa Fru Nche Sylvester's eldest daughter, of Ntambeng Mankon. I convey our heartfelt sympathies to the new Fon, Fon Angwafor IV and the entire Mankon Fondom.

Fon Angwafor III was such an iconic figure who left an indelible mark in the lives of the Mankon people, the Forcob family, and the Fru Nche family of Ntambeng opposite the Catholic Church. As holidaymakers on vacation in Ntambeng, I used to see from the veranda of Pa Fru Nche's residence this illustrious personality sitting at the back of his jeep, passing from the palace to or from Mankon town. When asked, I was made to understand he was the Fon of Mankon. I cherish some of the privileged occasions I directly experienced his leadership. His sense of judgment, dignity, and humility struck me as he put you at ease, and made you feel special.

I remember some of the encounters my family and I had with him which made me experience his greatness; because of his great confidence in late Pa Fru Nche Sylvester, he was behind his last appointment as a member of the Ngemba customary court in Old Town Bamenda. Stopping by the roadside in front of our house to have a conversation with my maternal grandmother Mami Agatha Muma (of late), whom he had known in Bambui many years before his reign, described who he was. Recognizing me as a Forcob daughter, the label of our extended paternal family, during a visit with my late father-in-law Pa Isaac Tassang and spouse Dr. Andrew Tassang paid to the Mankon palace in 1992, made me perplexed. He then asked Pa Tassang about the land dispute he had at his SONAC Street Mankon Town residence. I marvelled at his retentive memory.

In 2015 during the Mankon Cultural Development Association (MACUDA) general meeting, which brought Tiko, Buea, and Douala together at Brasseries Club Mutengene Buea Road, I felt special when he sent for me for a brief talk with him. The highest tribute we, the Fru Nche Sylvester family, pay to this great Fon of North West Region of Cameroon is the preservation of the value of humility we do cherish. You were indeed an epitome of humility.

I am proud to be a daughter of the great Land of Mankon, and I promise Papa Fru Nche's Sylvester children and grandchildren will be loyal to the new Fon, Fon Angwafor IV.

Celestina Neh Fru Tassang
Associate Professor of Sociology
University of Buea

HRH Fo S.A.N. Angwafo III, has called us to celebrate the end of his sixty-three-year dynasty on the throne of Mankon. A Nobel and great leader he was during this journey; He was author of the book, *Royalty and Politics: The Story of My Life*".

My earliest memory of my father-in-law dates back to December 1984. I travelled from the United States, with my husband, his son, Fru F. Asanji Angwafo III, and our three young children to take part in his historic NI-KWI celebration of 25 years on the throne of Mankon.

I remember how excited I was about this visit because it was my first time to Africa, the motherland and also because he was the King of the Mankon people. I had never met a King before and of course this involved many traditional protocols to which I was being introduced. The Fon, was a towering and impressive figure, dressed in his traditional attire, and he had a strong presence with a command of respect and that, he was given by all around him. I was a bit nervous, however, to my surprise he was very welcoming, conversational and overjoyed to meet his first grandchildren and I, their mother. Of course, after they were born, he named all of them according to tradition. My son, his first grandchild bears his name.

Immediately, I had to start learning the traditional system of rules, which were many, but I followed suite and although I made mistakes, he overlooked them. I had just met an African King, which was very different and historic for me. During the rest of my two weeks stay I saw the Fon as a father. The programmed celebrations spanned over several days and it was grand with a vast display of the rich Mankon heritage and culture on display, At the end of it all, and before our departure, my family and I were blessed traditionally by the Fon, our father.

Six months later, I returned to Cameroon for good and now, with four children, as I was an expecting mother with my third daughter during the trip. Over the next almost forty years of my stay and connection to Cameroon, my experiences and interactions with the Fon, were always one of a father and daughter. I soon learned that he was the father of all, a role he carried out so well as he embraced humanity with a deep level of understanding and helping those in need and making many others his family. I often wondered how he managed so many and carried out his other daily responsibilities as a father, farmer, paramount traditional leader, trouble-shooter, community builder and statesman. However, he did this well, and much more, as he worked untiringly, for his people from the grassroots in many uplifting efforts.

He had a profound passion for farming and animal husbandry, and he toiled the soil all the way into his twilight years. I was privileged in seeing him mentoring, coaching and instilling civic and community pride into the young ones he nurtured. He was a leader who bridged gaps and strengthened families.

His majesty, Fon S.A.N. Angwafo III, had a thirst for knowledge, learning, and development. He was a visionary leader who enabled many philanthropic groundworks for the educational development of schools, university, and health care facilities, to improve upon the social network of the people and communities of the North-West Region. As the times ebbed away, he was always adapting but he never compromised his traditional outlook and roles. He documented the story of his life, which also helped me and many others, to appreciate and understand his complexed journey.

Sixty-three years of a great journey in which he pledged and ensured that peace reigned during this dynasty. He ruled with his heart but concerted to reason as he built bridges around him and maintained brotherly love with his neighbours. How, fortunate I was to witness, partake and better understand the significance of many traditional celebrations, blessings and marriages in which my children partook. He was a great orator to whom I am thankful for the stories and history lessons passed on. The Mankon Palace museum is a masterpiece of rich cultural heritage and is second to none, in Cameroon.

Above all, I'm grateful for being blessed in carrying out very dutiful roles in his life as one of his children.

Rest well HRH S.A.N. Angwafo III, great leader, father, mentor, farmer, statesman and *keeper* of Mankon sacred rites and tradition. Your sixty-three-year journey of a great era filled with love, hard work and humility, will always be celebrated.

Charmaine P. Angwafo

There is the season for everything under the sun and this is the season of renewal, for new beginnings where the earth springs to a rebirth in joyful jubilation.

HRH Solomon AnyeGhamoti Ndefru Angwafo III, ruler of Mankon calls us to a celebration.

The end of a dynasty of sixty-three years on the throne, years filled with mastery and great history.

Let the trumpets sound, for the Father of all, mentor, teacher, orator tells us; sixty-three years and no more on this journey.

Sadness we feel as great memories must flow, but a rebirth is here and new seeds must grow.

Beat the drums for an illustrious father, farmer, historian, and nation builder;

Holder and caretaker of sacred rites and tradition, counsellor and bridge-builder; oh, what shall we render?

Play the harps and violins in honour of a statesman, one who worked from the grassroots to build his nation;

He stood for the rights of many, in all kinds of season, and within disputes, ruled with his heart but concerted with reason.

Ruling and managing seemed natural to this leader who hailed from the great school of lifelong learning,

What a long and historic journey, all filled with such great meaning.

Oh, what a beacon of hope and light, that shone through the darkest night

Yet a farmer he was, who continued his toil beyond his twilight.

Fon of Fons, great leader, with a mind so diverse, always so ready for the next discourse.

Dance the royal dance for a great Father of many, a role he did so well, indeed he was very Noble.

One who embraced humanity, as he welcomed and called so many, family.

Long live HRH, Fon Solomon AnyeGhamoti Ndefru Angwafo III, Long live a well-earned legacy, long live his great teachings and memories.

Charmaine P. Angwafo

Oh! My dear father the educator, if I can write my name today, it is thanks to you. You are forever in my heart. I join the world today to celebrate your triumphant entry to eternity.

Your son,

Che Cletus Awa

Dear Mbeh, your loss has been so hard to bear.

Dear Mbeh as my tears fall, I think back to times long gone when you would be the strength that my life was built upon.

I remember all the happiness you brought throughout the year and, although they are the sweetest memories, I can't stop my tears.

You were always my protector- my advisor and my guide. And life could never be the same without you to walk beside.

So, Mbeh as I pay this visit to your resting place today, I'd like to thank you for the caring that I never could repay.

Your Child and successor to late,

Chi Henry Ndefru (Alubalah)

Cheo Paul Ndefru

HRH Fo Angwafo III: The Sage

The word impossible defines the challenge of attempting to eulogise HRH Fo Angwafo III of Mankon in one page. In my personal opinion, his life and story can only be reasonably abridged in a capacious book.

If I were asked to encapsulate the Fon in one word, that word will be WISDOM. Wisdom in name and wisdom in nature as time after time he meted out this extraordinary gift to the immeasurable benefit of his people.

Although the Fon and I were related directly as first cousins, and shared the same grandfather Fon Angwafo II, we shared a particularly special relationship as confidants. It was a close relationship that came full circle in 1977 when I graduated from the University of Yaounde and subsequently when I returned from the University of London in 1982 with a PhD in Law. The news of my PhD success was received by the Fon with tremendous jubilation and celebration, reflective of a man who was an enthusiastic educationist and avid reader.

Whenever I visited the Fon at the Palace, I would often leave very late as we spent the moments talking away on all categories of issues which intersected law, sociology, religion, anthropology, education, management, tradition and culture. He was all-encompassing and neatly played the role of father, farmer, Fon and politician with such dexterity that left me in perpetual awe. He was my friend.

I benefitted from his benevolence and was knighted with the title Ndefru Atsum (meaning a place where people converge to fish – a fishing spot) in a grand ceremony in December 1998. He was

116

relentless in encouraging all who yearned for education as he firmly believed in the enlightenment of the Mankon man.

It was thanks to him that I was updated on matters that arose in the West Cameroon House of Assembly as he was a member of the House of Chiefs. I was also intrigued by his admiration for the oratory prowess of Peter Motomby-Woleta which he used to motivate my curiosity for savviness in public speaking.

My family and I were amongst the very few who were honoured by the Fon as he graced our humble home with his presence on very many occasions, often spending the night. This was an absolute pleasure for my wife and children who got to meet and interact with the Fon several times in person.

Nonetheless, like all great leaders, the Fon had his own detractors. This comes normally in politics and land ownership; hence he was not spared the trouble of contradiction. However, the manner in which he navigated and sailed through these challenges is another measure of his greatness and a lesson for the world.

To sum with brevity, the Fon embodied an unquestionably colossal persona the likes we may never see again. We, the people shall forever remain indebted to him for his wisdom, teachings, advice, and commitment to serve the people of Mankon and Cameroon as a whole.

Farewell Mbeh...

Prof Ephraim N. Ngwafor

A Royal Visit (Fo Angwafo III in Minnesota)

The years 2006 and 2007 were transformational for many reasons. First, the Mankon people in America, led by those in Minnesota, had decided to rekindle the flame of their umbrella organization, the Mankon Cultural and Development Association (MACUDA) America. Next, they organized a convention in 2006 that brought Mankon people to Minnesota to mark the rebirth of their organization. On the heels of this landmark achievement, the then Fo (king) S.A.N. Angwafo III of Mankon paid a surprise visit to his people in Minnesota in December 2007. The Mankon community in Minnesota at that time was youthful and not very conversant with the technicalities of hosting a royal visit. There was therefore much anxiety ahead and at the start of the visit.

Royalty is Simplicity

Needless to say, for those who knew Fo Angwafo III, he was of great stature. He dwarfed most people who stood next to him. His

117

stature and royal aura gave him a captivating persona to behold. During the visit to Minnesota, the local Mankon people did everything they could to bury their trepidation and increase their excitement. But once the Fo arrived, everyone realized that the anxiety that had gripped the community was unfounded. He held court and treated his people with exemplary simplicity. He would converse, crack jokes, laugh, and dance at every opportunity. But one incident, involving Mankon children, stood out clear during the visit.

The Father of Mankon Children

In one of the events that the king graced with his presence in Minnesota, the planned major points of the event were the elevation of some Mankon people to the position of Red-Feathered notables (*Beukum*) and the presentation of the new MACUDA Minnesota uniform to the king. However, no later had the occasion started than the children stole the show. The Fo had hardly mounted his throne than one of the children, with childlike innocence, broke loose and rushed straight into his arms. There was a gasp of bewilderment from the audience. What was going to happen? How would the Fo treat the child? Was there a breach of royal protocol and if so, what was the fine to pay or punishment to endure? Those questions and more were swirling in my head because guess what? The kid was mine!!! Her name was Miya!

A Giant Tree on the Field

Surprisingly, the Fo took the little girl in his big and warm embrace. He looked at the child lovingly. Spoke to her funnily. Stroke her hair gently. And most of all, he let the child tour his royal garb. She picked and explored a few embroideries on the Fo's Akohsi (the traditional gown famously worn by the people of Mankon and those of the Grassfields regions of Cameroon). The royal beads were not left out as Miya inspected each one of them. Many other kids soon joined Miya and for most of the time during that event, they never departed from the Fo. The king's charm and grace kept the kids around him like a magnet. Fo Angwafo III was a towering king with a gentle heart. Like a giant tree in the Savannah does to the animals of the fields, he provided comfort, protection, and rest to his people. Most of all, his love for children was unbridled, as the Mankon children in Minnesota were fortunate to find out.

Tangyie Elijah Che Munyong-abieri
(Fo Angwafo III in Minnesota)

The Royal Wind (Forever Blows)
(An Ode to Fo Angwafo III, and all the missing Fons of Mankon)

It was time to go, the ancestors beckoned,
Sixty-three years gone, that must be reckoned,
With all majesty, he took the final breath,
The body stayed, but the spirit left.

A mighty spirit, flew to the mausoleum,
In its sacred confines, a gathering awaited,
Every single royal, afore departed,
Acknowledged the arrival, of the Great One.

The ancestors, from Ndemagha,
Through Minwi Tingoreu, to Ndefru,
All twenty of them, on this special day,
As royals of Mankon, spoke without haste.

"What left you, for memory's sake",
"Unity and growth," Angwafo said,
"You did well. Now take your stool,"
And next to them, he sat as told.

Of a sudden, a gentle wind spanned,
From resting place, unto the land,
And covered it all, a royal embrace,
The land never, shall know disgrace.

The fields are green, the rivers rich,
The forests swell, with diverse beasts,
The rains plenty, the sun shines too,
And Mankon knows, Angwafo looks!!

Tangyie Elijah Che Munyong-abieri

Thank You Father
Mbeh,
I thank God for you, for your thoughts and deeds.
Words cannot convey what you mean to us.
Rest in peace.
Your Daughter,

Elizabeth Manka-Mafo Angwafo III

To my father-in-law…
There once was a man I admired
A man who cared
A man who shared
A man who knew life as it may seem
A man who was generous to all
A man with wonderful children
This man was a dad
This man was a grandfather
This man was great KING
This man was my father-in-law
This man is gone to rest.
And I'll wait for so long
Until the day I'm with him
With him up there
Where the lights are dim
And where I can show him my appreciation
that I've always cared.

Pa, I call you a great king because that is what you really are, more than words can describe. In your lifetime you made impossible things very possible because you practised hard work, perseverance and steadfastness. You approached every issue with tactfulness and wisdom, as a young Mankon man, you laid a very solid foundation for us by the values you inculcated as our King. You touched so many lives positively. When I first came into the royal family I didn't know what to expect, I was nervous and afraid but you gently eased my mind. You made me feel right at home from the first day we met, you welcomed me with open arms; that I won't forget. I was struck with such humility and love coming from a great Baobab, the greatest King Solomon. I couldn't have asked for a better father-in-law. Pa, you have been a great father to me and my family, thank you for raising such a beautiful and smart lady (my wife), I thank God for blessing me through you, we all love you but God loves you most. May you enjoy your stay in heaven, and may glorious rest be yours. Once more, I love you.
Son in Law,

Elvis Fonchingong

Once Upon A Leader: His Royal Highness Fon Angwafo III of Mankon

When news that His Royal Highness (HRH) Fon Angwafo III, had gone missing surfaced, like a brushfire in the savannahs, it quickly swept across the globe halting those who knew him in their stride, for his had been not only a long life but also a long reign on the throne of the Fondom of Mankon. It was obvious something major had happened, with people rushing to share or confirm what they had heard. The initial apprehension the news brought was palpable; it would seem the Fon's long life had made many to forget he would someday go missing. Yet it was true, fire had gone out of Mankon, even if only temporarily. Accordingly, I heard and read as many recalled and revelled about moments when they met, spoke with, or simply experienced this dignitary.

On my part, the first time I heard of him was in a song performed by a Mankon meeting group in Buea Town, sometime in 1964/65. My parents had taken me to this event where a family was celebrating the birth of a child and the group sang, giving thanks to "'Ngwa'fo," instead of the child's parents, and it struck me as strange. I wondered and questioned about this "'Ngwa'fo," only to learn from my dad that he was "our Fon," the Fon of Mankon, and my father spoke with so much pride and affection that it got planted on my mind. For a long time, our Fon, as my father put it, remained this mythical figure to me, until I was later to meet him in 1988 when I visited the Mankon palace during a research trip. I was to meet him again, many more times, especially during his different visits to the United States of America.

HRH Fon Angwafo III was an imposing and dignified personage, and after decades on the eminent, achieving, and distinguished throne of his forebears, one would have thought he would personify haughtiness and arrogance while being power drunk. On the contrary, he was down to earth and willing to grant audience to whomever, whether a citizen of his or not, and would never lose his calm during ensuing discussions even when the topic turned controversial. I experienced this of him when in 2010 or so, he was registering his dissatisfaction that, like many in the diaspora, I had left the country and seemed to be comfortable outside instead of returning home and giving a hand to our people. I was able to convince him that most of us are not away because we like it but are like Mankon citizens who have gone to the farm and must toil, plant, harvest, and then bring back home the fruits of our labour. I made him understand that we are aware of how much we are missing. For example, our parents get ill, and if we are fortunate, we visit momentarily and see them before they ultimately pass on, but we are not always that lucky, and so we return home briefly only to inter them, whereas, had things been otherwise and we were permanently at home, they would have transitioned in our arms, and our time spent serving our own people as he had wished. I also reminded him of the fact that a good number of us can and are doing what we can for our communities even from the diaspora. He agreed and indeed sympathized with my perspective. Like a great leader, therefore, he would not only engage his citizens about a particular situation and goal but would acknowledge it if he felt their perspective was in order. In like manner, with equal ease, he would remember the names of members of his Fondom he had met before who impressed him in one way or the other, or else he would easily recall with a slight hint.

This, without doubt then, was a leader committed to a higher purpose for his people, yet equally trying were the challenges he had to overcome to see this goal materialize. He started by protecting Mankon territory. He did this by making it hard, initially, for non Mankon people to own Land in Mankon, let alone be buried there. With foresight, however, realizing his village was growing exponentially in population and the cultural heterogeneity of the people flocking in, and understanding the benefits it would have on Mankon in the long run, he began relaxing this grip when he thought the time ripe, and the result is the enviable pluralistic city Mankon has become, but with his people firmly positioned in their territory.

With such changing demographics, to be accessible to his people HRH Angwafo III had an office on what is rightfully called, until today, Fon's Street. However, a mob that never understood the tight rope he had to walk as a member of the ruling political party and at the same time the traditional leader of Mankon, while trying to keep his people safe, burnt down this building during politically motivated uprisings in 1990. Not many of the cosmopolitan population he was now Fon of, given their presence in his Fondom, understood the caution with which he had to tread as a leader, and so expected tactless open declarations from him about political authorities. Even in this chaotic quagmire, when he and all he stood for were attacked and the annex of his palace-cum-office burnt down for political reasons, he never raised his voice indignantly, nor abandoned Mankon during the ensuing brutal state of emergency, not even when a full-blown war was declared against the entire region over a decade later, his Fondom being one of the major epicentres of military operations. Many failed to understand that frequently the decisions he had to make in the face of government, on the one hand, and his Fondom, on the other, called for profound discernment and enormous courage. On several occasions, therefore, he had to stand alone because of his convictions, the mark of a poised and determined leader in the face of detractors who are always present in the lives and ventures of such great men.

As a result of such towering socio-political exigences, HRH Fon Angwafo III, people argue, led Mankon during easily the most challenging epoch in the history of our attempted union as a nation. It was a time during which people had had enough, especially the marginalized English-speaking part of the union. As a nation, the entire country, especially the Northwest Province at the time, gave birth to struggles for true democracy and multiparty politics which, unfortunately, the government sometimes turned bloody. In the same vein, decades after, the Anglophone struggle in defence of the integrity of their institutions met with the declaration of war on them. These were, indeed, trying times as the Fon was caught between his people's desires and the government's, especially being a member of the ruling political party and having served in parliament for decades. To manoeuvre this situation well, it has been rumoured that Fon Angwafo III said one thing to the government but did a different thing when it came to his struggling people, to the dissatisfaction of the regime and some civilians who could not grasp his plight and perspicacity. Consequently, amongst other issues, it led to the government's declaration in 1990, of the so-called State of Emergency which was intended to teach the Province a lesson as the exercise was tantamount to a socio-political and economic chokehold. Even though this astute leader ended up being understood in the long run by most of the cosmopolitan population now occupying his Fondom and surrounding villages, it cost him so much in terms of property and his reputation which detractors always hungered to soil for selfish reasons as tension mounted with ephemeral political administrators trying to usurp his position and power as the traditional leader of Mankon. Nevertheless, Fon Angwafo III stood by his people and struggled to stem the tide to the very end.

As a true and exceptional leader, Angwafo III fought many battles in the background to maintain the territorial integrity of his Fondom, which is still under attack as malicious individuals struggle to side-line and relegate it to the background, despite its distinguished contributions in the migratory and settlement history of the peoples of the Bamenda Grassfields. These same characters have struggled to wipe out the name Mankon as nowadays it is almost always substituted with the "near meaningless" sobriquet, Bamenda. And so, interestingly, one will hear of Nkwen, Bali, Bafut, without hearing of Mankon, and where Mankon should have been obviously mentioned or written, it is "Bamenda" put in its place as if there is a traditional society called Bamenda. Indeed, but for the names of the neighbourhoods and the determination of Angwafo III, such malicious distortion of history could have prevailed totally. Yet listen to the names of some of the neighbourhoods in the heart of what detractors like to call Bamenda, instead of Mankon, and see what other proof is needed not only to expose their malevolence but to confirm the confines of this great Fondom Angwafo III had to administer to and protect effectively for decades until his transition: Akokikang, Ala'kuma, Ntamulung, Mulang, Musang, Ngomgham, Atuazire, Atuakom, and Ntarinkon, to name a few. It is not surprising then that in keeping with his struggle to uphold and accord Mankon her due, there was word going around that he once asked somebody from an institution in Mankon who came to invite him to an event on the school's campus which was said to be in Bamenda, instead of Mankon, to go and invite the "Fon of Bamenda" in his place. This was his subtle yet most effective way of decrying attempts at relegating the name of his Fondom in preference to "Bamenda." This Fon fought hard to keep the rightful name "Mankon" intact, like one would still hear of Nkwen, Mendankwe, Bafut, and Bali instead of its being replaced or at best used interchangeably with the moniker, Bamenda. Even the Lord Himself said, "Give to Caesar what is Caesar's" (Mt 22: 15-22), so let it be with Mankon and Angwafo.

And so, with these overt and covert challenges with which HRH Angwafo III had to deal, most of the decisions he had to make called for enormous courage which, in his always regal disposition and calm readiness, was never in want. It is this rare leadership quality of his that caused some to dislike and so try to defame him; hence, he sometimes stood alone when in his opinion his position was for the good of his people. It was having such strong convictions and being able to continue believing in and sticking with his people, the mood of the times, popular or unpopular in the face of detractors notwithstanding, that endeared him to many. Yes, there are so many conflicting views, some even damning of him as a leader, yet this would seem to me typical of such great leaders. The truth remains that he was human and therefore with the potential to err, for which reason he has had to suffer the effects of damaging comments proliferated about him, yet he was loved and respected by most of his citizens.

Beyond the overwhelming challenges at the home front, Fon Angwafo III forged on with his vision to position Mankon as a pathfinder and breakthrough people not only at home but abroad also. In this light, he made several trips oversees in a bid to link Mankon and what used to be the Mankon Urban Council, now decentralized, with Sister Councils overseas. He made it clear that with such unions and connections, such cooperating councils stood to benefit from each other. Again, he was part of the team that accompanied President Paul Biya to New Zealand when in 1995 the nation was accepted into the Commonwealth of Nations. He was a leader at home and abroad, therefore, as such endeavours confirm.

Here, therefore, was a leader who, like his predecessors, brought awe and respect to the dignity and authority of traditional leaders of the Bamenda Grassfields. He was a master when it came to pitting his people against hostile political authorities. As a result, his long tenure and life apart, people will remember him as a peace-loving leader who brought out the best, not only in Mankon people, but in all those with open minds who encountered him. With such an impressive background, armed with ambition, honesty, courage, and a delightful personality, it is not surprising he was greatly admired by his citizens, and those who understood his astuteness, even while being sometimes disparaged by those envious of him and his desire and ability to make his Fondom a key player and partner in so many ways. Achieving leadership like Angwafo III's is a lifelong endeavour, and it is attainable only with personal will and commitment to one's people as he demonstrated. His father, therefore demonstrated prescience in passing over the baton of the leadership of Mankon to him, as his tenure has, without doubt, proven. He had a vision for Mankon – keeping Mankon at par with the times – and did just that as he was able to make the people of Mankon believe in themselves, their dreams, and potentials, which instilled in them the will to succeed, the times and odds notwithstanding. His has been a long and challenging yet victorious reign as he epitomized dedicated leadership made manifest in his burning commitment to leave Mankon a better place. Like his predecessors, colossal in their achievements, he will be far from forgotten as his legacy will remain alive and well in those he served, those he inspired and in whom he stirred nascent potentials that worked for their good, that of Mankon, and beyond. All said and done, this was a great leader of a great people.

Emmanuel Fru Doh

To think that you are gone is simply a thought I fail to comprehend.

Who's going to gently laugh at me because I don't speak or understand Mankon?

Who's going to encourage me in school and remind me how smart I am and that I can do anything that I set my mind on?

Visiting you in the Mankon Palace was always a moment I looked forward to. Entering the different hallways and admiring the intricately designed statues and stools, wondering what each carving represents yet not daring to touch any. You always welcomed us with a lovely smile and hearty greetings, and we never left empty-handed. You took your time and spoke to each one of my siblings and I, and eagerly asked questions to learn more about our personalities. You were always concerned about our wellbeing and would send a bunch of plantains and chickens for Mami Ngu to make plantain chips for us to take to school.

Mbeh, you may not be here physically, but your legacy remains in each one of us. You taught us the importance of valuing and preserving our culture and you always wore our culture with pride. You celebrated with us, and you also mourned when we mourned. You were a father, grandfather, and great-grandfather who always took delight in his children and called us "the leaders of tomorrow."

As we bid you farewell and remember you in our hearts, we can only hope to be as gracious, kind, generous, articulate, and honourable as you were. Thank you for showing us what true leadership is.

Rest in Peace,
Your granddaughter,

Emmanuella Kiyieih Nyamnjoh

Today, I am remembering my dad and the great memories we shared. He provided for his family. He made sure his children had the guidance they needed. Dad was my hero. He was the most intelligent, courageous, and resourceful man I ever knew. Life is different without him, but I am grateful I got to call him my dad. One of my greatest memories with dad was when I invited him to the U.S.A. for the first time for my graduation from the college of pharmacy. After receiving my acceptance letter into the program in 1998, I called dad. He was happy and excited about my accomplishment. I told him that in 4 years, he will be coming to my graduation. He accepted the invite, but his biggest concern was leaving behind his responsibilities. I said "Dad, it's okay. You need a vacation because you have been working hard all throughout your life." And as he said and will always say, "Okay, by the grace of God." In 2002, I was blessed to send dad his itinerary to come for my graduation. It was a remarkable event. It was another version of the movie "Coming to America." Life is different without you, but I am grateful I got to call you, my dad. You will forever be in our hearts. Long live Fo Angwafo III S.A.N. (King).

Daughter,

Dr. Esther Angwafo Foncham

I find it very difficult as a blind man to describe an elephant very well by just torching a portion of it. My father survived as a lone child to my grandmother and became the heartbeat of our family, the Mankon fondom and village and a nation builder. As a sociologist, an economist, an agriculturalist and a person who lived generations before his peers, you made me the man that I am today. Because of your extra kindness and goodness as you fathered everyone who came to you without discrimination, God Almighty gave you all earthly rewards (long life and Abraham's blessings) above all, I am convinced that heavenly blessings you will receive. I used to tell people "take heart" but I never knew how it pains. Your grandchildren are asking me what happened to grandpa but I have nothing to tell them because you did not tell me. Old man, since you live in me your carbon copy, may you incarnate in me that I can do everything like you (objective, truthful and firm). Lord help me to thank you for these blessing bestowed on my father and family and to learn to accept your will until we meet in the heavenly choir. Adieu His Royal Majesty.

Son,

Professor Evaristus Ntoh-akoh Tsi-Angwafo III

The pain in my heart is more than I could fathom grandpa, you loved me from birth although I don't have any memories of it, right from the time I had complications from birth and was referred to Yaoundé for a surgery, I was told you visited me at the hospital and took care of me financially saying that nothing will happen to your grandson, I now understand why you gave me your name Solomon.

You showed me love and concern from birth, followed up my education from nursery school and gave me gifts of books and pens each time I came home with my results. When my mother and I visited you in Yaoundé in 2020 when you came for check-up, I came with my results of common entrance in flying colours, you were so happy with me and immediately gave 20000frs through my grandma to give my mother to take me immediately for interview at Sacred Heart College Mankon, to that effect, we travelled the next day for the interview, I did well at the interview and was admitted, currently in form three. My mother sustained a serious leg cut that same day from gunshots from the Anglophone Crisis, thank God my mother is a bit better now.

You will always say, "Oh my namesake, the big head with intelligence." grandpa I have been doing excellent as you taught me, rushing home since I must always present my report to you first, I saw everyone wearing sad faces and when I mentioned going to the palace to show my report card, news of your disappearance was broken to me that you are now with the angels. I recall it being announced in our school that you were missing but I didn't quite understand. It has now dawned on me that I will never see you again. oh no, as true as this is, you were my mentor, my real-life superhero, and my saviour from birth, how do I carry this big name now? I am alive all thanks to you, grandpa.

I promise you that as I continue to strive for success, in my educational pursuit, I will always remember your advice and will not disappoint you. I will be guided by the wisdom of SOLOMON and follow your exemplary footsteps and become the doctor you said I must be to take care of other kids as a" paediatrician"

I love and will miss you, grandpa. Rest well, I will take care of grandma and maintain the great name Solomon.

Your Grandson,

Fobisi Solomon Ndifor (Grandson)

My Name is Fon Emmanuel Ngang from Alamatu – a member of the Matroufon Clan, with our roots deep in Ndzummabueh.

Time is a double-edged sword. It gives and takes with the same effectiveness of purpose. We are witnesses of this double edged quality of TIME. Here we are just finished mourning the loss of our venerated Monarch His Royal Highness San Angwafor III, Time with its mystical quality is giving us the opportunity of celebrating the enthronement of not only A Chip Of The Old Block But The Old Block Himself!

I cannot pretend to say in here that I met with Fon Angwafor on several occasions. No, I did not but like every citizen of Mankon one did not have to meet him to feel his presence all the time. So, in a way most of us met him anytime we wanted even if not physically.

However, As God would allow it, I was blessed to meet and interact at a personal level with His physical presence in 1982 when I was elected President of the Mankon Students' Association (MASA). After my election I vowed to completely change Annual Cultural Week which the executive usually organized every summer holiday. The new program was to be a grand launching of that week at the Palace as opposed to the usual General meeting at Longla Commercial College Campus. So, we contacted the Fon's Secretary ad explained everything to him and he scheduled a meeting for us and the Fon at the Palace. God knows I had never met him at close quarters before and my deficiency in the language gave me the greatest fright I had ever experienced. The problem here now was meeting His Royal Highness to explain this new program and how it was supposed to be like. What kind of President is this who would not express himself in our language? This question was the demon rattling my mind. But I gathered courage and so early on that scheduled meeting day myself and some members of my executive arrived the Palace on time before His Highness could leave for the Town since he always had series of meetings almost on a daily basis all over the town.

I was really frightened because the program we had drawn up had never been attempted before by any executive of that Association. After a few minutes, he arrived in the reception hall and mounted his Throne as we all stood up to welcome him. He called me by name and I had to clear my throat because it seemed my vocal cords had suddenly rusted and no sound wanted to come out. But I managed to clear that stubborn throat. He did not have time for any long discussions with us. He requested to see our program for that day of

129

the launching. He glanced at it and saw that the SDO for Mezam was on the list of the invitees. He asked me if I had sent an invitation to the SDO but my head could not even move from side to side visibly enough to mean 'no', let alone an audible "No Mbeh". He continued to ask how I expected the SDO to know he had been invited to this program. I responded that I thought He would do that for us. He just laughed and asked me if he was the one organizing this program. And in his usual way of telling someone like me what to do he asked, "The students have chosen you as their leader and you surrendering your leadership to me Is that how it works Ngang?". I said No Mbeh. He ended up by saying the programme was good but we should be the ones to execute every item on the agenda as we planned. "You must start learning how to lead and not to be waiting for your parents to continue doing things for us until they die". That was the end of the meeting and that put us to work. But in the background He had arranged a deserving welcome for the SDO and his entourage - something we did not know had to be done. It turned out to be one of the greatest student gatherings ever to be organized by the students themselves in that Palace. And when the Fon Himself stood up to dance a few steps as the Mbaghalum from Asongkah was playing, it seemed Mankon was 'reborn' again that day. That is one greatest lessons I learnt from His Royal Highness. We grow up and learn by doing and not by asking for help from our elders and parents.

May His Great Soul Rest In Perfect Peace

Fon Emmanuel Ngang

To True Legend Fo S.A.N Angwafo III of Mankon who happens to be my Father

" Father" is the noblest title a man can be given. It is more than a biological role. It signifies a patriarch, a Leader, an exemplar, a confidant, a teacher and mentor, a hero and above all a friend." Your everlasting words that will stay with me at all times "Never Leave What You Can Do Today For Tomorrow, For Tomorrow Will Always Have Its Own Agendas."

Son,

Fondeh Angwafo

It is rather unfortunate that Pa Forngang Alphonsus Ndenge, who was the pioneer Chairman of the Mankon Traditional Council, is not here with us today. Incidentally, he left us last year at exactly the same age (97) as the disappearance of Fon Angwafor III of Mankon.

Being the great writer, researcher and promoter of the Mankon culture that Pa Forngang Alphonsus Ndenge was, he would definitely have been the right person to send in this tribute.

As children of Pa Forngang Alphonsus Ndenge, we remember some of the many great achievements that were performed under the collaborative efforts of our dad and HRH Fon Angwafor III of Mankon. In particular, we remember the great work those two put in the conception, and setting up of the Mankon Palace Museum which today stands out as a big tourist attraction and knowledge centre; and also, the reorganization and efficient transparent management of the different quarters in Mankon.

Mankon will always be placed honourably in the history books because of the creativity of their great minds, and the vulgarization of our traditions through writings and the organization of cultural events. Mankon Palace Museum will forever stand there to tell the stories of our people.

Those great minds have done their own bit, diligently, and have passed on the baton. Their vision for sustaining our culture will be seen by generations to come.

We stay extremely grateful to them.

The Family of Pa Forngang Alphonsus Ndenge

To My Father, Teacher, Protector, Mentor, Hero, HRH Fon S.A.N Angwafo III

To My Father, Teacher, Protector, Mentor, Hero, HRH Fon S.A.N Angwafo III Daddy! Daddy! Daddyyyy! Where are you? I cannot say and will not say that you have left us. You are just away with a cheery smile and a wave of hand showing us that you wondered in an unknown land and left us dreaming how very far you are and still showing us the love and care like you have always done.

Daddy, I will write the rest of my life if I have to describe the kind of man you were. You were a king, a father, a mentor, educator, teacher who lead by example. I can go on and on and I will never find enough words to describe you. I cannot be silent or play silence to hearing that voice which keeps echoing every minute "mantoh manghie! mantoh manghie!" When will I see you? Papa, I love you so much and missing you. I want to thank you for bringing me into this world and showing me how beautiful the world really can be.

You were our ever present father, my hero, my rock, my mentor, my shoulder to lean on with an ever listening ear!!!

Daddy you were so great a father, king, mentor, friend that I never knew nor imagine that this day will come. A man full of humour, selfless, loving, caring, empathetic like you would deserve to live forever but no one is above God. I thought and kept deceiving myself that you will forever be with us even though you kept reminding me that a day will come when I will not hear that voice again.

You were such a pearl but your transitioning into the other world just reminds me that there is a superpower "God" because to me, you were so divine and I never thought you will ever leave us even though I know death is inevitable. You were viewed by your subjects as a stabilizing influence in a country that saw numerous fights during your reign. You were a King and father who worked hard for his people and used your wisdom to intervene at times of heightened political tension, keeping your people at peace and holding them so dear to your heart. You embarked on a series of goals in Mankon and Cameroon at large and had your name to a number of developments, particularly in education and agriculture.

Daddy, your ability to reach out to ordinary people in Cameroon and the world, made you a wonderful ruler and has left us the Mankon people, stronger than before. On several occasions, you told me that, the day will come when I will see you no more but because of how gracious and loving a man you are, I was living in denial until that fateful Saturday when I got the message. Within a second, it seemed like I disappeared from this earth and reappeared in no time. So, what you kept telling me this past year has finally come to pass?? Wooooh! I rushed into my prayer closet to ask God for the grace and strength to receive the news. I held my bible close to my heart for comfort and kept dreaming thinking someone will tell me it is a lie, but no one till today has said so. Dad, is it really true that you are gone? God give me the grace to accept this.

Daddy, I want to thank you for making me the young woman I am today. Dad, you brought me up in such as wonderful way and I do appreciate it more, now that I am a parent and also running my own home. Growing up in the palace, my morning routines were centred on the palace duties, you and your visitors. The first thing in the morning was taking a shower and going straight into the palace where I served you, your guess and everyone. I would only return to my mother's house later during the day to take my breakfast or sometimes lunch because it sometimes got so busy in the palace that

132

I will only get back to our house after midday. I did that with so much joy, pride and love.

Whenever schools were over, I was so happy coming for holidays because I loved serving you in the palace and your guests. I learnt so much being around you and have incorporated the lessons from performing those palace duties into my own life. This has helped me tremendously with my own family, work, my community and the Mankon family as well. Thank you so much for teaching me to be a servant to all. Education was your number one goal for everyone, boy or girl. You stood by me and saw that I went to school and finished my course. You had a policy of no child left behind and educated all of your children. You were there financially, morally and spiritually to support all of us. For those in the Mankon community that needed school fees and support, you were there. You were a father to all and that is why we called you father of all nations. I remember when the Principal of our Lady of Lourdes summoned me to you that I was studying during odd hour (sports, siesta, late at night); you immediately came to school to have a talk with her about my study habits. I ended up doing very very well in my GCE and you were there to remind her how my hard worked has paid off. You taught us how to work for a pay check. We took on holiday jobs in the palace during summer holidays. When it was time to go back to school, you rewarded our hard work with wages.

Daddy you were a great accountant not by profession but by wisdom, teaching us how to balance income and expenditure accounts. It was fun, my siblings and I would write that out and present to you and even with your busy schedule, you made time to go over it to make sure we did the right thing.

Daddy, you are special. I keep thinking to myself, how you were able to do all of these given the fact that you had a very large family. This just adds to the way I see you and how powerful you were. I call you my "superman". I remember we would show up in the morning for name check and headcounts before heading to the field for the day's activities. That just became part of me, making time management and punctuality a very important part of my day. You taught me the importance of being on time in everything I do, which is key to my efficiency and output today. You taught us how to share with one another. Our mothers and the elders in the family will cook food occasionally and had everyone bring their plates and the food distributed amongst us. While in the fields for farm work, we shared a common meal during lunch and these are some of the things that kept us together. You thought and showed us love and the unity and love we have for one another today is testimony of the love you showed the family, Mankon community and the world at large.

Daddy, I am so thankful for the memories we shared both in Cameroon and USA and not a day goes by without me thinking about you and your words/actions of wisdom. It is hard to know that you are no longer there for me to call and talk with but I know you live on.

Dad, you were the guiding light in my life and your disappearance especially has reminded me how I was so blessed to have you as long as I did. That was a blessing that I now appreciate so much and even more. As much as I am not having you around, I am happy you are at peace and an angel in the Lord's kingdom.

Papa, we love you so much but your time was up. The Lord wanted you to continue your good work in his kingdom and I am happy, for you lived a good and God-fearing life. Your age is a true testimony of the blessings and reward from the Lord almighty for your good work and service to his people on earth.

Daddy, please shelter us from above that no weapon fashioned against us shall prosper. AMEN!!! Daddy, I miss you! I love you, dad. I know you leave on, and I keep hearing your voice.

Daddy, you were a great soul that served everyone at all times. Great souls never die and because you were one, you live on.

Dad, there is a special kind of feeling in my heart when I think about you. A feeling of loss but I know I will be ok because you did instil you in me and as long as I live, you live in me.

Papa, we love you and I know and hope that we shall meet again. Fare thee well, Papa!!!!

Your daughter,

Fru Mabel Angwafo

I came in close contact with Fo when I was the National President of Mankon Students' Association (MASA) from 1999-2000. HRM triggered the vision that I had for the students and Mankon at large. My leadership at the helm of MASA, stood out to be one of the most outstanding thanks to the input from Fo Angwafo III. HRM, was a multidimensional person who had a say in all domains of life and that is why His achievements are enormous and diversified. His love for motherland Mankon was immeasurable, and of course Mankon is where it is, National and International greatly thanks to Him.

In assigning and urging me to take the flag or star of Mankon to the nooks and crannies of the Country, he gave me a copy of the creation of the Mankon Post Office in 1961, to promote for everyone to know.

The Fo has gone, but his legacy will live forever and ever. I pray the Almighty for the repose of his gentle soul in perfect peace.

Tangyie Fru Venasius Kondze Tabe
Ndzumabeah-Mankon

I want to thank everyone gathered here today to celebrate my grandfather, King Angwafo III. I didn't really know my grandfather, and most of my memories of him were from 8-9 years ago. I remember him holding me in his arms when I was 2 years old and that pretty much was it. I remember a dog that we used to play with every day, and it turned out it died from a snakebite. The news of its passing made me unhappy and sad.

I didn't spend much time with my grandfather, but from what I've known, he was a very great man who ruled over his people when he was still living. He has ascended to a greater place up in the heavens and he rejoices with God and God's fellow angels. In my grandfather's time of living, I remember we used to go outside in the backyard and get chickens to cook for dinner, then after that we'd go outside and play with the dog every day when we were in Cameroon. My grandpa was loyal to his citizens he was a very honest man, he was kind, caring, and very supportive of his kids.

My grandpa is my role model because not only is he a great king, but he brought one of the most amazing people in my life which is my dad. I asked my dad "what was one thing his dad taught him that he taught me" I wasn't surprised by his answer because these are the things my dad impacted in my life which was education being a successful key in life, being honest and showing kindness towards others. He has taught us many things that have been passed down through the family generation, an example is that he always wishes for peace no matter what it is, this trait has been passed down from his children to his grandchildren.

This impact on all our lives in the Angwafo family is colossal, he really made us into the people that we are and it's not just the Angwafo family he also impacted other people's lives with his delicate socializing skills. I thank my grandfather for what he has left for us, and the mark he has made throughout the world, because of his good deeds he can be remembered, as his wish comes true, this was a peaceful time for him and us.

Grandson,

Frunwi Fletcher Angwafo

"Dear Grandpa, I am blessed to have spent a lifetime with you. While we never communicated as effortlessly as we may have wanted to; I always felt your love, aspirations and hope for a better future for me and everyone in general. I take this time to revel in the joy and great memories I have of spending time with you; especially during the holidays when we were chanced to do so. One regret I have is, my children came so close to meeting you but unfortunately couldn't. On the other hand, one of the joys we share is our love of dancing (or affectionately known as "make nyanga" by Grandma). As leader and steward of our people and our family, you have done so much - especially when it comes to education, modernizing our culture and empowering all those who dreamed and worked towards a better future. I hope you find solace with our ancestors especially in the wake of all that you have done. While I cannot hope to measure up to all your achievements; as your first grandchild and namesake, I hope to carry on that trailblazing spirit, fervent hope, peaceful determination and everlasting hard-work for a better tomorrow for us all."

Grandson,

Ghamoti Anye Angwafo

Mbeh,

The wonderful memories of knowing you as my father-in law are those of a father who would not come to Buea without stopping by the house to see how the children and I are doing, especially when Francis was out of the country for long spells of period. I reminisce the deep conversations on world affairs on topics that caught your curiosity and a keen interest in knowing about the different countries we lived in. Coming home to visit you from Botswana, Senegal, Holland, and South Africa, I was always amazed at your knowledge of these countries and your inquisitiveness to know more about the people, politics and especially about agriculture. Coming home also inspired me to prepare mentally for an engaged conversation with you. I recall vividly how pleasantly surprised you were when I told you I have gone back to study, your encouragement was phenomenal. When I informed you, I was going to Pinyin for fieldwork, your first reaction was to send me to the Fon of Pinyin, "tell him you are my daughter". That message was enough to cushion my stay in the village gathering data. I still remember your visit to South Africa as if it was yesterday!

You left a lasting legacy and memory not only to the Mankon community, but to whoever you encountered and those who came asking for help during your sojourn on earth. Your generosity was without bound, especially when it concerns education and Christianity. I recall vividly your one million FRS CFA support to Caroline to attend World Youth Camp in Brazil that was organised by Pope Benedict.

It was very humbling when you came to my father's funeral (cry die), exemplifying what family is all about.

I know you are up in heaven right now, running an extensive farm for everyone who comes through those pearly gates. It was my greatest honour in life, to be the daughter-in-law of such an amazing and generous man.

While you are physically gone from our lives, we are grateful that you are never gone, for we know that all of your energy that was known to us in your human form exists now in other forms.

You are here with us all, here with us in the memories we have made of you, here with us in the children, grandchildren, families you have helped to create, and here with us in the friendships you forged, here with us now as we all are, together as one.

Adieu.

Dr Henrietta Nyamnjoh
Cape Town, South Africa

The seed can only grow if the farmer plants the seed and takes care of it to grow. If the seed is sowed and proper care is not given to the seed, it may grow wild and be lost in the bush. But when suitable care is given to the embedded seed it grows into the intended plant and it becomes productive the way the farmer wants. I am that seed that was planted by my father. My father did not only sow the seed and let it grow wild in the bush, but he enriched it very well that it becomes the biggest and tallest tree in the forest. That's who my father is. He never gives up any task that is presented in front of him. He is a man of all weather and the only goal he has in mind is to get

137

it to the finish line and continue standing tall as the winner all the time.

As a young man growing up in the palace, I will follow my dad to the farm all the time to help him. But many times, I will ask myself this question; "Why is my dad working this hard"? Even if it is raining, he will not stop working until he is done with whatever job he is doing. My dad will tell me many times "son never give up on anything you chose to do because you will encounter many ups and downs in life, son always try to compromise, and it will serve you better in life."

In January 2008, my dad was in Houston, Texas. I drove together with my wife - then girlfriend for 9 hours from Midland, Texas to visit my dad in Houston. My dad called for me and asked who that young lady is to you? I replied, Mbeh a friend. Then he said, "just a friend?" and I answered Mbeh. He smiled and replied in the native tongue "argh kung' ntaw" (she has entered the palace), everyone was laughing. A week after arriving back in Cameroon I called my dad and he told me "I have already married your wife". Then I asked which wife? Mbeh and he replied saying "the young lady that you presented to me as your friend in Houston". I love my dad so much because he is very serious and incredible in everything he does. In 2014 his grandkids had the opportunity to spend about two months with their grandpa in the palace. After spending time with his grandchildren, he said "I have passed the baton to you now make sure you take care of my grandchildren the same way I did you."

One early morning I woke up very sick and went to the palace to tell my dad of my condition. The moment he set eyes on me, he called me "Sick man of Europe", I answered Mbeh. He asked, "do you know why I sent you to Technical School?" I replied No Mbeh. He said, "because I want my own technician, I want my own electrician and I want my own Engineer in the palace. If you are sick now, how are you going to be that my technician, electrician, or engineer that I'm training?" These words from dad are not ordinary words but words of wisdom because what he saw in me for the future has become my reality. My dad is my hero and my supreme role model. I am standing tall today because I am my dad's technician, electrician, and his Master of Electrical engineering. He is more than a biological role model. He signifies a patriarch, a farmer, a teacher, a hero, a politician, a leader, and the greatest king. I am proud to say that I and my family are living with his legacy today. He was not only a father to me and my siblings but the greatest King to all Mankon People and beyond.

Your majesty Fo Angwafo III, The greatest King of Mankon. Our Father was not only our father but the father of all Mankon children and beyond Mankon. One of our father's greatest passions is education. One of his goals was to ensure every child in Mankon had the opportunity to go to school. Because he saw education as the weapon that will change his people's life. By doing so he invested the skills to establish many primary and secondary schools all over the entire Mankon Kingdom. He will provide lands to missionary churches and the government to build schools. That was his dream, to make Mankon people become more scholarly endowed and for Mankon Kingdom to become the educational centre of the NW region with the best primary and secondary schools and University in Mankon.

Our dad, our king, my dad, my teacher, and my hero I will miss you but the greatest memories we shared live forever, and we shall live and celebrate your legacy forever.

Son,

Hycent Fru Angwafo

Milɨŋnə Mbɨʔə Mbyiɛ Fɔ Aŋgwaʔafɔ III, Fɔ̀ Máŋkûŋə.

A nə adzəŋnɨ zə wi, nkɨə mbé ntsambi ŋpfú ambo mé aŋdzuʔu ŋgə Fɔ̀ Máŋkûŋə a tsô bo nyom ntsɨ keʔé bŏ zɨ bə saʔá.

Kɨfɛrɛ a tswírə afɔ atɨ atɨʃé !

Mbyiɛ Fɔ Aŋgwaʔafɔ III, ô faʔa ambo Máŋkûŋə, ɨfɔtɨ alaʔa Cameroon.

ô kɔŋə anuə áŋwaʔanə bé tɨsɨŋə.

Má waʔatɨ ndánwaʔani tsɨ wi, ɨfɔtɨ tsɨ kɨʔɨnɨ tsa ô tôkɨnɨ Government a ŋaʔa nkɨə ŋkorə amû Máŋkûŋə.

á ŋé alôm ŋtsûʔu nɨ ŋkɨ tsinɨbvûʔə nɨ mɨwúm minɨbvûʔə (1990), mbyiɛ Fɔ Aŋgwaʔafɔ III atəmə mbyi, Goverment aŋaʔa ndánwaʔani sa tsinə a ntaʔa ŋgubɨ bɨ tɔŋnə sɨŋə nɨ G.B.H.S Mankon la. A nɨ ndánwaʔani za ɨ doŋkɨnɨ ɣan ma bé ŋwon sɨŋə ɣé.

Má waʔatə Tsázɨ mbyiɛ Fɔ Aŋgwaʔafɔ III tɨsən tɨsən mbɨʔɨ mɨɣam tsô;

1) mɨkɔŋ tsɛʔɛ ŋkarə.
2) ô zuʔə anuə Máŋkon ô kwətɨ ɨwə. mə mɔʔɔ kɨ mbvurə.

ɨtiʔi lwitɨ, anuə tsumə a tsi la ŋtsi nɨ ŋpfú ziə. ŋpfú za nyɔ̂m á saʔa nə, ŋpfú za nyɔ̂m á tsɔ̌nə ɣé .

á ŋé ŋpfú ŋtsɔ̌ nyɔ̂m zɛnə, má tiʔiɛ ntsáʔtə Ɗwiŋgɔn a fɔməbvurə ŋgɔ́ á kubɨnə ɣô a diʔi wa ô tsi nɨ nɨ bɨgharɨ bə fɛmnɨ tsô mbaʔa mángubɨ a kubɨtɨnɨ ɨbobi ambô a təwəm la.

Ivense Fru Tadzong (Nkyaŋtɨ)

I worked with the Fon of Mankon from 1962 as a customary court clerk in Mankon. He was instrumental in my employment at the court. He was a very powerful man and did everything to foster progress in his community. He has ruled Mankon for 63 (sixty-three) years and within these 63 years every Mankon man has enjoyed peace. His death to us was a great surprise.

I want to thank him for using the same "eye" his father used to select him amongst thousands of children. He has equally used that same eye to select our new Fon Angwafo IV of Mankon. I pray that he should stand behind him to rule the Mankon people better than what he did.

Long Live the King,

Fru John Aborungong
(Nitob I – Mankon Bamenda II)

Memories remind us that nothing lasts forever.

Our father is in heaven now and we should celebrate the 97 years that we had him on earth. His achievements are enormous and go beyond the Mankon Kingdom – his legendary and visionary leadership has improved the lives of Cameroonians.

I will always appreciate the guidance and fatherly role he played in bringing our family together during some challenging times. Papa, you were a great role model who made me proud to be a Mankon Man and I will always be proud of you.

Rest in Perfect Peace, Papa! I will miss you very much!

John Nji Chi, PhD
United States of America

In Honour of Fo Angwafo III

"Return with the knowledge you have gained from other nations and build your homeland. If you don't, who will do it? " Fon Angwafo III, on several occasions.

His exceptional oratory and deep insight meant he was easily recognizable - increasing his sphere of influence not just in the North West Region but throughout the country and around the world. He was Fon Angwafo III, the erudite Fon of Mankon who needed no interpreters when interacting with World Leaders and other Dignitaries. He was an Icon of Mankon whose *LEGACY will LIVE ON Forever.*

For me and others who grew up less than a mile from the Palace, we referred to the Fon as "Fo" but responded "MBE" during conversations, which the Fon typically initiated. As I grew older and began having conversations with MBE on a range of topics, MBE was consistent with his message that those who currently reside abroad should eventually return home and contribute their knowledge toward the development of our homeland. Instead of trying to reinvent the wheel, it was MBE's position that those in the diaspora should return home with the knowledge gained from those nations and work with the community at home to develop our homeland.

I am grateful to MBE for the vast range of opportunities he enabled and made possible within Mankon- enhancing and changing lives. For example, thanks to the efforts of MBE, I and many others were able to attend secondary and/or high school at "Ntahngub", very close to home. This meant that we did not have to incur additional expenses needed to attend school far away from home. This is just one of many.

As MBE has clearly outlined, future developments in Mankon will require collective effort from those who reside at home and the diaspora, so that together, we can follow in MBE's footsteps and continue to develop and enhance lives in our Fondom.

Long Live Mankon!
Long Live the Fon!
Long Live the Fondom!

Jones Nkimbeng

I received the news of the recent demise that befell the Fondom of Mankon with His Majesty Fo Angwafo III missing and moving to the ancestral land to join his ancestors with total shock and consternation. First I was confused and overwhelmed with feelings of disbelief, yet it turned out to be a reality. Mbeh, you showed unreserved and unqualified love for us your children. As National

President of MACUDA, I was privileged and singularly honoured with your commissions of Royal Errands to some Fondoms, other royal assignments of total confidence notwithstanding. Thank you Mbeh for counting me worthy and trusted to work with your numerous sons and daughters. You have disappeared from among us, but your indelible signposts in the domain of education and development of the Mankon Fondom will always remain green in our memories.

For instance, as Director of Paul's Computer Higher Institute of Technology, and for over ten years running, we were beneficiaries of your Royal Scholarship scheme which enabled vulnerable and underprivileged Mankon sons and daughters to acquire professional knowledge in the various ICT specialties that the school offers. It is our greatest wish and expectation that our present father, Fo Angwafo IV will continue with this important educational scheme given that he is an educationist himself and his Fondom is replete with needy and unprivileged children yearning for professional education.

May your ancestors give you warm embrace while the Heavenly Angels cushion your soul into God's bosom. Adieu our beloved father.

Joseph Mumbari

For My Missing Dad Fo S.A.N Angwafo III
Three Things My Dad Taught Me:

1) Laugh Often:

I am struck with the memories of Dad, how happy he always looked. He had one of those smiles that always reached his eyes, and he was a very kind father who could find humour in any situation. I always loved that about him because it made my being with him so easy, and it taught me that, no matter what life throws at you, a good belly laugh can make even the darkest moments feel more manageable.

2) Be Kind To Others:

My father always showing me that, no matter what a person's sex, age, race, religion, village or socioeconomic status is, they are human beings just like you and me. So, he gave a beautiful smile.

3) Love Your Kids Unconditionally:

Most people assume my father being a king, his passion in life was his job a traditional ruler since he dedicated so much of his life to it, but what few people realized is that he took his role as a father much more seriously, he often knew more about what was going on in my life than my closest sister and brother.

Goodbye:

I never got the chance to say I love you, Dad. I never got the chance to say I miss you, Dad. It hurts I never said Good – Bye. I will remember you each day that I live.

You were such a nice father with so much to give.

Such a privilege to have known you to be my father, no one can deny.

Goodbye father, I will keep with me the good times we shared together.

Till we meet again,
In God we Trust
Love you, I miss you
GOOD – BYE
Your son,

Jude Fru – Nkwah Angwafo

Oh! Grandpa is this a dream, why now when u promised me a great future if I made it in flying colours in the GCE Ordinary Level? My heart bleeds as I write grandpa because you were more than a grandfather to me, you said you were waiting for my results, so who will see my results and encourage me to go ahead in school?

Your advice, care, support, and love for education, please watch me and give me courage as I sit for my exams, give courage especially to my mother and grandmother to continue from where you have left, you always called me "nyongfor" who will call me that again?

Grandpa, I promise to do my best in the exams even though with tears in my eyes and to take care of my younger ones, proud to be among your first granddaughters. You were always so generous and kind, I will miss you always.

I love you, grandpa.

Your granddaughter,

Kien Mafor Ndifor Gracia

My Father, friend, mentor and leader HRH S.A.N Fo Angwafo III of Mankon is my hero, my motivation and my inspiration. He was the most courageous, goal getter and resourceful man I knew.

Growing up, he made me understand that EDUCATION is my first husband, that hard work pays and that, I shouldn't feel limited in pursuing my dreams because I am a girl child.

You nurtured me the way a girl wants to be groomed to fulfil dreams and become the virtuous woman that she should be.

He told me he owes me a debt and that is education that the knowledge I acquire no one can take it from me and that, I should not look forward to answering yes sir/madame but rather become an entrepreneur just like him and create more jobs.

I vehemently would say that he indeed paid that debt of education for me and I'll forever be proud of you, Dad.

At a very young age, you taught me how to be responsible like, keeping the place clean, respectful, welcoming your guests, tilting the soil, to plant pears, plums, mangoes and watering the garden.

Whenever I did something wrong, he corrected me in love yet I still faced the consequences of my action by punishment.

He never spared the rod and spoiled the child. I must say, his parenting skills were unmatched.

I paid him a visit on the 26/12/2018. When he saw me he shouted Mami England I answered Mbeh, he continued you have made me proud I knew you wouldn't go for long you will always remember home. I fell down at his feet, tears rolled down my eyes seeing the happiness on his face and knowing how proud a father he was melted my heart.

He told me 'don't be a stranger in the white man's land'. That when I have achieved what I wanted, I should come back home and build AMERICA in the palace so that he and my mothers can also enjoy America while at the palace.

These may seem like just mere words however, there's a strong message being passed.

I was on the video call with HRH and my siblings on the 18/10/21. We had such a great time and a good laugh with him. He kept asking us when we are going to be home. I told him I'll be seeing him in December 2022.

After pouring showers of blessings on us, I told him I love him and miss him so very much. His response was oh yes, thank you.

He further said, 'you have my address, how can you miss me while I'm in my Palace? We all giggled.

He added, 'I am aged now anything can happen, are you sure you are going to meet me when you come?.

144

I said yes and rejected it in Jesus name that nothing will happen to him that, I'll meet him strong and healthy he replied with an Amen. Little did I know that the former would be my reality.

The last time I spoke with him, he asked me if I have spoken with any of my siblings. I said yes. He said that is good. That I shouldn't leave in isolation, unforgiving-ness, anger or hate. That I should spread love and peace always with my brothers and sisters and then came him his famous quote

"Mukong tse'eh akare" meaning Unity is Strength.

Same message of love and unity he would pass to the Mankon people. He was indeed a father to all who encountered him.

I am honoured being a part of life sharing in his love and values.

Father you left a legacy that will live on in me forever. Mbeh I Love you. You ran your race so well that you deserve a Glorious rest.

Your Highness continue to rest in perfect peace in the bosom of the Lord, Amen.

Daughter,

Kien-Ngum Angwafo

Dad, for all those times I left it unsaid...thank you for always being there for me. You will always be the first man I ever loved, the first hand I ever held. I know I don't say it enough, but you are amazing, and I am so lucky to have you as a father. Growing up was often hard, dad, but your presence lit my way. You led me along life's path besides me all the way. You taught me how to catch fish and not just see fish and begin to eat. I want to say I love you, for all the years together we have had, I cherish deeply. Fare thee well, I shall see you when our paths cross again.

Daughter,

Lum Florence Angwafo Ndenge

Rest on My Hero and legend.

Some Memories just can't get off our minds and hearts.

You were a Lion, a hero, a King and Most of all a shining star to all. A father to Everyone whom you came across, and you blessed us all with your wisdom.

One thing about you I won't forget is the wisdom you instilled in me. My Legend, I know you are still very close guiding and watching over us and the best we will do in return is to instil your teachings in our kids, loved ones and the world at large. Thank you for being just the best. You will be missed, my Legend. Rest in power, Grandpa.

Your Granddaughter,

Lum Kab epse Akosah

Farewell Father
Tsazui Fo Mankon

I have no words for this. No real way to prepare for this. No prose beautiful enough, no speech pointed enough to describe the essence of my father, Tsazui.

Grace and wisdom he exuded. Strength of character and perseverance he displayed. But do we have a measure for the depth of his goodness?

We do not only grieve your disappearance, but also because this sphere of existence has lost so much goodness.

Warm and bright. Convivial and stern. No matter the storms whipping around Tsazui, he stood unwavering, shining his light.

Tsazui spent his life taking care of his people, his children. Even now the truth is, he is still taking care of us all. Father of all.

I will miss the little things, hearing him fill the palace with his healing laughter, his face beaming with that smile that told me everything.

I remember that even though he has transitioned now, his goodness lives on, the father lives on in his Emi, bangyiebuntaw, bontaw, his children's children, oh yes in his people, in his deeds, in his dreams and aspirations, in every sacred *miyeh* he offered all and sundry, every piece of advice he gave to the myriad of people he mentored, every seed he planted, every soil he tilled, every life he improved.

Father, I feel you in the warmth of the sun, I hear you in the ruffle of the wind in the trees and I will look for you among the stars in the heavens where You are, You are in every breath of air I take.

Daughter,

Lumnangah Angwafo III

Dear Father,

Your demise has left me searching for words to describe the great king you have been, the exquisite personality you possess and the unique relationship/bond you created. I fumble at my own words

146

because simply put, you were a "rare gem." I could never fully describe who you are or what you meant to me, the Mankon community and the world at large because words have failed me but, in an attempt, ...

Dad, I have cherished every single moment spent with you and I will forever long for more. You were the father that ensured we had everything to be successful and never know lack. You were a constant coach and a steady adviser, you ceased every opportunity to encourage, teach and educate. You were ever so joyful and effervescent (high-spirited). Your approach to life was unique and easy, filled with so much love to give. You treated everyone that encountered you with so much kindness and love. You had an all-inclusive approach that left even children longing for your presence. Your open-door policy and hospitality encouraged so many people to stay humble and feel at home even though sometimes away from home.

Dad you were my friend and a very generous one, I remember early 2008 while you were in America, we came home for the holidays and you had kept specific tasks for us to do as our usual holiday assignments starting from cleaning Ntawbargh, cleaning the palace, all the visitor's rooms, and farming the garden by the pig fence. We did such a great job and when you returned from your journey, I placed a call from school asking if you could pay us a visit as we had missed you over the break and you said of course. The next day during afternoon preps to my greatest pleasure, you had come, right in front of the principal's office, I was so happy to see you and ran straight to you, you had brought us so many goodies. You visited all our classes and gave each student an allowance through the class head girl in our respective classes. You were never impressed by me taking the first position in class, but by how what average I had and what difficulty I encountered that stopped me from getting an average of 20.0. You always asked us who the top 5 students in our classes were, who their fathers were, what ethnic group they came from and will go further to grant scholarships to those classmates who excelled in school but had little financial support.

One of the group video calls initiated with my siblings, left you excited seeing more of your children in one place and you said, "Can you have everyone together so I can see them?" I saw the delight in your face that day and the next several group calls we had. Cognizant of the network situation at home, I decided to make a birthday tribute video in your honour instead with most of my siblings, your

147

grandchildren, and our mothers, and when you watched this video on your birthday last year, you were so elated that when I called, you said "Ngwetsi, wonderful! I have had a nice day and heard my grandchildren talk as if they are my elders and father. God seems to be with us, but you must take care, if you don't know what gold is and you are given, you will destroy it. Life is short, when it is time to act, if you don't act it is gone and gone forever. You are not only acting for yourself, but you are acting for your family and for your country, and you are teaching. Because if people are impressed with your actions, they will transmit it from generation to generation, then you will live forever. You did all this from a different world, everything you do to impact will never die but live forever. Thank You!"

These words give me hope looking back and knowing that just like you stated, your legacy will never die, the footprints you've left behind will never be erased, your teachings, counsel, love, encouragement, and laughter will stay with me forever, oh! How I cherish all the sweet memories we created and long for more!

I vividly recall you asking me several times on every call, "when are you coming home? When am I seeing you? Remember your father is an old man. I told you by December and you were a little worried, but kept the faith by saying "well, I don't feel very well but the doctors and your mothers are doing an outstanding job", and my prayer for you was that of *strength*, a *peaceful mind*, some *good rest*, and *joy* to which you said a huge *AMEN!* And then you turned to my sister and asked, "How long did she say her school will take?" and when she replied to you, you turned back and stirred at me for a short while and you said "Kabfor, your father is an old man, are you sure to see me when you come?" then with a bright smile as though you noticed the sadness in my eyes, you said "well, the Lord has been good to me, and by God's grace I will see you when you come but make sure you don't come alone." You were always very meticulous when it came to me and you showered me with great love, I pray you know how much that means to me and I love you very much.

Dad, the news of your disappearance left me distraught, it has been the most painful and difficult time of my life, somehow you managed to comfort me with the sweet memories left behind and I trust that you are watching over us from heaven. I have two shooting stars from above, please tell mama Magdalene Kien what a brilliant and wonderful woman her little girl has turned out to be. Thank you for being a friend, a mentor, a disciplinarian, a counsellor, *an absolute wonderful father, a great King,* and above all the stamp of love and kindness you have left in our hearts. I love you forever.

Daughter,

Lumnkap B. Angwafo
(Miss, Ngwetsi, Kabfo!)

Memory in Honour of my Grandfather

My grandfather, His Royal Highness Solomon AnyeGhamoti Angwafo was a peacemaker. He loved conversation and dialogue. There was nothing he couldn't talk about, and for hours.

As a child, he would ask very adult-like questions to which I would answer timidly with a smile. He had such a broad smile and laughed very loudly. He either melted every room with his personality or kept the room alert for his next move.

My grandfather loved to dance. I got to witness this on two occasions. 25 years ago, while I was in secondary school, I had heard so much talk about the Fon's dance *"Abungafo"* and I was eager to attend. I was 13 and homesick. I decided that I wanted to observe the ceremony. I obtained permission from the school administration to go for the Fon's dance. My thoughts were while I was in the area for school, it was probably the only substantive chance I would get to experience this dance.

When I got to the palace, I went straight to my grandmother, who looked surprised to see me. After a warm embrace, she asked me why I had come. I told her I wanted to witness the Fon's dance. She looked surprised again and said I had missed most of it and had arrived the day before the finale. She didn't say anything else about the dance, but sent a message to the palace that I was around. I later went to greet my grandfather who was entertaining another Fon. I met him with that broad smile on his face. He asked me how I was doing, and I said I was doing fine, very sheepishly. He asked why I was not in school, to which I answered that I had come to watch the dance. He asked why I decided to watch, and not dance. He said, "if you came all the way here then you should be in the dance." His guest took one look at me and asked where this little "Hausa" madam had come from and whether I could dance since in his words, I was very frail-looking and skinny. His guest continued to tease me and proceeded to ask again who I was, and my grandfather loudly said to him: "she's my granddaughter and not a Hausa girl, and she will dance with me tomorrow". I ran off to my grandmother and the next day my grandfather sent for me. When I arrived, there was a line-up with several queen mothers and princesses holding different traditional pieces. I was handed one and we were ready to go. We walked out to the grandstand and we stood behind him on a big concrete stoop. Several dance groups presented their dances. Their footwork was impeccable and the musical instruments were loud and congruent. Then he arose, descended the stairs and we followed. The dancing continued with him dancing with and around the various groups, usually in one spot. The women chanted praises, and clapped with their hands to their mouths. He had a very broad smile that never faded. That was the first time I saw my grandfather dance. He had the crowds mesmerized, chanting and jubilating. I felt entertained watching him dance. I'll never forget how exciting that moment was for me.

The second time I had the opportunity to witness his love for dance and being in the presence of joy and celebration was during my traditional wedding. This was 12 years after the last dance experience, and just 13 years ago. At some point during the reception, as the dance was finishing, my grandfather who was enjoying the dance bolted from his throne and tuned the song again. Everyone jumped to their feet and started singing and dancing. He then sang louder with a smile, and began to move forward in dance, as everyone started dancing backwards and out of the house into the courtyard. Before my husband and I knew it, the whole courtyard was full with dance, merry-making and cheer and my grandfather was in the centre of the dance, again with such a broad smile. The smile on his face never faded. I knew from that smile how proud he was to be part of my special day. Everyone present felt his pride and joy.

My grandfather was very adamant about the younger generations being educated, and particularly the girl child. He believed that education was our meal ticket in society. That was always the second question out of his mouth when we were in his presence. It was always how are you doing, and how is school, or how did you do in school. As such he defended the female child attaining higher education, at any level, and supported female entrepreneurship, and females in administration. He always said, "there is no dull child", and that the teacher just needed to figure out how to teach, motivate or encourage children to learn. As a child, I was never excited to listen to him talk to adults. Those conversations with adults were usually held over hours of dialogue and questioning. He was very inquisitive and loved asking questions about society and development, different cultures, norms, and other perspectives. He was never hesitant to ask anyone a question as long as he thought he could learn something. He was well-read and always knew what was going on somewhere in the world to ask about someone's thoughts or opinions. He always seemed to have experiences to share, opine, and to ponder.

He was a family man and loved being in the midst of children. I remember I was about six, or seven years old, the first time I saw him fellowship with some of his children and grandchildren. It was a sight to behold. He was watching the evening news in his library, and some of the children asked if they could watch a movie. The thought was the older children would organize the movie night when my grandfather left the library. What ended up happening was a movie night in the library in his presence, and all the young children sat around him while the older children sat in outer circles to watch the little TV. As he aged, he still loved being around his children, particularly his daughters. Again, during my traditional wedding activities, my aunts and I sat in one of his parlours to eat, and he sent extra drinks to the parlour and came by and made merry with everyone. He loved seeing people happy and loved celebrating his family.

There is a lot to highlight, and many instances which I remember fondly. There were quite a few as a child. As an adult, I was away for so long and only saw him on three occasions. The second of those three instances was when I was getting married. During my traditional ceremony, my grandfather had sent for my grandmother and we went together. I experienced a sentimental moment between the two of them that I will cherish forever. He called my grandmother by her first name in such a loving and tender manner and it felt so special to me. I could tell there was a special bond that had never faded over the years. The third time I visited was with my children and husband and I felt so blessed that my children got to meet their great-grandfather, and were in his presence and welcomed.

When I was leaving for college 21 years ago, I went to visit him and he asked me what I intended to study. I said environmental science. He looked at me and asked me what the subject entailed. I started to describe the lines of study, and he looked astonished. He then asked, "Why DO you have to go so far to study nature, it is all around us here. I have virgin forests and lands here!" He then added, "I see you want to be a farmer!" to which I answered timidly, "Not quite". He said, "I see!" Little did I know, 15 years later, as a hobby

I would be ecstatically tending to fruit trees, gardens of vegetables and herbs, and recycling produce for composting.

It was an honour to have known and experienced my grandfather, and to watch from afar the legacy of a man who wore so many hats and filled so many shoes. He was a father, a farmer, an organizer and builder, a proponent of female education and empowerment, an administrator, and so much more.

Granddaughter,

Maatsi N. Ndingwan

Knock knock knock, grandpa, here we are at the palace gates, please open up. You told us to study hard and bring to you good grades, here we are with our report cards, also eager to listen to you because you tell the best stories but everywhere seems quiet. We love the books you always give us, the best part about going on holiday is spending time with you, grandpa. What type of sleep are you in? Where do good people go to? Are you with the angels? Will you forever remain silent? We saved up some money and bought you a present, please how do we hand it over? Our parents and grandmothers are all sad, are they hiding something from us?

We miss you, grandpa
Rest well, grandpa
We love you so much.
Grand children,

Mafor Joy, Caleb and Harley Bemnji

HRH Fo S.A.N Angwafo III visited the United States in 2007. I met him for the first time in December of 2007 when he visited my city of Chicago. I was in awe of being in the presence of such a giant of a man. Within minutes of our meeting however, he put me at ease with his gentle nature and his great sense of humour.

On that cold December evening, he enjoyed and appreciated our dinner at one of Chicago's most exclusive hotels where he was hosted like the true royal he is. The hotel personnel had never had the opportunity to serve such a dignified African (Cameroonian) Royal – a King. They had been specifically instructed as to how to welcome and to serve his majesty. The staff were heard to whisper that they felt as if they were on the set of the famous movie "Coming to

America" where an African King is received at the Waldorf Astoria in New York, no less.

This great leader of Mankon found all this excitement interesting but his mind remained steeped in plans he had for the development of Mankon such as encouraging those in foreign lands like America to return home and contribute to the development of the Fondom. Specifically, he brought with him plans he had drawn up to expand and modernize the palace museum. He wanted the knowledge of arts and crafts to be taught widely and to be highly developed, both for artistic (in museums) and commercial value. Remember that the Afo-Akom was once on display in the museum of Natural history in Chicago.

I came to Cameroon in 2009 to be part of the 50th Anniversary celebrations.

Over the years my communication with him centred on moving his people forward in every way possible – education, agriculture, the arts, and culture. He was a man with a great vision for his people.

I thank him for his leadership and for reaching out beyond the boundaries of Mankon to see that his visions would come to fruition.

Mbeh, for 63 years you worked single heartedly to move your people to the head of the line, now you can rest in peace knowing that your job is done.

May your reception in the hereafter be grand as befits a loving father and a great leader of his people; May peace, and joy be yours eternally.

Mafor Marie Ebie

My big brother, my father, my strong support. I recall firmly our journey through life. I remember when you were sent to work in Bambili, you took me along and insisted I enrol in school, but I refused because I had younger ones and needed to back them while my mum goes farming and about her activities. From Bambili, you were transferred to Befang, and as usual, you took me along. I remember this particular journey being so tedious, stressful and difficult. I boarded a truck carrying benches, we moved so slowly, and when we got to Mbuhting, it got bad, and I was bound to spend the night in an open mosquito infested truck. I fell terribly sick and was given a vaccine which eventually left my hand swollen. When I finally got home, you felt so bad about my looks, so you made a special bed just for me, where I was well attended to by the best medics till, I got well. That notwithstanding, I insisted on going home to lend a helping hand to your late mother, Mafor Manka and Nimo Ntambeng. You were a father and senior brother to me, and I became much more attached when Mafor and Nimo Ntambeng eventually passed away. Given the position I held in your life and late Mafor's, I was given the privileged assignment to put a life fowl in the bag of the most cherished royal masquerade dance (*Alubeh*) during Mafor's funeral.

I flash back to when you were enthroned Fon of Mankon. I moved around crying and looking for you with your specially requested menu in my basket (boiled plantain and groundnut). I couldn't sleep without seeing you. Eventually, each time I thought of you, I will immediately take off to see you so as to have a peace of mind. You called for and scolded at me severally for allowing the children spend the best part of their lives in the coast. To this effect, I often sent them to you for the best counsel. Whenever I fell sick, the whole Santa community would wonder and marvel at my closeness to you, due to the powerful non-stop delegations you would send over to cater for me and settle my hospital bills.

It is really sad to say that I have gone to untold number of places just to seek a solution to your health, but it seemed it was the appointed time for you to go home. I am saddened and heartbroken at your demise. I beckoned on GOD almighty to preserve and keep you at his right-hand side and pray you continue to guide and take care of the family as you have always done because, in this solitude, I no longer have anyone to turn to because you did virtually everything for me. Rest on Mbeh.

Mama Awa Anna (Mama Santa)

Love leaves a memory no one can steal but death leaves a memory no one can heal. It's sad to know I will not see you again nor listen to your wise saying, but again it is a loving memory when I think of your life and all you did for us.

Mbeh, I remember you as a disciplinarian. As young as three, I recall a day you got me well beaten for crying and following Nimontaw to the palace something I did often, never repeated the act again. I also recall when my siblings and I were well beaten for destroying a small palm tree at "nkafo" because we wanted to produce brooms for handwork for school. Not forgetting the beating and punishment to replant mangoes as my siblings and I harvested mangoes and plums without your permission which you considered it as stealing.

Dad, you taught me to be disciplined, respectful, accountable and hardworking. Right from a tender age while we were keeping the palace clean, you would sing 'little children come on girls, little children come on boy, come on little children 2x' to encouraged us, which made us work relentlessly. As early as 5 years old you started teaching us to be hardworking and duty conscious as we fetched pear (avocado) for the pigs every morning and a register was kept to record our progress and assiduity. You also gave us goats to tend to at this tender age teaching us a sense of responsibility. Immediately we enrolled in secondary school you started teaching us the value of money and accountability. This can be seen with the holiday jobs we did with 500FCFA daily pay from 7am to 3pm with an hour's break. You made sure you inspected the work done to ensure the hours of work were respected and the work done deserves the 500FCFA for a full day or 250FCFA for half a day's work as you always say, 'there is no food for a lazy man'. You taught me accountability and record keeping as I accounted for every cent that was given to me in my account book making sure all receipts were well kept. You made sure I understood the value of money and that it should be diligently spent and whenever you gave money for my needs you always say, 'what I give you today you will give your children tomorrow and even more than what I am giving'.

Dad, you always stressed that education is my first husband and what is yours is yours and the only thing you could give me is education so I should not joke with my studies. You always told us how you fended for yourself while growing up and by so doing teaching and training us to be independent. Dad, I never understood what you meant by the saying education is my first husband until I became my own person. The person I am today is all thanks to you because you did all you could to make me a better person. All through school I never lacked any didactic material nor got driven from school for fees. You gave me all what was necessary to be a success. You went as far as organising evening classes for us and preparing a conducive study room for us and will pass by unannounced to make sure we were actually studying.

Health and education to you were paramount. There was never a light headache for you as you insisted that anyone ill must be consulted, and drugs consumed must be prescribed by a doctor/nurse.

Dad your hospitality cannot be overemphasized as no one came to the palace and left without a bite or a drink.

Daddy, my heart bleeds each time I remember that you are gone, but your loving and caring fatherly role will continue lingering in my heart. You lived for others, always helping others. I will do my best to carry on in your footsteps. I am happy that I'm one of your children. Your memory will not die in me…. Thinking of the time spent together brings a smile to my face and I remember and miss your simile. Dad you are my hero and always in my heart. I will always love you and miss you. Continue to rest in peace dad. Adieu!

Your loving daughter,

Mambo Neh (Tahkar as you always call me)

Though growing-up was far away from my fatherland; education about Mankon, the people and its language took central stage during school vacations particularly in my teenage years. My father spared no effort to stock every contemporary literary work on Mankon in our home library. Amongst, many such works was the book titled "Becoming of The Fon of Mankon", which leveraged our magnificent culture and gave a glimpse of the great leader of our 20th dynasty, Fo Angwafo III of Mankon. Meeting your majesty personally for the first time was nothing short of scary, exciting and remarkably godly. Destiny had me your daughter-in-law, rather more properly described, your daughter. Your contagious healing smile will be missed over our land. Your legacy is alive in us today, tomorrow and will continue to light future generations. We greatly miss and love you.

Your daughter-in-law,

Mangyie Alia Tawbargh

Fo Angwafo III A Myth Beyond Reality

Father, my Ibadan of knowledge, beacon of time, my mantra of Success etc. We went through all our drafted stages together. You put me on my marks, I was getting ready to go and just then you rather chose to be my guardian angel. Daddy, I wish I marry a man just like you. **QUANCURUM (quick and steady)** will remain your word for me. I love you my best friend and my first son. You will forever be 25 years old for your Benjamin is 25 now. I Love you more than my Life, my love. Rest in Heavenly Royalty.

Anye Solomon Angwafo III

Men could not fathom your Personality.
The Great untouchable
A man who sacrificed his life for his people.
A man of wisdom and forecast
A man awarded Best Man of the year.
A King most prominent in this century.

Your virtues were kindness, love, peace, patience, Hope, joy, charity, Understanding etc. In all you were the fruits of the Holy Spirit in its fulness.

Your Principles were; " Your future is what you do today", "A man should never run away from a battle , but face and defeat it", "Do for Tomorrow Today", "Education is a father's gift to a child", "Agriculture should be your preoccupation no matter your occupation", "Eat to Live and don't live to eat", "Trust in God"," While in an ant hole or bee hive, keep your dignity to the optimum".

Father, you taught me to be humble, content, how to fish, love for God and humanity and hard work.

All above is only proof that your Highness' Legacy lives on....

The King Is Missing,

Long Live The King.

My Father

How could I live on earth without you?
You are as precious to me as gold,
As unique as a Jewel
As caring as an angel
As sweet as Marsala
Without you oh! What will life be?

When I was discomforted,
You comforted me
When I was full of gloom,
You Covered me with glint
Oh, father how men admire your ways.

How I wish I Can father my children the way you do. I dedicated this to you on your 91st Birthday Mbeh. I just want to Say Thank You For Being A Super Man....Live On Daddy.

Your lovely Benjamin and mother,

Manka Mafor Angwafo

157

My grandfather, my father. You were a man of peace and social justice. You led by example and dexterity. You once told me, love is what overcomes all. You told me to love all being men or woman. You told me to love my enemy the most and see how forward life will be. You were a legend of humility and simplicity. Farewell father.

Mankah Grace
Daughter of late Pa Ndefru Paul Musongong of Musang
(Ma Nde, as the Fon always called me)

As a toddler, I never understood why everyone clapped in your presence. Or why I never saw you eating. I know I was most excited to see you because you always had a broad smile, a soft drink and called me Mafo (your mother). Of course, I thought it strange to be under 10 years old and also be your mother, but I knew I could not ask you why you called me that. The realization of who you were and what you meant to us came much later.

In the summer of 1998, Nimo Maatsi and I were tasked with cleaning the palace in the mornings. At the time, I would grudgingly wake up early to sweep the sacred grounds. But Nimo Maatsi and I would also sneak around after cleaning to see what else was hidden in the sacred grounds. We thought you didn't hear us. One day, we had cleaned the palace and went about our usual exploits and then suddenly Nimo Susanna called my name. She told us to go greet you. During our discussion, you asked me about school and what my objectives were for my holidays. When I said I didn't have any in particular, you bellowed, "it definitely shows!" That evening, when Tata Asanji came home from greeting you I was certain Maatsi and I would be punished, but it turns out you didn't tell him anything!

As time would have it, I now long to hear you call me Mafo one more time. I wish you would remind me of why I am both your mother, your aunt & granddaughter. I wish you would tell me stories again about your time in Ibadan and Befang, the farms and how much we can learn about ourselves from the quality of our soil and the type of farming we do. I wish to see you rise up and dance one more time during *"Abenghe fo."*

When I told you, I had quit my job to go into Agriculture. Unlike everyone else, you applauded me and encouraged me to keep at it. When I moved to Ndop and needed help, you were sure to guide me to your counterparts in Babungo and Baba I. In our last discussion, you asked me about business and chastised me for working alone.

158

You reminded me who my great grandaunt was and why I could not continue to walk alone. It was a tough discussion, but I know you left us knowing that I heard you.

We knew this day was coming, yet nothing prepared me for the deep feeling of loss. Grandpa, thank you for giving me strength to keep going. Thank you for staying true to yourself and showing me to do the same. May we all continue to make you proud and continue your legacy.

Your granddaughter,

Manka Swiri Angwafo Ngundam

Grandpa Mbeh, we wished you a happy birthday on your birthday only to wake up the following morning and mommy told us that you have gone to heaven to meet Jesus Christ. We asked mommy if Jesus Christ will send you back after healing you, because we were looking forward to spending this summer holiday with you, only for mommy to tell us that we wouldn't see you again until we meet in heaven. We love you so much grand pa and will miss you and all the nice things you used to give us.

Your granddaughters,

Mankah Keziah Nde and Kien Neriah Nde

To My Loving Father Fo S.A.N Angwafo III

My Amazing Father,

My Hero,

My Jewel of Inestimable Value,

King Solomon the Wisest King,

The most Courageous and Resourceful Leader of all time,

Rock of Ages, Ancient of Days,

Our Encyclopaedia,

The Nation's monument,

How do I eulogize you when your story is still being written? The thought of me never setting eyes on you again makes tears roll down my cheeks. Creating beautiful moments with you was my favourite thing to do and the moments we shared remain my sole consolation and will be forever cherished. Our fond memories remain the highlight of my life.

I vividly remember when as children, we struggled to wash our legs and faces to get set for school in the frigid hours of the morning in Mankon. Out of the blue, we would feel a serious whip on our backs from you during your morning rounds with your radio on your neck listening to news, insisting that we take a complete bath before heading to school.

Going to farm with you was fun. Behind our Toyota Pick-up were drinks, rice and stew which you provided for our elder sisters to cook, and you tailed us to the farm in your famous "0614", as we fondly called your ride. There on the farm in the scorching sun, you taught by example in your large cowboy cap.

Contrary to popular belief at the time that a woman's place was the kitchen, you gave equal educational opportunities to all your children -both girls and boys alike. You encouraged hard work and academic excellence amongst your children by giving prices to meritorious students. I can still remember how I proudly wore my raincoat and rain boats to the farm which were my reward for excellence.

Early July, we greatly anticipated your return home after the June session of the National Assembly. Those who made it to the next class upon hearing the growling noise of your car made their way to you singing "mato Fo ye eh, mato Fo ye eh" with their report cards in their hands. And you rewarded each child accordingly.

As a teacher, you helped us improve on our reading skills by getting us books (pacesetters which I loved so much) during holidays. Your eagerness every morning to listen to what I read the previous day galvanised me into reading more and I always looked forward to telling you a story.

We looked forward to back to school with a lot of enthusiasm thanks to your family spirit. We called it last supper. We lined our plates in the dining room where food was served with each person having a bottle of Coke or Fanta and you watched us eat while giving us pep talks and ensuring that we were well groomed, set, and ready for the school year. You taught us the value of hard work.

You always had a way of protecting us. Thank you for being our safe place. I recall once in "Ngoh" when we went to plant Guatemala grass. My sister Adela and I sneaked off for adventure only to be chased by a cow. We ran and came and sought refuge behind you. You laughed and said, *"Do you expect this cow to know I'm your father not to hurt you?"* Keep watching over us from heaven, Dad.

You were a provider. You always came through for your family in our points of need. You were such a remarkable personality, kind-hearted, a pacesetter, a father, my best friend, my teacher, my mentor, my confidant, and my greatest model. I could call you any day any time and you never failed to show up for me. That's what a father does. You were always in good spirits even till the hour of your death. You eased the burden of those you loved.

Your largesse knew no boundaries. Not only were you the founder of Nkah Ni kwi Ni Mankon, which has as objective to foster girl education, but you equally provided land for its activities and training centres. As the current president of the Yaoundé branch, we promise to keep the ball rolling.

Your intelligence was beyond measure. So much so that we thought, as a King, you were also a spirit and omnipresent. We sneaked into your orchard at "Ntah Fo" literally 'the Fon's hill' to steal plums, mangoes, and pears that we nicknamed "affair" so you wouldn't know. Only for you to summon us later in the courtyard to ask what "affair" meant. Dumbfounded, we could only admit our guilt and of course assume the consequences.

My professional life could have been nothing without you. I am because you were. I remember calling you after a very difficult week at work telling you I want to resign. You said, *"Daughter, winners don't quit, and tough times don't last but tough people do. Moreover, quit when you find something better, and not because somebody made you to quit"*. You always reminded me of the bright side of things and gave me reason to press forward. To this day, I strive to remain the winner you saw in me. You moulded me into a fine, organised, and hard-working woman. Thank you for always believing in me.

My boss whom you took as your son, and who held you in high esteem and took care of you in the very best way mourns your loss. Also, my colleagues at Afriland First Bank equally got the chance to see what a great man you were. The memories and moments you shared with them every time an occasion presented itself will forever be remembered.

As if the work you called "*my first husband*" was not enough, a few years in my professional life, you started requesting for a son-in-law. I told you I had a friend, but we are still getting to know ourselves. Amused by what I said, you told me "*Daughter can you ever say you know a man? People change in space and time and the only constant in life is change. So, learn to adapt. More so, a sip is enough for a wine taster to know if the wine is good or not.*" Thank you for accepting "*my choice*". These have remained a beacon guiding my way.

I envied the relationship you had with my husband: it was a love filled relationship. You took him as your very own and bonded with him in every sense of the word. He too reciprocated in a like manner and you both shared a lot in common, spiced by lots of jokes. I recall you telling him during one of your cosy moments *"Joe, this your woman na small girl"* and you both laughed. I wonder what that meant. All this strengthened family ties and ultimately helped us build our families like that of Nazareth. My darling husband who knew and did what a caring Son should to a father always shall greatly miss you.

You were slow to anger and abounding in mercy. Never have I seen another as compassionate as you were. You lived by your slogan *"Unity is strength, love and forgive one another"*. I can still remember your own children standing against you, some illicitly taking your property and you telling me on your sick bed in Yaoundé *"don't hate them, they are your brothers, and remain my children, vanity upon vanity"*. Your dying wish was to see your children united. I pray we live by this principle so you will be happy forever with your Maker. You were indeed an instrument of Peace.

The third generation (our children) were not left out in your selfless quest for human wellbeing and education. I can still visualize you under heavy rain pour behind the Mankon Metropolitan Cathedral waiting to ensure that your granddaughter is admitted into Lourdes College. This even caused you to postpone your trip to Yaoundé. You answered present during landmark ceremonies in their lives in school (First Holy Communion, Confirmation, Jubilees). They proudly introduced you to their friends as their grandfather and the generous provider of the land on which stands two great colleges in Mankon: Our Lady of Lourdes Secondary School and Sacred Heart College.

Your departure has left a void in my life that only God can fill. I will miss your counsel and your encouragement on the days I hit rock bottom.

If we had forgotten to show our gratitude enough for all the things you did, we're thanking you now. And we are hoping you knew all along, how much you meant to us. My heart is deeply grieved but my soul knows you are at peace. We love you, and we'll always remember your love, your life, your laughter, and your good counsel.

You are the HERO of my childhood and my later years as well and every time I think of you my heart still fills with pride. I know you are up there looking down on us, watching over us and guiding us as we navigate through life. I take comfort in knowing that you will always be with us in spirit. I could go on and on, but I'll end here. Till we meet again Dad! Love you always. Farewell My Hero!!!

Your daughter and mother,

Mankah Mafo Doris Angwafo epse Malegho

The Lion of Mankon: Fon Solomon AnyeGhamoti Ndefru Angwafo III

His Royal Highness, Fon S.A.N, Angwafo III, Grandpa, you are our irreplaceable jewel, and we celebrate you, Gramps.

From childhood, I heard most of your wise words as tales from my mothers. And, I believe, that these set the foundation of my life's core values.

First, I learnt that you taught your progeny to work hard, and not count on the fruits of others as theirs. Also, I learnt that you taught them to fear God and never Men; which, I always saw directly portrayed in your charisma, your eloquence and firm conviction on addressing turbulent squabbles wherever they arose.

Your mother, Mafo Angwafo III, told me that her first and only Bible (which we still use at home today) was given by you. It is from it, that I carved out unto my heart that children should make their fathers and mothers proud of them; give our mothers that happiness (Proverbs 23:25). Thus, everything I do grandpa is to stick to this phrase and make your name known, by my deeds.

Mbeh, your mother also told me how incredible their upbringing was. Stories of how they nursed your palm plantation under your careful supervision and how primarily she is a farmer before any other "occupation" sticks to the back of my mind, when I do anything in life. I know that I belong home and that the future depends on the seeds I sow today.

Grandpa, you were a man of integrity; and wherever I went to, I heard leaders respectfully speak of you. Equally, I saw you exercise your authority heartily, humbly and wisely. Most remarkably, Father you cared about the future of your offspring and made sure that your legacy lived on.

On August 28, 2021, you happily shared with us the professional achievement of your last seed and celebrated your 70th anniversary of solemn matrimony with your "Mamie", Nimo Nanga-Maatsi Emilia Angwafo, our Professor Sebiso. There, I heard you sing jubilantly "Oh, what a happy day, what a day, what a beautiful day eh….Oh, what a happy day, what a day that the Lord has made". You held her hand and cut your anniversary cake and a few days later asked me; who I aspired to become and what I was up to!

Later, on April 24, 2022, I came home with my mentor; H. E. Richard Bale, who had evidently heard a lot about your wisdom and resilience, and at the end of this event, you again asked me, what I wanted to become and what I was doing towards attaining that goal;

which again, I told you. Alas! You told me Congratulations, held my hand and we parted. That was the last word and the last time, I saw you gramps, before May 21, 2022 gave you rest.

From your life, I deduced three major ingredients for success and fulfilment. To be: perseverant (dying but never surrendering in the face of difficulties), maintaining and strengthening good ties/relationships (loyalty) and above all taking everything with a smile, patiently and peacefully being oneself.

As much as the transition from adolescence to adulthood brings identity issues/crisis and all, Grandpa, you have given me exemplary and wonderful fathers and excellent mothers who always maintain the composure of "women of iron" amidst difficulties. I am immeasurably grateful for them. You worked hard, played hard and loved hard. And, if anyone is to challenge that, then history will speak for itself. Martin Luther said, "He had a dream", Barack Obama transposed dreams from his father into his life and Michelle Obama shared with us ladies, how to become "her", then pricelessly, YOU, our legend topped the list with "Royalty and Politics- the Story of my Life". Mbeh, we are privileged to have seen your "dream", received your "dream" and been challenged to become better Angwafos, following "the Story of your Life". However, Mankon, misses and mourns your disappearance; not because of your abundance or the fame you acquired nor your political sturdiness; but because of the lives you transformed.

You are our hero, and we deeply appreciate you!

Grandpa, I love you so much, your selflessness, your rigour, your sense of justice, your audacity, everything about you; really appeals to my conscience to always look at my elders and copy their virtues, correct their mistakes and write a better story for the future. I cannot thank you enough, and I would not cease to make sure that your legacy lives in me!

Live on, Gramps, the Great Boma Tree in the Mankon Fondom,
Live on, Father of the Mankon people, and Pride of Cameroon,
Live on, Courage of the Belittled,
Live on, Voice of the Voiceless,
Indeed, when we lay our beds, we confidently lie on them; because it is most refreshing that you taught us how to make this bed!

Your Granddaughter,

Mankah Mafo Ndibe

Your highness Fon Angwafo III of Mankon Fondom and kingdom. A perfect and mighty king. King Solomon the wisest king. I can vividly recall how on a Christmas morning many years behind you asked me to sing a Christmas Carol for your entertainment. I sang about the 3 wise men that presented gifts to baby Jesus in a manger who was to rule the world. Your question to me was if the king was really influential than you. I must admit that you are a great ruler that many generations shall resonate with my lord.

In the eyes of many people, you were their king, to me you were a daddy. Your highness, you encouraged me to invest my energy in education because it shall be my first husband. As your highness always emphasized, "a woman who doesn't study has no advantage over a man who can't read." You groomed us so well your majesty. As you always said, "unproductive days quickly become unproductive years if you don't sharpen your focus." So many sweet memories daddy. Your legacy lives on and we shall continue in the spirit of togetherness which you exercised and encouraged. Watch over and protect your children and the entire Mankon Fondom your majesty. We love you. Forever in our hearts.

Mankah Ngonguru Ntaralah

You were my hero, mentor, model, and wise king Solomon. You imparted a lot of knowledge in me, teaching me farm work, problem solving skills, politics, how to build a home. Work in the palace, church, and community just to name a few. You instilled in me virtues such as humility, love, gentleness, patience, wisdom, forgiveness, and generosity. You were a peace maker, respected and valued by all and your beautiful smile will forever remain in my memory.

You gave me so many sweet memorable names; Viz, wife to my secretary (then Angu Ndenge Sylvester), Nkum (Notable), President (Akongne group and inter church committee), my child and my wife, warder, and Bishop's wife (for information for the church).

I was very happy and proud to call you my King, father, husband, and caregiver.

Oh!!! How I miss that sweet voice. You gave me a lot of hope when I came to you with the project to build a centre for the Mankon language, and bible translation. You even went further to appeal to the government and the Archbishop of Bamenda to encourage the teaching of the Mankon language in schools. I pray this dream will one day be realized.

I highly believe you are rejoicing with the angels in heaven because you were blessed (a few days to your disappearance) by the Archbishop of Bamenda (Bishop Nkea) during the pontifical mass in your palace. You joined my husband, your former secretary (Angu Ndenge Sylvester) who worked devotedly for you for 36 years. May your gentle souls rest in perfect peace.

Margaret Khien Ndenge,
Wife of late Angu Ndenge Sylvester,
Former Secretary of Fon S.A.N Angwafo III

Your Royal Highness,

Father and King, most people have measured your greatness with respect to your work to the Mankon people and the country at large. To me your greatness was your time you gave to us the children of Mankon. Our access to you directly and the advice we received from you is immeasurable, for that we say thank you very much. As you live on our King, we shall continue to put all your words into practice. Mbeh, you live in us.

Martin Nche Nde Gashu (son of Pa John Nde Gashu)
We live in Atu-Azire
(Currently in Birmingham, England)

It is with deep regret, waking up on Saturday 21st of May 2022 to learn that Fon Angwafor III, My Father, my benefactor and mentor who hugely shaped my view during my educational life, work, and many other things has disappeared. Many things immediately propped my mind and I puzzled for a moment wondering if I will ever meet someone as impressive, smart, peace loving, grounded and filled with a lot of tenacity as the Fon.

Each and every one of us present here will join me to attest to the fact that it is not that common at this stage of our careers to have a father like the Fon; full of King Solomon's Wisdom, who has shaped our intellect, interest, and life in general. But HRM did all these for me.

Most of my work with him started at my very youthful age, when I was in Sacred Heart College and CCAST Bambili respectively. His RM being a trained agricultural engineer inculcated this spirit in me and I assisted in his farms during this period and this gave me the opportunity to learn from his views, perspectives and his wealth of knowledge/experience that marked the fundamental for my understanding of the world.

Thank you HRM for continually standing by me and inspiring me to do my best. You helped me strive for goals. I vividly remember how much you instilled in me when I was President General of Mankon Students Association and subsequently President of Mankon United. Your insight and strength as a resounding Father helped immensely and I feel much more confident in being able to make the right decisions for a potential change in the lives of others.

You have been the brain behind my political achievements. As first vice president of the ruling Cameroon People's Democratic Movement, you have inculcated much in me since 1989 till your exit. Getting through to this level with my political career is not just thanks to the greatest support and wisdom you shared but the fact that you continued to be there for me. You were generous with your advice and made it practical by sharing personal experiences of tolerance, perseverance, hard work, humility, good sense judgment etc. Indeed, I found guidance, direction, friendship, discipline and love.

A Hero of the Mankon Fondom has passed unto glory! This man who had changed many lives, I hope that everyone who has passed through his paths, never take him for granted, I certainly never did and never will.

Our great party, the CPDM will miss your experience and technical advice as the First Vice President of the party.

You carved your name on hearts, not tombstones. A legacy is etched into the minds of others and stories they share about you.

Rest in Peace His Royal Highness

Matoyah Cletus Anye
SHESAN

Although I didn't have many opportunities to spend much time with my great-grandfather, Fon S.A.N. Angwafo III, I remember every visit was highlighted by the sweet drinks he gave us to drink, which I thoroughly enjoyed. After we had finished drinking, my sister and I would chase each other around the courtyard while the adults spoke. He often gave us a chicken to return home with which, I might add after my aunt prepared, was very delicious. While we were saying our goodbyes, we fondly played with his dog until the time came for us to leave.

I remember there were some extraordinary things about him like the fact that I neither saw him eat in public nor saw his head. I asked my mom why this was, and she told me that it was customary for the Fon to never be seen eating or participating in ordinary activities of daily living. These things I observed impressed upon me a mystical quality about my great-grandfather and I realized there was a lot special about him. I wish I could have seen him when I last visited Cameroon a few months ago, but unfortunately only my mother could see him because it was too dangerous. The ongoing conflict since 2017 often got in the way of our plans to see him. Reflecting on the last time I saw him five years ago I wish I could have seen him one last time. I wish that I could turn back time and relive the moments I had with him, but this time I would not take them for granted. Even though I don't have many memories with him those I still have I will cherish forever.

Great-grandchild,

Mbongta Nanga-Afuuanwi Awantang

The Exit of an Uncommon Patriarch

Life is but a pilgrimage for mortals who after their sojourn on earth must return to their maker.

Death truly remains the common denominator of all humans reason why our own very legendary, magnificent, brave and sovereign king too disappeared at God's appointed time.

Today we celebrate the life of a hero, a great ruler who reigned for more than half a century with honour, dignity, splendour, and charisma. A leader who had a moral, cultural and intellectual influence on his subjects.

His Royal Highness Fon S.A.N Angwafo III was a rare species whose imposing presence and smile lit every environment in which he found himself. Mbeh carved his name on hearts and not tombstones reason why today he has etched a legacy in the hearts of many with incredible stories to share about him.

With a deep sense of honour, I can pride myself to have not only been born and lived during his era, but personally associated with the Fon from childhood where I occasionally spent holidays at the palace with my grand Aunt Nimo Ntoh, during MASA, numerous visits to the palace with my mother and my husband.

I cherished and relished every moment spent with the king during these visits and directly experienced the impact of this great ruler who vividly struck me with his desire to see the Mankon girl child educated.

Yes! The Fon of Mankon encouraged parents to defy gender boundaries and biases at the time by sending their daughters to school to become women of calibre and timbre. He reiterated during all MASA gatherings that a woman's first husband is her job. His advice yielded so many fruits looking at the prestigious positions held by many Mankon women today.

Mbeh, hard work was your watchword as you often said " without hard work nothing prospers and no food for a lazy man". As an agronomist, your passion in giving back to your community was highly displayed with you leading by example. Your usual rounds around the palace with your children and holidaymakers for clean-ups was always fun as I still have good memory of this, especially going to Asongkah for work at your different plantations.

Mbeh, I hold so close to my heart our last visit to the palace, less than two month before your disappearance where you crowned my elder brother with the great title of KUMALAH- AZHWIŋƏ-M+NTSÔ.

We had an intimate discussion with you, wherein you advised us to walk the road of honesty, sincerity and dignity in all our dealings as lawyers, reminding us that an apple never falls far from its tree thus we should be true representatives of our mother, your faithful servant whom you lamented passed on so soon. Who could have told us that those were our last moments with you?

You were a great man in every sense of the word, the king Solomon of our time who left the world and Mankon a better place than he found it.

We feel extremely naked with your disappearance Mbeh, but at the same time overwhelmed with joy for though you left for a deserved rest, you are still seated on the throne with the ascension of Fon Angwafo IV whose coming gladdens the hearts of your subjects as evident in the mammoth crowd all clad in plantain leaves who gathered to mourn you and welcome the new Fon on June 7th 2022.

This historic event made news all over the world and you sure watched with pride from the forest, the unique, Solemn yet exhilarating event which showcased our rich and enviable culture leaving everyone with a sense of belonging and unity, truly our strength.

We can't be more proud of you King Solomon, and for who we are. We promise to tenaciously hold on to the great values you inculcated in us, especially in preserving our culture which is our identity.

Adieu His Majesty Fon S.A.N Angwafo III.

Barrister Miranda Muluh Akumah

An archive, encyclopaedia, museum and a brain box in the entire Mankon land has disappeared. The above attempt to summarize what Fo Angwafo III was cannot give a real picture of the monarch until you had time yourself to interact and understand him.

Keep aside any human weaknesses he had; he was quite knowledgeable with the history and events in Mankon from his childhood to old age. His brain never failed him. What a memory box. Till date, I ponder where did such supernatural skills and knowledge come from. Being a traditional ruler embedded in customary and cultural values he was open to Christian values and embraced all churches in Mankon.

The wisdom of Solomon that he had has given us a visionary Fo Angwafo IV to complete what he left undone. Long live Fo Mankon.

Muama'ah Nguti J. C.
Alankyi Mankon

To the Go-Getter Fo Solomon AnyeGhamoti Angwafo III

The Mankon Fondom has remained an island in the stream where all and sundry throng for refuge. To test the strength of a bridge, water needs the collaboration of the rain. This Fondom has been tested over time dating back to pre-colonial history until hitherto. The dexterity and the tenacity of its leaders epitomized their rulership and this was characteristic in Fo Solomon AnyeGhamoti Angwafo III.

He was the incarnation of the customs and traditions of the Mankon people and nipped through the language with such fluency and knowledge. His magnanimity, charisma, decorum, demeanour, appearance and tone commanded respect. His legacy will live on in all the facets of the life of this Fondom.

Cognizant of his philosophical prowess, he sought to empower the youths in the propagation of the Mankon language and culture over the media. This was done by replacing an Octogenarian Teuh

Avwontom Malufah with Nimo Mujum Helen almost a decade ago. This ties with the Mankon adage that 'the eyes of the Kwifo are found on the leaves of the 'nearby bushes''. This voice has remained distinct as the people remain glued to their wireless sets every Monday at 4: 15 pm over CRTV Bamenda.

All the Mankon Language broadcasters in the implementation of the Royal Act will continue to remain deeply indebted to you as the driving force to reckon with in fostering the Mankon language on CRTV Radio, Foundation Radio, Radio Evangelium and the Christian Broadcasting Service radio.

Given his sixty-three years of rulership, the Mankon Fondom has evolved from a village into a Central Business District while maintaining its cultural identity. The king will forever live.

Long live the king.

Nimo Barrister Mujum Helen

Mankon and the world mourn the passing to glory of Fo Angwafo III. His passing to glory arouses in us feelings of tremendous sorrow and loss. He was a great man and ruler of his village. He was a far-sighted politician and an outstanding statesman who shouldered responsibility for the destiny of his people and of other people. As a ruler of a village situated at the convergence of many other villages he turned his village into a bridge of understanding and cooperation between all other villages, our tradition and the new religions. His life was devoted to improving the lives of his people and to the development of his village. His active presence on the national scene and his authority made it possible to discuss and resolve many extremely important problems relating not only to the village but to the entire nation and the world.

He was a great teacher by example. Especially in the field of agriculture where we had a lot of fun time and strategy for the new generation. He was an advocate for peace, mutual understanding and tolerance. His contribution to peace-building and the establishment of a spirit of friendship, cooperation and mutual assistance contribute an integral part of his invaluable legacy.

I am deeply honoured to share with everyone the sadness and gratitude for the life of a great king, father and brother in my humble capacity as Muma Angwafo III.

In an age when many people wrongly identify natural values with anger and violence. He showed the world the true face of a dedicated ruler of his nature, a face of wisdom, tolerance and moderation. He was a wise man, a refined politician and a remarkable statesman.

He passed on at a time of hopeful change in the village, country and the world in general. I regret especially that he has not lived to see peaceful resolution on issues affecting the society on which he and I closely worked together but I have every hope that we shall be able to complete the job with his successor whom we will support sincerely for peace stability and prosperity in a United Mankon. mɨkoŋ tɛʔɛ nkárə. Mankon will forever remember and miss you.

Muma Anye Nsoh
(Successor of late Muma Angwafo III)

Many, many, many years ago, judging it to be a century and a half back, a people from Bum under the leadership of their Grand/Great Grand Father Mbanga Augustine alias "Adamu" was wandering from the northern grass field towards the East.

They and their Hausa migrants found a piece of grassland suitable for farming and grazing. On investigation, they discovered that it was the land of the great King called Ndefru of Mankon. They prayed the King to allow them to be his tenants. He allocated a settlement area for them called Nta'ambag which has evolved with time to be called Abakwa, the Old Town with a large portion Bum Quarter.

The gesture of the King to offer the piece of land for free, but with one condition for it not to be sold, showed his kindness and love for a people, as Fo Angwafo III upheld this gesture and showed kindness which today has been proven through inter-marriages.

We, the Bum people shall always give our respect, gratitude and allegiance to the King and his people.

Our main regrets will be that we will lose his wisdom, his approach to solving problems, his wisdom in addressing issues, his way of connecting and communicating and above all an inspiration to many of us.

For the descendants of the Bum people in Mankon/Mezam, and by the people of Bum Quarter in Mankon

Long Live the Kingdom and welcome the new King.

Nji Mbanga Mbaswa E. Joko
(Compound Head Bum Quarter Mankon)

Legends don't die but their legacies live on, Dad. Though you now dine with our ancestors, you are undoubtedly still amongst us as manifested by the leaves of trees that you planted, whose fruits now blossomed in the full swing of the rainy season. You have always been a kingpin in the lives of many and as such; 'End of Span is not end of Legacy'. It breaks our hearts to part from a great figure like you. You were such a baobab cultural phoenix for posterity. You were so loving, caring and all-knowing. You were a 'colossus'. Your brain was replete with wisdom of unimaginable proportions. That's why your words were always well refined, apt and succinct. Much pain and difficulties accompany your passing into eternal glory.

Taking cognizance of the fact that; 'a journey without an end is not a journey' and 'every beginning must have an end'.... Your transition to dine with your ancestors is without doubt, a great one. Your son-in-law (Justice Timah), your mother (Mafo), your namesake (Anye) and Nkyante will all miss you.

Fare thee well...

Your daughter,

Nanga Angwafo Linda Epse Timah

Dear Father of the Mankon People,

My heart bleeds to know that you are missing. How I wish I could turn back the ends of time to those good old days after my anointment as Ndifor-Angwafo II of Mankon when you made me understand during my visits to the palace that as a successor, I do not have brothers, sisters, stepbrothers, stepsisters or stepmothers and that they are now my children and mothers. I remember in 1999 when you recommended me for recruitment at the University of Dschang and refused to recommend your own biological son Prof. Tsi Evaristus Angwafo III for the same recruitment for the reason that children are one and that more than one recommendation will carry weight. Rest in perfect peace, your majesty.

Professor George Ndiforngwafo II Ncheh

Why does it take absence to value presence, and sadness to know happiness?

In a sudden fit of nostalgic longing, I got off the (237) call and headed to my study.

I was grappling with the realities of time and change while poring over an archival collection of grainy black-and-white photos neatly preserved for posterity in an ancient photo album whose crusty crumbling covers were desperately clinging on to an unyielding metal ring binder.

Having survived the physical trauma of years of temperamental storage, the battering of travel, the vagaries of weather, and the untamed restless fingers of my children seeking to connect with their papa's past, the album is a veritable family heirloom, a repository of laughter, celebration, intrigue, and occasionally-sadness.

Flipping through the laminated pages I found what I was looking for. It was one of the few colour photos in the album. I stared at it for what seemed like an eternity.

The gist of the phone call that triggered my archaeological excavation was the sad announcement of the disappearance of the only king I have known personally; a quintessential leader, and most importantly, a father to me. Fon Angwafor III.

I shared a brief narrative about the photos with my wife Joanne 'Manwi'.

One of them showed my uncle Daniel and I at the palace in 1983 during a brief respite from my medical studies.

Then in a moment of focused introspection, I thought about my own journey through life and how the king had played such a pivotal role in my formative years at the beginning of a trajectory that has ultimately led me to my current neck-of-the-woods.

I had just graduated from secondary school, with an eye on furthering my education on a different longitude and latitude. Upon hearing this, my father recommended that I discuss my aspirations with our king.

A visit to the palace with my belated uncle Daniel left me inspired and motivated by the possibility of realizing my career ambitions despite overwhelming social and financial travails and insecurities I was confronting at that time. During our visit, the king spoke at length about life and barely broached academics. Primarily, he focused on personality, attitude and behaviour. That day I left the king's palace with an enviable set of survival tools which have enabled me to navigate the sometimes-daunting challenges on my circuitous journey in this thing we call LIFE.

Among the plethora of life's pearls, I acquired on that visit decades ago was something that still resonates with me today and I

174

must say that over the years I have shared this philosophical gem with thousands.

In essence, the king stated that how high I would climb in life would depend not as much on my academic prowess but rather on my attitude, behaviour, and conduct.

In short, Attitude, NOT Aptitude, will determine Altitude!

Fon Angwafor's tenacity, leadership skills, and commitment to human service are legion and timeless. A critical thinker and listener with profound emotional intelligence and a unique sense of situational awareness, he was a man imbued with an enormous capacity to absorb uncertainties and foster collectivism.

In a world of rugged individualism let's be mindful that his legacy lives on in each of us-sons and daughters of Mankon and in the lives of those around the world impacted by our attitudes and aptitudes.

As we celebrate his transition and the ascendancy of a new king, we must never forget that wherever we are in this world, somebody helped us to get there.

On my part, I owe it to him for the magnificent view I enjoy from the vantage point of his gigantic shoulders where I stand!

It takes absence to value presence, and sadness to appreciate happiness.

How I miss him!

Nche Zama, MD, PhD
Servant, Humanitarian, Author, Cardiothoracic Surgeon

Mbeh,

Oh life, what is life but a walking shadow. How illustrative of this are all the early stories you told us. One of them begins with Mafor Mankah Angwafor III and her lone brother, Nchewah of Munkyi, she getting betrothed to Ndefru III alias Labere (another laughter of the people), whom destiny had hoisted to the highest post in the land. Ndefru III could rely on his brother, Atso'oh Nta'ah who became Muma Ndefru III.

Muma's son, Peter Nche was a Second World War veteran who had seen action in Tripoli, Libya. After his return, your father Ndefru III anointed this dynamic young man to the position of Muma and he thus became his aid. Inspired by Peter Nche Muma's tales of his travels, Ndefru III decided to expand the town from the Ntambag hill to the Azire hill on which The Fon's Street and Commercial Avenue are located.

- He accomplished this through communal labour every Zakob. The Mankon people refer to works of constructing the roads, bridges and halls and other communal infrastructure as *Atsangha community*.
- Pa Peter *aka* Muma Ndefru III got his friend Maximus Chibikom, a teacher to note what he was doing. Using his steps and some workforce to put limits with bamboo pins; he mapped out the Commercial Avenue and the Fon's Street neighbourhood following what he had seen in Tripoli.
- Mbeh, you kept asking us why we could not follow the example of simple determined people to change our surroundings. Today, this is the only planned part of our city. ***This is the people's power!***
- Oh father, unforgettable are stories you told us of the early days. Stories about you, Akuma Lawrence Atanga and Alphonse Forngang Ndenge starting life on a narrow path. You first built a hut at the present City Chemist site to live in and attend school then a second at Atua Azire, at the present site of the Community Hall on land donated by Pa. Gashu. Taking footpaths every weekend in search of food from your mother in the palace of many people in the early thirties was rife with challenges and full of lessons.
- Mbeh, you told us of your school life from one Mission School to the other and finally finishing at Native Authority School Up-station where Mrs. Ngeng of Ngeng Junction was your bench mate and your brother, Stephen Awasum *Alias Awasum C.N.U* sat behind you.

We marvel at you going to-and-fro up the station hill between Atua Azire and N.A. School Up-Station every morning and diligently coordinating food supplies and carrying out bookkeeping duties for Mafo Ndefru III's enterprise at the Bamenda prison.

- Mbeh, who shall tell us these interesting stories again about the trailblazing Mafo Mankah Ndefru III who bought a Land Rover in 1924 to facilitate the food supply business and named it ***Aghahnwi*** (God given)? This was the first vehicle popularly called Nyam Timusong in the Grassfields.

176

- Mbeh, who could tell that your destiny had been mapped out in an innocent play by young lads in the early forties? You played the part of the Fon and your brother, Ndeh Ntumazah played Winston Churchill, then British Prime Minister visiting the land. This play later turned into reality, with you becoming the FON and the name Winston sticking to Ndeh Ntumazah who later on became a politician, not unlike Churchill.
- Mbeh, you told us about Angwafo II building 30 huts at Ntambag to accommodate the Hausa traders who were compelled to leave the market site Up-station where the Germans intended building a fort in 1901. Always the father, Fo Angwafo II subsequently settled the first Bum family besides the Hausas. Effectively the market moved to Ntambag and that was the beginning of the expansion of our city.
- Mbeh, it was so enriching when I told you about Prof. Sama Doh and you told me they were your children: Mrs. Lucy Gwanmesia, Prof Sama Doh and Ni Sama Doh Finley. They were the children of your neighbours in Befang, your last post of duty as an Agric officer before ascending the throne. Pa Doh was the Health Officer at the time.

Again, the story of the making of businessmen. Your uncle Pa Gideon Angwafo II of the CDC Bota Labour Camp, Pa Gregory Nsoh of the Messelele labour Champ, who intervened in the Ngemba Union, to save their child from embarrassment by the then CDC Manager (paying into the CDC account £.15 sterling due to accounting errors by the then accountant Daniel Awah Nangah in 1955). CDC then decided to separate with Pa Nangah. Pa Gideon sent him with a note to Pa Wangia of the P.W.D Bamenda carpentry workshop. He said Nangah shall supply timber to P.W.D. and that it was better to start from Befang. Guess who was giving timber, Solomon Anye Ghamoti Ndefru III. Even though the union did not last, it paved the way for the beginning of Nangah as contractor. The rest is history.

- Mbeh, as a missing Fon, you are now in the venerable line of great men who for over 800 years have moved their people from Sa'ah Nyom, Ngambe Tikar - Donga and Mantum plateau-Upper Noun Valley (Ndop plain) - Babadjou - Balessing - Bafou - For Ngu Tenghor (Fongo Tongo) - Bamumbu - Ntarinkon in Atezwirikum (Widikum) and Alah Nyki (the present site), in quest of better pastures, more fertile soils, more game, more clement climate and avoiding Islamisation that was halted at *the great river* and by tse-tse fly, thus scattering the people in various directions (Around the 1200/1300 hundreds).

You gave us the background on the people who never rested on one spot. Most were traders (Atangha) dispute settlers (Asah), Titleholders (For). Recognition for deeds and important events and situations are reflected in our names: *Ngeh, Maghine, Andze, Atso'oh, Ako'o, Asso'o, Ama'ah, Na'ah, Nda'ah, Mbue'eh, Tchieh etc.*

Those that were named after great deeds;

- Asanji Manya'ah who after the war (1900) was the first to father children that opened the way for baby boom.
- Ntohmambang, great emissary of Angwafo II to the Fon of Kijem-keku (Big Babangki) to grant protection of the women and children during the German invasion of Mankon. This exiting population was led by Teh Meso'oh (Brother to Formarah of Alakuma). He never returned from this expedition with others with whom he went. That is why up to the present day, Mankon can never forget the protection of the Kijen Keku (Big Babangki) people in time of need (1891-1900).

Who will open for us the annals of ages gone by? Again, I remember how you told us of Atangha Tabah **Nde Angu** losing one eye at the warfront. That he was a road trader with friends buying palm oil from Teze to sell in the big market at Banyo and cola nuts from Kumbo to sell in the great market of Kano in Northern Nigeria. All this they did on foot through Mayo Binka, Bali in Nigeria to Kano. They brought back salt and from Banyo goats.

Ah! Mbeh, the lessons from the stories of the early brave Mankon men who were German soldiers;

- Ottou Ngang (Alias Kasarah) who came with cassava from Santa Issabel (Malabo),
- James Macaba (who came with cocoyam's from Santa Issabel), the above two came home by 1916.
- Pa Akumchi and Pa Marcus Ngang, Pa Pheih (Felix in German) Akuma Ntumnah and Clement Ngwa (They opened the church in Alamatu (1924)).

How Ottou Ngang and James Macabah after landing in Fernand de Po (Bioko Island-Afueh ne tzuh) saw cassava and macabo (brought in by the Spaniards to the Island of Santa Issabel from South America). Took samples through Kribi-Mvengue, Bokito, Bangwa, Baffoussam, to Mankon. All this on foot and planted what we have today. A lesson to all, especially those in the diaspora?

- Mbeh, always Ntambeng. Ntambeng, Ntambeng. The stories of the Bafut people not happy with the Catholic Church, the building of huts at Ntambeng. The relocation of the school to the spot with all the people living in the area. This was the first boarding school in the North West in the early 30s by Ndefru III in consonance with the example of Angwafo II in Ntambag.

- Mbeh, we cannot forget R.C.M Ntambeng on Saturdays in the early 60s at the beginning of your reign. Sport preparations for the Empire Day to be held at Up-Station.

- The school football league; Basel Mission (Mbengwi, Bafut, Bali, Batibo and Azire). Native Authority (N.A) Bamenda, Santa and Ndop. Roman Catholic Mission (R.C.M) Mile4 Nkwen, Big Mankon and Ntambeng.

These schools met on Saturdays at the school field of R.C.M Ntambeng. R.C.M Ntambeng had great football names such as Stephen Chi, Nsoh Bang and Peter Forbah. From Big Mankon; Nche Gardarme, Plumber and the great Chi Bandeh. The school field was the best to play in the early 60s in the area and was centrally located.

Again, in 1966 when Father Harold Percey and some Sudanese students were running away from war ravaging Sudan, were asked to be stationed in Ntambeng. He being a master builder succeeded in building the present church and father's residence.

In the early 70s, when the Bamenda Diocese was created and a Bishop named, only Ntambeng had a conducive area for the Bishop to reside. No wonder Ntambeng has continued to be associated with Bamenda Diocese in the Catholic System.

- Mbeh, your early life coupled with your difficult road to education made you a pillar of our development. You ceded royal land for schools (Sacred Heart College), negotiated for others to let go land for Our Lady of Lourdes College, Longla, Baptist High school Mankon, GBHS Mankon, GBHS Ntahmulung, Technical schools and others.

Your children have not failed you in this aspect and are all over the globe representing you and the village.

We say the Fon is missing because he is always with us.

- Mbeh, you are a general of unparalleled brilliance. Your size, smile gives everyone in contact with you the feeling of being around power and a great personality. Those that know you up close and personally know you were a youth full of life and camaraderie.

You refer to those up close by their initials, and many times we heard your friendliness and peculiar dynamics of interpersonal relationships.

In all of this, you told us on a serious note that we were lucky. You always asked if we knew what it meant to confide in a sister?

Mafo Mankah, Tatah Nchewah the mustard seed had grown to become a great baobab that shall last centuries.

Nche-Fortoh Atanga

I was in Standard III in primary school when HRH S. A. N Angwafo III succeeded in 1959 his Father, Fo Ndefru III, the Fo of Mankon and the paramount ruler of the Ngemba people. Mankon was a typical grass field kingdom. The hills were pure savannah and the valleys were either lush forests mixed with a scattering of raphia or covered completely with stretches of raphia palms from which palm wine is produced. Quarters were interconnected by a network of footpaths and river crossings with bridges constructed of timber and bamboos designed and built by the people of Mankon. In the palace, the women quarters and some other buildings which he inherited were roofed with grass. A large majority of the house in the then Ntahmbag not to talk of the rest of the kingdom were grass-roofed. Today, the situation in all aspects is radically different because Fo Angwafo III adopted and applied a modernization strategy anchored on the following pillars: education of the people, infrastructural development, socio-economic empowerment, and political involvement of the people.

He recognized that an ignorant population was a danger to itself and that education of the population was a powerful tool for its transformation for development in a rapidly changing environment. In this regard, he wisely sacrificed his hunting ground, Ngomgham, for the construction of Sacred Heart College Mankon and essentially at the same time he gave land for the construction of Our Lady of

180

Lourdes College, and the Women Teachers Training College (WTTC) which later became Presbyterian High School; and then the land for the other mission colleges, government primary schools, government secondary and technical colleges was allotted as the need arose. It is from his ascension to pilot the affairs of Mankon that Mankon children started going to college in large numbers. Colleges in Mankon today have become centres of educational excellence. Education was a fundamental strategic policy objective at the core of his societal transformative efforts.

Regarding infrastructural development, except the Atsum, "the holy of holies in the palace" which has stayed the same, the palace in several areas has been totally reconstructed and modernized and a museum that houses Mankon art objects and other cultural artifacts has been built. Grass roofing of the palace was an annual ritual involving the entire village during which primary schools had to cut grass around December each year, tie it in bundles and take to the palace. Now, the children know nothing about this because of the reconstruction of the palace in durable material. Thanks to the modernization effort of the Fon.

Between 1960 and 1970, the network of footpaths was reconstructed through purely Mankon community effort as motorable earth roads and bridges were progressively built by Mankon people. Travelling from one part of Mankon to the other was made easy. The current road to Mbengwi was built during this period and it replaced the old road through the palace. Without the inspiring leadership of the Fon this could not have been accomplished.

As a trained agronomist, the Fon introduced in all areas of agriculture and forestry new farming techniques and led by example. Those who believed in him and followed him in his various agricultural and forestry efforts increased their income which enabled them to sponsor their children in schools as well as improve their living conditions. He was present in the life of the people and through varied farming projects showed them how to improve their economic status.

In the political arena, HRH S A N Angwafo III upon becoming the Fon of Mankon quickly realized the strategic position of Mankon and its historical situation as well as the then prevailing local political dynamics. Mankon was the heart of One Kamerun (OK) party allied to the UPC, the nationalist opposition party which the government of the Federal Republic Cameroon was bent on its total destruction.

This placed Mankon and its people in the eye of a cyclone. HRH S A N Angwafo III correctly came to the conclusion that he must be involved in partisan party politics. As a consequence, he fought parliamentary elections as an independent candidate; he won the elections and became the first and only independent parliamentarian in the West Cameroon House of Assembly. He remained in politics until his passing on. To the Mankon people, his decision from inception to be a politician positioned him to anticipate and block all the machinations and malicious forces that rose now and again against Mankon. This was indeed perceptive and proactive leadership.

During the past 63 years of him as the ruler of Mankon, the demographics of Mankon changed profoundly as a result of the massive influx of populations from other parts of the North West Region, the West Region and other parts of the country. This influx progressively transformed Mankon into a cosmopolitan area thus creating a complex sociocultural environment. Compounded by the old historical conflicts with some of its neighbours, this urbanization created a difficult environment for a leader. While other leaders like him had to lead only their indigenous population he had to contend with a mix of cultures due to a determined and ambitious heterogeneous population. He was unlike any other Fon subjected to complex human interactions and varied interests seeking to settle and carve out their niches in the Mankon space. He successfully managed and survived in a minefield. We thank God that because of his education prior to his becoming the Fo of Mankon he was able to meet the challenges of his office and became an effective and efficient leader.

In 1970 I won a British Council scholarship to study engineering in the UK and as part of the requirements to travel I had to present a medical certificate. When I did the medical examination I was given a medical certificate which stated that I had Tuberculosis. Of course, I knew this because I opened the envelope. I was frightened and confused because I realized that I would be taken off the scholarship list. I knew that I had no tuberculosis. I was inspired to realize that the Fon was the only person who could understand the gravity of my situation and promptly come to my rescue. I was not wrong. I went and presented the certificate to him. He instructed that I should sleep in the palace; the next day he took me himself to Acha-Tugi Hospital operated by Presbyterian Church in Cameroon for another examination. He told the doctor that I have been coughing severely and since I had to travel out of the country for studies, he needed to ascertain that I did not have a serious health problem. The X-ray taken showed that my chest was clear. It was only then that he showed the doctor the medical certificate. His swift action left a lasting impression on me. I am not the only case where he acted same, promptly.

In November 2003 when I graduated from the infamous and notorious "university", Nkondengui Central Prison, Yaoundé, after four years of detention for crimes I never committed and following due process (trial and acquittal), I presented myself to the Fon. His joy on seeing me was indescribable. He firmly grabbed me on my upper arms and shook me and declared that "Ndefru, the State turned you upside down and nothing fell out of your pocket. You are therefore the cleanest man in Cameroon". He encouraged me to be strong and courageous and move on with my life. He had made several efforts to visit me but this was not possible because of his position. His compassionate and encouraging words strengthened and preserved me.

In one of my visits to the palace, the Fon after the usual salutations asked me: "how was the *Aqwara matoh*" (the harlot princess). I was taken aback because I had never heard of such a person. He laughed heartily and then told me that that was how my mother was known in the palace. My mother was the daughter of a prince and grew up in the palace and got married as a princess from the palace. She got this name as a result of her determination to get married only to my father. She threatened to remain single if she did not marry my father. It is a love story that ended well for I and my siblings are the fruits of that union.

That is the Fo S.A.N Angwafo III, I know. He was a distinguished and accomplished leader of his people, the Mankon people, and is one of the founding fathers and builders of this nation, Cameroon. He was strategic, innovative and transformative in leading and managing the affairs of his people in very challenging circumstances. He was an efficient and effective Change manager-a task for the strong hearted. He was an intelligent, brave, and courageous man. A compassionate leader in every sense of the word!

Nde Ningo, Forla

His Royal Highness Fon S. A.N. Angwafo III was a father figure to all and sundry, but to me in particular, he laid the foundation stone and provided the blocks of my post-primary education. This valuable assistance provided a springboard for my career as police officer. I shall eternally be grateful to be him.

May the love and peace of Jesus be with be with him as he journeys home to go to receive his Royal crown and have eternal rest granted on him.

Adieu, my beloved father.

Ndefru Daniel Chi Ndifor Angwafo III

My Hero Goes Home

My dear Dad, where do I start, where do I end? How do I express what I feel deep down inside of me?

As the days go by, it begins to dawn on me that my Hero has truly gone home. It is very difficult to hold back the tears, but one thing that reassures me is this: although my Hero has gone home, his spirit still lives in me. Your unflinching support and mentorship throughout my life's journey have been very present and deeply rewarding. Consequently, I find it very difficult to refer to you in the past tense. Your transition is a colossal blow to me and I am still grappling with the huge vacuum you have left in my life. When you returned from South Africa in 2014, you narrated a story to me about how you almost 'went home' but for the grace of God. I made a prayer of thanksgiving then and asked God to give you a while longer so we could continue to tap from your wealth of knowledge and wisdom and you 'disappeared' eight years later.

I am thankful for His grace and mercy. You have been my rock, a Dad and a Hero to me. You helped me stand even when I wanted to give up. The fragrance of your wisdom will linger on like a beautiful orchid that God allowed many to share but did not allow me to savour for as long as I wanted. I guess I could never have enough of you. Though I miss you and shed tears, I cannot complain because your spirit lives on in me.

In the year 2002, exactly twenty (20) years ago, you took me to the United States of America for a one-month working visit. During this period, you imparted a lot of knowledge as we toured the states of Texas, Massachusetts, Maryland etc;. I can vividly remember the day you sat me down in the palace at Worcester in Massachusetts and addressed me by my real name NGWA and not my nickname 'Betterman' as you usually called me. You gave me the following basic principles of life:

- Never be a beggar
- Remain humble
- Remain honest
- Always be ready to reconcile

These life nuggets will forever be etched in my memory.

My Hero! My version of King Solomon! Have you truly 'disappeared'..?

Your son,

Ndefru Linus Betterman

"Grandpa, I am short of words. What I know is like King Solomon of the Bible, you applied wisdom in everything you said or did. You lived all through your life listening to people and applying wisdom in talking to your people, wherever or whenever there was any conflict, you will water down the tension with your calmness and gentle words.

Grandpa, I pray that this kind of wisdom stays and lives within your children, grandchildren, great-grandchildren and amongst your generations yet to come. I am pleased to have spent part of my childhood with you, I felt so comfortable and with you one knew and understood what being at home means.

You have lived in the Palace during the high and low times of the crisis, the armed conflict that has driven many families and youths away from home. You stood by your people, sat on your throne and you always assured them of your presence and support. You protected your dignity as king and kept your head above the waters even when everyone felt like drowning.

I remember when we came to interview you once as a team of Journalists, you still singled me out in your old age and presented me to my colleagues as "your daughter", I felt proud and loved. Your words gave me reasons to continue to do things differently and to pull through no matter the storms of life. You are a true Hero.

Thank you for all your teachings, truly you have written your name in the sands of time. We will miss you, we will read about you and continue to write more about you. Rest with Our Ancestors!!!"

Grandpa as you rest with our ancestors, I wish to say that I have witnessed first-hand the blessings you left behind for us to enjoy. Your people mourn the fact that you will not be seen anymore and mourn that they wouldn't hear you but again rejoice because you left a legacy for all to enjoy.

Mankon Children can sit anywhere across the world and be proud to talk about home. You were a rare king, a dad with a golden heart. Continue to watch over us, your family, your people, wherever you are. Guide our steps when we seem confused and help us remain united so we grow stronger to preserve the beauty of the Mankon Culture. Amen

Your granddaughter,

Ndefru Manka Mafo Melanie

Anybody who knows Ndemuafo David (Pamero) will be waiting to read what he has written about Mbeeh (His Royal Highness Fon S.A.N. Angwafo III) Fon of Mankon. Your eyes are on my ink, the DNA witness of what I term SSS (S^3) *Solomon Supernaturally Surprises.*

Solomon, like King Solomon in the Bible, he manifested the wisdom of king Solomon in his Judgment of issues among his children and people. It took me more than three decades (since 1985) to understand the judgment he passed among us his children, that he/she who failed exams should be consoled, that merry-making without consoling those who have failed is wrong.

Supernatural: Some people will be mourning for land, money, food, title, etc. they were getting from Mbeeh but I am mourning and glorify God for a mentor God placed me under his guidance. He trained me by instructions and signs. He supernaturally protected me with hardship and hard work through the umbilical cord of servanthood. He lived a simple and humble life. He was the source of hope to many but unfortunately for him, he was the source of energy to an ecosystem of many national and international food webs and food chains that surrounded him and operated with the modus operandi of grabbing of what he had and he supernaturally lived a successful and impactful life. He understood with whom he was living and dealing. He who understands the supernatural controls the natural.

Surprises: He drilled me on how things that happened to him came as a surprise. This drill is not up to one year old. Mbeeh has surprised me right to the marrow of my bones by putting men of God at the central stage for his way forward.

Oh God help protect, guide, feed, heal, teach, deliver and direct your people. Thine will be done.

Solomon Supernaturally Surprises the people with a just come.
Son,

Ndemuafo David (Pamero's strategist)

21ˢᵗ of May 2022 will forever remain the darkest day of my life, for it was this day that the Almighty God took you our father away from this sinful world unto himself.

I did not believe what I was told but it came time. Father, you were a living encyclopaedia not only to the Mankon man but to the whole Nation at large.

My family and I will always be indebted to you, for I am what I am today all because of you, father.

You taught me political tolerance and cohabitation with other political opponents. Father, I promise to keep all your enriching advice.

May the Good Lord grant you intentional rest till we meet to part no more.

Son,

Ndisah Philip Fon

Why were Angels not made to Physically live on Earth forever?
Biologically, you were my Father.
Physically, you were my Protector and Guard.
Spiritually, you were my Inspiration.
Emotionally, you were my Comfort.
Theologically, you were my King Solomon.
Practically, you were my Teacher and Mentor.

Politically, you were a Development Activist and thus impacted the lives of your Children, grandchildren, great-grandchildren, Mankonians, Cameroonians, the international community, and the world at large in such a way that mankind will live to remember.

You showed humankind love beyond boundaries. Your care and advocacy for the underprivileged, the downtrodden and humanity, sets you apart in a class of your own qualifying you, *Our Angel*.

Because you completed the task our Heavenly Father sent you to perform on earth and more, even in the most arduous conditions and because we understand that no one lives in human form in perpetuity and that there is reunion after life, we are hopeful.

Because we always made known to you how special and how much of a blessing you are to us and the world at large, we are consoled.

Because we know that you carried all the beautiful moments we shared, we trust that we are not separated but that you are in a better place to exercise your powers of ancestral intercession with your forebears over us.

I know that I will see you physically in your son Fo Fru John ANGWAFO IV while carrying your wise words of advice and drive everywhere I go.

We do love and miss you, DAD. Till we meet again to part no more, I am forever indebted to you in love. Rest well legend.

Your daughter,

NEH Tabo Angwafo

Fo Angwafo III leaves a huge legacy for the people of Mankon and the Chingang family in particular. The Fon was more than a father to his late friend's children, even after the demise of his bosom friend. The Chingang family will forever be grateful. As one of Cameroon's most educated traditional rulers, Fo Angwafo promoted culture and education in all domains, especially the education of the girl child. That is why Mankon will forever remain the pacesetter in the grass fields because he gave the right to the girls of Mankon to be landowners and heirs.

As you join your bosom friend, Pa JC Ngang, we know you are watching over us.

Long live the king.

Ngang Prudence epouse Fuh Wung

Gone At A Ripe Age
Gone in his nineties
Missed by all parties.
Gone to his ancestors.
Mourned by all benefactors.
Born in the month of May.
Gone in the month of May.

All night long Mankon cries
Tears run down her cheeks.
All friends mourn the demise,
Of her king in all the streets.
All Mankon is full of grief,
Yet no one to lend her relief.

No one comes to the temple now,
To worship on the holy days.
Nor are there people to bow,
Who come to the palace to say,
Long live the King,
Gifts to you we bring.
But you, O LORD, are King forever,
And will rule to the end of time.
And this, O LORD we remember,
That our earthly kings will live to die.
And gifts of praise and worship to you LORD,
We bring as we live these days to mourn.
Daughter,

Ngum Adela Angwafo

"Don't grief for me, for now I am free; I won't be far away, for life goes on. Life is eternal and love is immortal, and death is only a horizon". Will I ever get to see you again? Who will tell me those sweet old tales? Who will call to ensure my new family is fine, and the children's education foremost? Who will teach me the key marital traits? Who will take me to the orchards, fishpond, poultry, piggery et al? who will run behind me to tether the goats? Oh! A diversified father who will take us up the hills during the holidays and pay us wages as we work, all to inculcate in us the spirit of hard work and discipline. The life of one we love is never lost. Dad had a heart that cared completely.

Oh! The reality of life has finally dawned on me. My role model, friend, confidant, source of hope and defence mechanism has left me at a crossroad. Dad, you held my hand tight as I walked down life's journey. Your words of advice, encouragement, love, peace, humility, and unity still echo and have moulded me into the lady you have always wanted me to be. You prioritized my education, health and feeding. OH, how I flash into that fateful afternoon you drove to school after you heard of a riot on campus, just to ensure I was fine. I would always wake up to your driver's knock at my door each time I expressed a lack in school. You often told me my first husband is my job and that, you ensured I had. You called me up severally as a teen to check on my social lifestyle. You often applauded me for being one of your least expensive children. You fought tooth and nail and did everything within your powers to recover my documents and redeploy your little girl from Garoua after the train incident. Farming was a lifestyle you embedded in me. When I brought home my D.I.P.E.S and first degree, what you gave me was a hoe and a farm, telling me to equally defend the certificates on the farm. I vividly recall the tender love and affection with which you gave me into marriage. A dad who did not relent in his efforts to secure me a home assistant after my first child. You had always been an ever-present support to my husband and me. You encouraged and promoted my zeal and love for business by offering to us a shop to ensure that, the business spirit never dies. When I came home a few months back, little did I know it was the last. It was a very memorable time spent together and I enjoyed your fatherly tales, counsel, and constant encouragement, though in bad health. Where do I tell the children grandpa has gone to? To whom do I tell my story? Rest on our guardian angel. I know you are happy in your mother's arms. Your legacy lives on. Those inner core values you taught me were well assimilated. I am proud of you and will never fail you. Love you my hero, good night.

Daughter,

Ngum Angwafo eps Bemnji

Fon Angwafo III was a true father with a unique ability to encourage and acknowledge growth, independence and responsibility in all his children.

I clearly remember his frustration during one of my visits to the palace, when it was announced to him that Pa Wangia's son was there to see him.

"Mr. Americain, welcome! You come to the palace in your own right, not as your father's son. That you are your father's son is even greater. I knew and worked with him for a long time and he did a lot of things in Mankon. If you came to the palace as your father's son, then who is going to help me with all the work your father started and the work that there is to do? When I meet your parents again, what do I tell them?"

I sat with him in the palace while he received visitors and he proudly introduced me to them as "my son, the engineer from America"!

This, and many other lessons the Fon masterfully communicated to me will always keep me grounded and steadfast in all I do.

Hail to the Fon!

Ngwa-Nkwenti Wangia
Dallas, Texas

Knowing this life is part of a greater journey cannot prepare us enough for the void left behind once we transition onward.

The childhood memories I hold of my grandfather, H.R.H. Fon S.A.N. Angwafo III, are very rich, joyful, and full of colour as my long-term holidays from school meant I got to spend time with him and my grandmother among several others in The Mankon Palace, Bamenda. Every year, I looked forward to the only time during the year when I got to experience life on the farm with the curiosity and eagerness only a city child could hold. It meant mornings tidying the palace, imbibing traditions and customs from aunts and uncles while improving my fluency in the Mankon language by full emersion. Vivid memories of going with my grandfather to the farm at Asongkah run through my mind's eye. He had a passion for farming which was contagious, and I would ride along with several others in the back of the truck on windy bumpy roads with such excitement listening to stories told by the older passengers, mostly folklore full of metaphors, which were interrupted by the occasional gasps as the leaves of the palm trees brushed and beat about us as we got closer and deeper into the plantation.

Alas, these innocent childhood memories would give way to more concrete, interactive, and deductive encounters as I would later visit him as a young adult in secondary school, college, medical school, as a young bride with my groom, and later as a mother with his great-grandchildren. My grandfather always emphasized the importance of formal education with practical utility. He often celebrated our academic successes and encouraged the pursuit of education for the purpose of societal advancement. As a medical student he would often ask me if I could use local resources within my scope of training to improve the public health of the community without heavy reliance on the technologies or systems in which I trained. He constantly challenged me to think outside the box and return to improve the delivery and standard of health in Bamenda and Cameroon.

My most memorable visits are from 2008 when I visited three times from the U.S. with my husband. During our first visit that year, my husband who was then my fiancée accompanied by his father went to ask for my hand in marriage from my father who advised them to obtain permission from my grandfather, the only one who could grant such grace. I would learn from my husband that my father informed them that he was only the "babysitter", but they would have to seek permission from my real father, my grandfather.

This mild encounter was followed by a beautiful introduction for my husband and his family to the palace during which they experienced the nature and persona my grandfather embodied. During the 2nd visit, we were honoured and privileged to have had our traditional wedding with ceremonies and palace rites presided by my grandfather. On our third visit that year, we would celebrate our wedding in the local Catholic Church which he attended followed by a reception at the palace the next day with ceremonial traditional dances with hundreds of guests in attendance of this celebration. His advice to me and my new groom was simple. He said to us, "…in our language, there is no word for divorce. You need to make it work and manage each other." Fourteen years into this sacrament, we continue to learn and grow in consideration, compromise, sacrificial love, recognizing his advice that day was some of the best advice we both could have received at that time.

Over the years, we made several trips to Cameroon with our children to visit their great-grandfather. As a great-grandfather, even though he was the Fon and lived within certain procedural constraints, he was always eager to embrace his great-grandchildren and carry them as babies on his laps while engaging in conversations with them about every and any subject. It was my greatest joy to see him each visit with each additional child as our family grew. Our oldest two children have vivid memories of their visits to the palace with their great-grandfather and I find solace in knowing I took none of these moments for granted having seen him only a few months prior to his disappearance.

I am saddened, grieved, and no longer privileged to experience his physical presence again. However, the values, life lessons and memories he impressed upon me could only be accomplished by he who lived a life well and to the fullest. *What more can be expressed in losing the only grandfather I ever knew?*

We are never fully prepared for transitions, but peace comes in knowing the work of the journey is complete. I am grateful for the time and space we shared on this part of the journey. I continue to find inspiration and direction from those remnants within which I rely upon for guidance to tread the road I have yet to travel while looking forward to that place and time where and when I too shall transition, *onward*.

Dr. Nimae Ngumna'ah Awantang

There where so many beautiful moments we've been able to share with him, promises we've made to him and lessons that we've learnt from him.

If it wasn't for his support, words of wisdom and encouragement surely, some would have been doubting themselves today. It's then important to remember the Fon (grandpa Mbeh) did not only give us protection, love and support but also the strength to always keep going, to have faith in ourselves and we truly appreciate that, It will never be forgotten.

He was so particular about our education, encouraged us in going the furthest we could in life and truly fulfilling our happiness.

Our grandfather will forever be missed.

Grandkids,

Njom, Tarnu, Muaze

Fo S.A.N Angwafor III the Politician: Our contact and the unseen part of Him in the Public Eye

As a UPC Party Political Bureau member and an aspirant for the Parliamentary and Council multi-party elections of 2007 in the Mezam and Bamenda 11 constituencies, I had the opportunity to interact with the Fo from a different angle, not the Mankon Village and its challenges. I expected a very rocky encounter from what I knew about Him and Politics and the persistently repeated advice from my entourage. A few weeks before campaigns started, I contacted the Palace for a meeting with the Fo. The immediate reaction was he readily granted the audience I solicited. *First surprise*.

Knowing the Sphinx, my next feeling was, where is the trick? Unlike the general opinion, the Fo was very open to other political schools of thought. Then, during the audience, I outlined my intentions, approach and where he could come in for me. When he took over to speak, I was very keen on all aspects of the Fo: body movement, gestures, facial expression, tone, etc. Compared to what I knew him to be, I realized all was in order and he reiterated his determination to make sure the ground was level for all protagonists in Mankon. Reassured me of his availability wherever I thought he could be useful. *Second surprise*, the Fo was a genuine democrat but firm in his Political Party through conviction and reason, assuming his people will see that he is right. That had always been Him, but the public eye painted a different picture. I left convinced about his sincerity not to interfere in the expression of the right result of the political race. Obviously, around him there were some radicals, and I knew a few, who wanted the Fo to be high-handed and facilitate only the presence of his party on the ground. He insisted and said all his children had an open political arena for the best to win. *Third surprise*, before my departure he said I was very free to carry out my campaign everywhere in Mankon including the Palace. And I organized two campaign rallies in the Palace and Ntingkag Square. We separated, and he wished me well by invoking the God of our land to guide and protect me.

During the campaign, counting and proclamation of results, I watched the Fo. *Fourth surprise*, He was consistent with his declaration to me, no attempts to move or regulate polling stations, no rigging effort initiated by him, no out of order campaign from him, no biased use of the administrative authorities, etc. It all went peacefully.

I rediscovered the Fo, very firm and determined in his political camp but making sure the ground was open to other dissenting groups. The Fo was a genuine democrat, misunderstood because of no effort or inherent bias to get closer to him to know his modus operandi.

Nko'zhum F.M. Mantohbang Tsagineu 1 (Douala)

A pillar of stability in an area which was no stranger to conflict. I remember vividly how resourceful you were in keeping my family in check. What an honour to witness your great transition; Although physically unheard, I thank you for always being there.

Farewell my King, Your friendship was a blessing.

Thank you for your unwavering service to the Mankon people. The whole kingdom will miss you and mourn the disappearance of a figure so special. We have your precious memories and words of wisdom you gave us to hang on to during this transition.

Nkumfo'o Ntseh Awa

The Baobab Tree and the Lion of the Mankon Fondom. Your disappearance took us by surprise! For 28 good years that your right-hand Pa Nkwenti Angwafor III left us, you took over the baton of command and ensured we never lacked anything. You also waited patiently for us to become independent before disappearing to meet our ancestors.

The Bible in 1 Kings 1-11 predicted you were the Solomon of our Time. Our King Solomon (Fon of Wisdom). Through your wisdom, you picked a befitting successor with so much gentleness, kindness and finesse to pick up where you left off and rule over the Mankon Fondom. Thanks to this fervent action we are certain the Mankon Kingdom will preserve its honour, power, culture, wealth and respect.

I promise to provide my continued support to ensure our beloved fatherland upholds its values. Through us, your legacy lives on.

Through understanding and discernment of our King Solomon may God grant unto us great riches, honour, and longevity just as it is written in the bible(1 Kings 3:11-15, NIV).

Nkwenti Angwafor III

Our great lineage Head and Father,

His Royal Highness,

Fon Angwafo III, Solomon AnyeGhamoti Ndefru,

You were not only the Icon of the Mankon Fondom but also that of Cameroon. Your "missing" has created a palpable political, educational, agricultural and cultural vacuum in this nation that can hardly be filled.

You became a politician in the 60s as a young Fon and your contributions to the political evolution of Cameroon have left behind many important pages of history. Your participation at the Fumban Conference that brought true multiparty democracy at the birth of this Nation in 1961 will remain in the hearts of true Cameroonians. The unity, justice, and peace that you and late President Ahmadou Ahidjo cherished for our beloved Cameroon are today facing many seemingly insurmountable challenges. We pray for you beyond there to intercede for us so that God can bring back holiness to this fatherland.

As a great king who knew the importance of development through education, His Royal Highness, bequeathed substantial land and other resources for the construction of private and public primary, secondary and higher institutions like no other in Cameroon. He encouraged education for all children, and any child who is uneducated is largely to blame. As a long-time parliamentarian, His Royal Highness gave meaning and content to the Political slogan of

"Green Revolution", initiated by Ahmadou Ahidjo. By this, all parliamentarians were charged with inviting all Cameroonians to cultivate the land and own farms. In fact, the "Green Revolution" killed hunger in Cameroon and made this Nation the bread-basket of French-speaking Central Africa. Fon Angwafo III demonstrated the practicality of this political Slogan by opening large farms of palms, plantains, bananas and many other subsistent crops. He was often found working on his farms, where he even attended impromptu to issues brought before him. Culturally, His Royal Highness did more than our tongues can tell. His vision for many things was like a thousand miles ahead in the eyes of many. He modernized the palace without sacrificing cultural institutions. The modern museum he conceived, constructed, and equipped in the Fondom's Palace bears eloquent testimony.

Our dear Father and greatest Fon the Mankon Fondom has ever seen, you did many things with me. I was privileged to serve as a royal emissary relating to various developmental issues, the tarring of the road from Ntambeng to the Palace, in particular. Even though, the authorities kept assuring us with unlimited vain promises, we, in your absence, will continue to give hope a chance that one day our dream will come true and this road will be tarred. Although a handful of our misguided children brought an insignificant conflict between us, I still uphold the values of truth and justice, you planted in me while pouring palm wine into my hands in 1981 when President Ahmadou Ahidjo commissioned me abroad for a special diplomatic mission.

I promise His Royal Highness, Fo Angwafo III alias King Solomon, to adhere to these values till we meet beyond there to part no more.

Your son,

Dr. Nkwenti Ignatius Ndefru
Descendant of Fomukong

Fon Angwafo III, you were a truly inspirational hero and fighter to me. The Mankon community has lost a great man and a great leader.

The Mankon people and the country as a whole mourn your passing but celebrate your legacy and achievements. Your Royal Highness, you will not be forgotten that easily.

From a small schoolboy when I was in primary school, you took care of me making sure and insisting that I remain with you in the palace and made sure I went to school till completion.

Before passing on, you kept on reminding me not to relent in making sure the woodwork machine became operational because of my professionalism in that sector. Rest assured that as soon activities resume around that area, I will not relent.

I will remember to use your fatherly approach as inspiration to keep going. Thank you for touching my life.

Nkwenti Wilfred Anye

The mirror is broken, the mirror at which I looked at myself, and now that you are gone my life is so empty.

You never made a fortune, or a noise in the world where men are seeking after fame; You lived a Righteous life. We'll forever remember that special smile.

We'll always remember You *MBEH* because There'll never be another one to replace you in our hearts.

That wonderful gift of Education and Honesty etc.

Your most cherished words, "*Unity is Strength*"

Adieu! My hero, the Man Fon, Farmer, Politician and Nation Builder.

Your Son,

Ntawmu Nwi Angwafo III

Dear Father, I am at peace and my soul is at rest. There is no need for tears. For with your love, I was so blessed. You taught me the Hard way and I made it the Hard way. It started with Tears and ends with Tears but am very sure I have gained so much from you when I face the world today the Challenges I overcome with echoes of your words:

"Nothing Good Comes Easy";

"Being a man is not a day's Job";

"No food for a Lazy man";

"Don't keep what you have to do today to do tomorrow";

"Life is in the living";

" Who born dog?" ;

"Time waits for nobody".

Just to mention a few.

You built in me a positive mind set:
"Never you pay evil with evil";
" Don't fight back, fight only your Future";
"Love all and trust none";
"You must live with everybody, they are God's People".

I may not say it all now but trust me I really appreciate the way you raised me because when I look behind what I have done singlehandedly as a kid till date I now understand you had prepared me for difficult times and not times of glory.

Yes, difficult times because when you departed I immediately started thinking of the difficult task you left behind following our last conversations. Trust me, your legacy will always live on. You taught and showed me many things and said:
"live like a fool but know everything";
"Speak when the right time and opportunity comes";
"Talk and act for change and not for your interest";
"People should not know what you know but what you know should help people".

Dear Father, it is today I can see what you saw and I promise you that I will live up to expectation. You were such a great man and will always be.

The unforgettable number is 97. Full of history yes. It was going to come to an end, but you did not promise that it will not be painful of course. You taught me how to endure all pain that it will always end with success. But this pain doesn't seem to have an end. But comforting memories of your wonderful school of thoughts. It cuts through Agriculture, Tradition and Politics the core of a nation. A pillar on which the future depends.

Thank you so much, you brought so much and took nothing. The best lesson we, your children should learn from. What a great Father you were.

May God grant you the perfect rest in peace you deserve.
Son,

Ntseh Tangie Angwafo Nfo Mukare

Eternal Glow Sangmantha
Nil non aut lenit aut domat diuturnitas

As I reminisce about the lessons on duty, integrity, hard work, cultivating one's understanding and compassion You taught us, it becomes clear how my being is permeated by You, Tsazui.

Sangmantha, there cannot be any Saying of Goodbye.

The experience is forever etched in my mind's eye. I was at most five when I learnt that little or nothing about Tsazui Fo S.A.N. Angwafo III was ordinary. In the company of similarly aged boys, a much older boy, an outdoors expert whose acrobatics at tree climbing and plucking the juiciest wild berries and fruits were unmatched, led us surprisingly one day to a carpentry workshop. A stern-faced elderly craftsman, pencil behind his ear and taking a break from his work asked each one of us our names and those of our fathers. At my turn, I spoke. In a mixture of anger and befuddlement, the stranger scolded me for laying claim to everyone's father. Menacingly he impressed on me to desist from ever repeating what I had just said. But just who was everyone's father?

Any attempt by a blind man to probe an elephant, the *leopard of Fozan* let alone the *chameleon of Alankyi* is bound to be incomplete. How else can one get the whole without first gathering the pieces? Can it be otherwise growing up interacting with greatness? Words seem so hollow.

To You Tsazui I feel an enormous sense of gratitude and appreciation for the extraordinary life journey, for giving us so much of Your inexhaustible, pristine and seminal essence. An impeccable encyclopaedia of wisdom, Tsazui would casually delve deep into philosophy while demonstrating with stunning dexterity some agricultural technique.

You impressed very early on us that sacrifice, hard work and humility position one for greatness and that adversity breeds character. Admirable how even mired in a sea of malice, incompetence, and intrigue, You always stayed the course and steadfastly took the high road. There is no alternative to doing the right thing. Daily Greatness, Simply lived.

You were generous with your profound insights and the fruits of a bafflingly retentive memory. Your discourse sparkled with a subtle blend of wit and that your distinctive brand of humour that charmed many and disarmed the most hardened critics. You were a pace-setter admired by contemporaries. You taught that how one played was more important than winning.

A great champion of personal responsibility You were. Devotion and diligence in all you do was Your anthem. Now in my adulthood, not a day goes by without Your mellifluous voice cautioning, *"A little thing is a little thing but faithfulness in a little thing is a great thing"*.

"Of what use is it to be noble of birth but base of spirit?". The greatest influence in my life. Period.

Personal responsibility and independence were central pillars of our upbringing predicated on the knowledge that all are interconnected and thus interdependent. An interdependent whole that consists of individually viable independent entities is a vibrant community. Anywhere. Anytime.

Innumerable and unforgettable moments abound. Being in the comfortable position of having older siblings who catered to most of my material needs, I rarely had to bother You. On a rare occasion of me putting in a request at 18 years of age, your answer was classic: *"Do you think I get my own money from my father?".* This, I understood as an expression of esteem and confidence in the ability of a child. An admonition for me to pull my weight. I was not unprepared. You had been meticulously doing Your bit to lay the foundation, diligently laying brick after brick in the wall. Had You not made it abundantly clear to me that *"the best thing a man can give a child is a good upbringing, a good education"*? Had You not explained to me in the presence of my Mother why my first earnings while still in Primary School had to go to fuelling Your car and nothing else? Any better way to impress that a life without contribution is empty? From You, I learned that it is better to light a small light than to curse the mighty expanse of darkness.

The fact that Mankon stands out as a citadel of learning in the whole of Cameroon is due in no small measure to Your resolve that no child shall have to go through the ordeal You went through to get an education. Your abolition of **Ashebbe** on ascending the throne of Ndemagha and the drive for the education of all children especially the GIRL CHILD in Mankon have no parallel. It is claimed, rightfully so it would appear, that never have so many owed so much to a single individual.

Tsazui, You took the Town Planning and road construction initiated by hallowed Tsazui Fo Ndefru III in Mankon Town to new heights with the visionary work carried out personally with youthful zest in the 1960s. There is hardly a town in these parts for which Google Earth serves up more pleasant and well-structured aerial views as the Fon's New Layout at Azire. As the first maverick, You achieved a landslide victory in a hard-fought election into the West Cameroon House of Assembly in 1962. Besides being a task best left to historians, an attempt to treat this and Your tenure at Mankon

Area Council cum Bamenda Urban Council is beyond the scope of this script.

Long before environmental issues captured public attention, a Royal Edict banned the age-old practice of burning **Ankara**. This was enlightened, courageous and disruptive leadership pitching the right choice for posterity against the foreseeable discomfort of popular discontent. How You masterfully condensed tending the Fondom, Animal Husbandry, Farming, numerous construction projects, Forestry and Gardening in one life ranks up there among the wonders of modern times. The catalogue of Your activities, engagements and themes is as expansive as it is timeless.

Learning was always Your priority. Life-long learning You exemplified and encouraged. *"Read Son, read! There shall come a time when you will want to read but won't be able to"*. Yet there were moments and activities for which You counselled more restraint. Unsurprisingly, Goethe's admonition *"In der Beschränkung zeigt sich erst der Meister"* like so many other insights from the "great philosophers" would come across as not particularly original to any who attended Your Great School.

Your pragmatism, dreaming with Your feet on the ground was unparalleled: *"You visit your friend and find his estate well-kept, his children well-behaved and all else impeccably put together. Do you roll out a mat on his living room floor and take up residence there or do you return home and do better?"*

In an age of confusion and delusion, a good many Africans instinctively measure success by how far they deviate from that which is unmistakably and characteristically African. Your philosophy of traditional modernism is a flashing beacon of hope for a people in need and in quest of authenticity. You never settled for less than the best. You lit the fire, we can but only strive to sustain it. When the doors of perception and understanding are open and cleansed, everything appears to man as it is, infinite. Thank You for unveiling God to us, the indestructible and sacrosanct Force binding the departed, the living and the unborn.

At Your Growth and Rebirth, Your transition into the Babrvua Realm has You in sync *inter alia* with Grandma, whose love and brilliance demonstrably continue to illuminate the worlds. Tsazui, You left Your mark on all You met and continue to inspire many. Tutor-in-Chief and the One, this pupil will not and cannot be weaned off You.

Zeus once quipped that the trouble with being God is that there is no one higher to pray to. In like manner, You posited a few months prior to your disappearance, *"Shouldn't the farmer who has tended his farm go home at evenfall?"*

Sangmantha, Ati andzong-ndzong, Uhlargh ta ashweri, Ako'o bu kwigne, Azaba nda toam-toam, we draw strength and take solace from our unshakable knowledge that You are There with us.

Great Father,
Grant Your wearied ones Peace,
Grant them the Force
Grant them the Serenity to forge on
advancing the cause of man,
stoically in the footsteps of the Father.

Ntsewah Fobuzshi Angwafo III, *Dei Gratia Tamuhlargh*

I hide my tears when I say your name. The pain in my heart remains the same although I smile and interact with people. There is no one who misses you more than me.

His Royal Highness, you brought warmth, happiness wisdom and love to every soul that you touched. I am grateful for having a wonderful father like you. Your memory is my keepsake with which I will never part.

My utmost prayer was that God should bless you sail out with Mankon Fondom, in love, peace and unity that which you did during the hurdles of the immigration periods as from the Widikum, Ngemba, Mankon, Bamenda Urban councils of which we are now a city.

The life of His Royal Highness, S.A.N Angwafo III, Fon of Mankon whom we love is never lost. Its influence goes on through every life it ever touched. Hence, in memory of the late Fon and prosperity, liberations are poured at the palace shrine once a week.

God has you in his keeping, I have you in my heart. May the soul of our legend, rest in the Lord forever.

Ntsuntaw Ndisah C.F.N
Former Clerk to the Fon of Mankon

Dear Father, Dear Pa'ana, Dear Wise man,

What I am today: *a farmer; a trader; a storyteller; a disciplinarian; an educationist/teacher*, is all thanks to you.

I am a farmer. I remember when you bought new cutlasses for both princes and princesses. With this, you demonstrated to us how farmers cleared their farms. You gave us measuring distances from one plantain sucker to another as well as the distance between one palm tree seed to another and that is how we worked in the plantations in "Ndieni and Asongkah". You planted the following fruit trees: pears, plums, mangoes, guavas, paw-paws, lime and other fruits in our various orchards and so we had all sorts of food and fruits. You taught us how to prune coffee, plantains and palms. You taught us as gardeners how to produce compost manure. As great harvesters, in our maize farm in Fumndjug, presently the site of the Bamenda Airport, we harvested hectares of maize farmed by our tractors.

I am a trader: You taught me marketing. Our green pick-up car with the late Tse Oscar ("L'Enfant Noir"). The driver carried us with basins of guava during its harvesting season, dropping us at strategic points where we sold these fruits. 6a.m. was the kick-off time.

I am a storyteller. You usually gathered us together as you narrated your life, your educational life, your studies in Nigeria, despite the odds, you succeeded and ended up as Solomon of old in the Bible, and that was your name.

I am a disciplinarian: You taught us to be disciplined as you never spared the rod to spoil the child. You once had me severely beaten as I did not tether my goat and it went loose.

I am a teacher/educationalist. I am a teacher today because in my early days, you put in my hands a register with the names of all my siblings as we went to the various farms. In your usual Cowboy mood, you taught me how to mark the names of those absent and present from 7am to 4pm. As an educationist today, it all began in our palace library, where you taught us how to read and write. You provided study material to all of us, and equally sent us to good secondary schools, high schools, professional schools and universities. "Paana", "Wise Man", were some of the names we fondly called you with. You taught us this song as we built embankments to stop water from entering the plantain farm at Asongkah:

Get on board little children
Get on board little children
Get on board little children
There is room for many more

All of this was to encourage us to work harder. "Wise man", life was not a bed of roses as we both understood ourselves especially when it became very tough between you and me. As children united by you, I remember how we sang the whole night disturbing your peace, we used to gather in our mothers' kitchens and you will quietly come late into the night to stop us from shouting and playing.

"Wise Man", you would have stayed longer so we could revise all these lessons before your departure. This pen will continue flowing till this book project is completed.

Your Daughter,

Numfo Beris

His Excellency Fon Angwafo III of Mankon left a memorable legacy. Our King succeeded with determination in laying the foundation of prosperity for the Mankon people through educational, political and cultural openness. His intelligence and political vision brought Mankon and North-West Region to a privileged place in the concern of Cameroon and many nations. 'Gone but not forgotten'.

Odette Swirri Ade

In the bible in Revelation 2:19 it says "I know your deeds, your love and faith, your service and perseverance." His Royal Majesty Fo Angwafo III of Mankon was the epitome of righteousness; the man who impacted the lives of thousands, regardless of social rank or clan. His service and love to his people is vastly beyond the scope of a tribute. He will forever be remembered, loved and missed.

Oliver C. Fonteh

To My God-Given Father
My Father, Fo Ndefru III entrusted me to Fo Angwafo III, my God-given father well before he ascended the throne of Mankon. He enrolled me in school in Bambili where he was working at the time. Following his decision to pursue further studies at the University of Ibadan, he, Nimo-Ntaw *(then Mrs. Emilia Nanga Ndefru III)* and I left for Nigeria. Alongside his studies, he had several flourishing practice and demonstration farms on which Nimo-Ntaw and I worked after school. On his return to the Southern Cameroons, he was sent to head the Agriculture Department in Befang.

Tempted by the "free-life" my brothers were leading in the palace, I abandoned school and left Befang for Mankon. On becoming Fo Mankon, Fo Angwafo III once more sought me out and sent me again to school. On completing Standard VI, I learnt to drive for a profession. Working in Kumba and Buea, I was always at the side of the Fon when the House of Assembly was in session in Buea.

When I returned home and was deemed mature, he gave me my wife with whom I had six children. Whatever errors or mischief that happened in my youth did not dissuade him from taking care of me as usual. He allocated a plot for me to build my house. I later took a second wife with whom I have four children.

My retirement brought me even closer to Fo Angwafo, I had the honour to carry out several important functions alongside and with the Fon. I was the only male child with Mafo Angwafo III and Bangyiebuntaw at the side of our father as the days darkened.

Hard work, especially farm work, is essential for life. Learning from the elders, obedience and forgiveness have contributed greatly to structuring my life. My gratitude goes to my departed God-given father whose unconditional love has been the centre pillar of my life.

Peter Schofield Tse Ndefru alias Isahfo

To a Hero Who Now Rests in Power

I doff my hat to your royal majesty, His Royal Highness Fon Angwafor III. I bow before your ever-present Royalty because of the legacy left behind.

Great was your reign, great was your Wisdom, great is the legacy you left for us to cherish. You were a father to a family, a village, a community and a nation as a whole, Because your children, the Mankon children are spread throughout the nation and even abroad.

You carved and nurtured for yourself an imposing position in the socio-economic and political landscape in our nation. With these , you have been able to rule the Mankon Fondom successfully. You have encouraged many to go to school, you have influenced the creation of many schools so that children could acquire knowledge. Thanks for providing land for the then GSS Mankon, today GBHS Mankon was built on the hills of 'Ntahtintoh'. That is where I acquired knowledge and set the gateway to what I am today. Thank you.

You encouraged modern Agriculture in Mankon to give a Sustainable activity for our parents to earn a living and care for us.

You encouraged Petty trading with the facilitation of the creation of the Mankon main market, the food market, the Ntarikon market, the mile 8 market and the Fon's market in Ntingkag. We say thank you.

You promoted the cultural values of the Fondom. I remember attending the Fon's dance on many occasions. You also paid a listening ear to the youths. I remember the yearly visits of the Mankon students Association MASA to the palace and how you always advised us your children.

Being Paramount and First-class Fon, you stood out tall among your peers in the Grassfields area because you built a personality that goes along only with nobility. You were highly respected. At the mention of the name Fon Angwafor III many people honour you because of that personality.

Today many of us are basking in the glory of your great name. All Mankon sons and daughters rally under the umbrella of your name because you have proven to a father to them. Your name makes Mankon people proud.

97 years of existence you have played a vital role in the political process of Cameroon. You were one of the few remaining witnesses of the Fumban conference, the reunification of Cameroon, the democratic process and the days of political upheavals. Before your departure you witnessed how the land has been torn by war and conflict. We need your ancestral intervention for peace to return to the village.

Like the biblical Solomon, you have shown proof of great wisdom. You have ruled the Mankon Fondom with the kind of wisdom that God gave king Solomon. At the time things almost fell apart, you brought back your children into one fold.

Your disappearance made us weep and feel lonely, but it was not for long because you left behind your perfect replacement in whom we see you. Thank you for the choice of your successor.

HRH, the Mbeh of Mankon the wise one of the heart of the Nguemba people, you will be remembered for what you have done. Your legacy lives on and we bask in the glory of the great name you left behind.

Priscilla Lum

To my father, my grandfather... our Mbeh and the guiding light of the Mankon Fondom whose unflinching love paved the way for all and Sundry

His Royal Highness Fo Angwafo was an incredible ruler and father at the same time. He wore the crown of armour effortlessly. He was our voice, our feelings, and our heartbeats. The goals, dreams and aspirations you set for your subjects and to me in particular made me who I am today.

From my childhood days in .1959 when crossing the station hill was a Prestige, you gave me the honour to travel to Victoria out of my comfort zone to experience the world. You paved the way for me to become an independent and hardworking woman. You showered me with so much love, care and affection and provided the guidance I needed to sail through the hurdles of life! I remember staying awake till 10 pm just to listen to your counselling. You were a fundamentalist who taught me not to take life too seriously.

You were and are till my knight and shiny armour: you instilled in me the spirit of waking up early to plan for the days ahead. You were the most courageous and resourceful. I never questioned if you loved or cared for me because you made it so obvious: you provided a land for me to have a roof over my head, in 1984 you entrusted the Nikwi in my hands and gave your accord for Nkah Nikwi Ni Mankon to go operational... I can go on and on.

As I remember the teachings you gave me through the parable of 1frz I just want to let you know that I am grateful to call you my father, my grandfather and my HERO.

Long live the KING

Daughter,

Prudencia Ngum Angwafo

On May 21, 2022, which coincidentally was the day of his birth, the disappearance of a Colossus made rounds on social media and was subsequently declared confirmed by the Kwifo of Mankon. I bow down my head in disbelief. I only realised unconsciously that tears ran down my cheeks followed by watery nostrils. I soon mustered some courage and continued my task while remembering that I have missed a traditional ruler of repute. Someone who promoted education in his Fondom. Today, Mankon should have the highest number of educational establishments be they public, denominational or privately owned. He encouraged every parent to send their children to school. Fo Angwafo III's open-door policy also gave room even for foreigners to construct in the Fondom. As an agriculturalist by training, he encouraged sustainable farming and was ready to sacrifice his own land for anyone who was in need. He stood against the selling of family land whereby children will grow up and be wondering. That is why he frowned at any family head or successor who thinks he could sell even farmland to the detriment of other family members or children.

Fo Angwafo III, was what many think was a political Maradona. As a politician, he knew how to play his game even though he belonged to the Cameroon Peoples Democratic Movement, (CPDM) where he served as National First Vice President. Mankon became a political battleground for several other political parties, thanks to Fo Angwafo III.

There is so much that can be said about HM, Fo Angwafo III, but like every human being, he had his own flaws, which even fetched him enemies within and without. He was accused by many for positioning only his biological children in positions, while other qualified sons and daughters of Mankon were not favoured.

RIP Your Majesty

Richard Nde Lajong
(Publisher, *The Herald Tribune* Newspaper)

Papa, forever you loved me, despite all my wrongdoings, you still loved me. I didn't deserve all this love. Will miss you forever.

Roselynn Muma Mbah

I only saw my great-grandfather once in Cameroon. I visited him in 2018, and he blessed my shoes with his cup, and poured my blessings from his cup. I now have only these pictures of this memory about him. I will never forget this visit.

Great-grandson,

Samuel Azunwi Tsifo Ndingwan

The aura of his presence, his clairvoyance, his mastery of contemporary issues, his inquisitiveness in asking pointed questions, his demeanour and openness to listen to the opinion of others, are only a few of the attributes one can ascribe to the legendary Fon

Angwafor III. He was born a prince, trained as an agriculturalist, and reigned as a custodian of the tradition of the Mankon Fondom for over 63 years. It takes an enigmatic and charismatic personality to be the leader of a people who by historical account are "warriors". He went into politics because of his conviction that it was the best way of putting Mankon at the centre stage and making the voice of his people heard on vital contemporary, development and humanitarian issues at the highest level.

In his majesty's reign, Mankon was greatly transformed from a rural community to a semi-urban community. He was foresighted and his clarion call was always for the Mankon man to shun pride and embrace unity to be a more potent force to reckon with (*nikong nteh nkare*). This remains a key among the many other doctrines he advocated for that need to be embraced by the next generation. Every moment with Fon Angwafor III was a course in leadership, anthropology, and philosophy. In my last visit to the palace to carry out a reconnaissance visit and designate an area for the construction of a proposed public sanitary facility, I was held down for over 3 hours in a treasured deep and broad discussion that remains indelible in my mind until this day. What a storyteller and an encyclopaedia he was.

Fon Angwafor III may be "missing", but his legacy remains perennial. A baobab has fallen, and it will take a forest to replace the fortress that his leadership encapsulated. Unlike his predecessors during the precolonial and colonial era when Mankon was built through communal efforts, there was a shift in dynamics during his reign. During his reign, the Mankon people expected the government to play the leading role in development. Grassroot support that was a historic pivot of the Mankon man's prowess dwindled.

As a peacemaker, Fon Angwafor III was strategic and did all to resolve most of the land disputes that the Mankon Fondom had with its neighbours by demarcating the boundaries of the Mankon Fondom with concrete posts: this brought peace which is a prerequisite for meaningful development. He did so much to modify and adapt Mankon customs, cultural and tradition practices by enacting Royal Acts. He revised the administrative map of Mankon to ensure more grassroot participation on issues of administration and development.

The visionary Fon Angwafor III had great plans and assisted to establish private and public schools; plans to provide potable water, provide health facilities and all-season access roads to all nooks and crannies of Mankon. He expressed a regret that the funds were lacking, and the current generation needs to show more love for country and be more entrepreneurial given the circumstances. Fon Angwafor III had great concerns for the many educated and prosperous Mankon people scattered across the globe and longed to see this intelligentsia avail themselves to help in building the Mankon of our common dream.

Fon Angwafor III was therefore caught in a wedge; with a supposedly rich government on the one hand not meeting up with his people's expectations and a relatively impoverished people on the other part; expecting much from the government and from him. Calls from Fon Angwafor III for the return to community development and for total involvement might have never been heeded to during his reign, but he did lay a solid foundation for the future. The mammoth crowd that showed up in the palace to celebrate his transition, testifies this axiom. In his own words: "Comparatively, we are doing better. Home is home! Mankon is a beautiful home. Tell the Mankon children whether here or there, this is your birthplace. Come and build it."

By design or by fate, some of us happen to have been privileged to be involved in some projects that the' Fon Angwafor III had at heart but might not have seen these happen in his lifetime. He was always open to suggestions, ready to give advice and support any developmental initiative. As a student in the 1990s, he supported us in MASA (Mankon Students' Association) in a proposed project to put up a Community Library for Mankon. He valued education of all, without discrimination. The road from the Ntambeng to the Mankon palace, water supply in rural Mankon, construction of a sanitary block for public use in the Mankon palace are a few of some of the developmental projects that I was privileged to be passively or actively involved in the conception that Fon Angwafor III had wished to see accomplished. These were a major concern to him in every discussion I had with him. Seeing these happen will epitomize the eternity of his legacy.

May the legacy of his majesty Fon Angwafor III continue to blossom from generation to generation.

Samuel Fonteh
(Makwuswiri clan)

To that Great Son of Mankon, Prince of Peace, and King

His Royal Majesty King Angwafo III, SAN, for 63 years, two weeks, and three days (4th of April 1959 - 21st of May 2022) spared no ounce of his energy for the welfare and wellbeing of the beloved Mankon people whom his dear father, Fo Ndefru III, entrusted to his custody.

I first caught a glimpse of this now legendary prince on the morning of the 4th of April 1959, a great day in the history of the Mankon kingdom, when their beloved and venerated Fon returned from a long and tedious journey. He was presented in a brief colourful, traditional ceremony in the palace plaza by the kingmakers to an anxious, impatient, and a jubilant mammoth crowd dressed in a circumstantial traditional attire called Adzag. There were also delegations from friendly and brotherly kingdoms, the local, national, and international media, some state authorities, and some individuals who came from far and near just to live and experience the rich Mankon tradition and culture. When the king emerged from the palace escorted by a special traditional procession, there was general commotion, a symphony of musical instruments was playing, shouting, singing, dancing, etc. This was to express joy, happiness, and gratitude to welcome the new king from a journey from the land of his ancestors. "Mbeh, Mbeh, Mbeh welcome, we have missed you for too long. Long live the king."

I was lost in that sea of people at the royal palace plaza in Mankon called Nsamne. All eyes were focused on the new king. He came back looking younger, stronger, more energetic, and traditionally well equipped to serve his people. This phase of the ceremony was very brief because the squad which brought the new Fon allowed him to dance for a few minutes and the juju called Mabuh tried to arrest him. Holding the long staff decorated with two red feathers of the turaco bird, he raced back to the royal palace. As part of the ritual, symbolic pebbles were thrown at him as a sign of authority, empowerment, and blessing from the population. This signified the very last time any person born of woman shall ever lay hands on him. The population then returned to their respective homes to throw away the Adzag, wash the wood ash from their bodies, then put on nice dresses and then went back to the Palace Plaza to welcome their new Fon. The population came back rejoicing, singing, dancing, and celebrating the return of their new King who was then dressed in his royal traditional regalia and a full traditional protocol dispositive due his rank was put in place. This was his first official public appearance as the king of Mankon. This marked the beginning of a long period of celebrations and festivities of the reign of the new Monarch.

This period was undetermined in view of the plethora of the involvement of various families, quarters, clans, associations, socio-cultural and professional groups, brotherly & friendly Kingdoms within and without the division, Mankon sons and daughters in the diaspora, foreign friends, politicians, the Administration, and many others. The Royal Protocol was responsible for booking audience/appointments for visits to the Royal Palace for various reasons; to congratulate, pay respects, present gifts, chat, encourage, wish the Fon well in his new function, etc.

I met the Fon again when I had to go to C.P.C. Bali. My father took me to the palace where I received from the Fon traditional blessings and words of wisdom highlighting the virtues of obedience, respect for elders, all authorities, hard work, wished me well, and faith in God Almighty. Finally, the Fon poured palm wine from his traditional cup into my palms to drink as the final blessings from the palace.

While I was working in Buea from 1967-1969, the Fon always came to Buea for parliamentary sessions, and I made sure I went to the palace to pay my respect. After each visit to the palace, I returned home very happy and satisfied because I always learnt a lot from the Palace, and I was traditionally blessed and encouraged to serve the state faithfully. The Fon encouraged me to improve on my level of education. These words of wisdom and encouragement meant so much to me. I worked hard and I was able to go for further studies. This pleased the palace and was a legitimate pride for the Mankon kingdom.

After my studies, I returned home, and I was recruited to teach in Government High School (lycée) Maninguba Nkongsamba after which I was transferred to C.C.A.S.T. Bambili. I was now at home and could be more available to the palace from where I was constantly drinking from the Fon's fountain of wisdom.

The Fon was the section president of the ruling party and there was much work in his secretariat. When I discovered that, I offered to give a helping hand in the secretariat, in treating some of the files, running a few errands, drafting speeches alongside the Chief of the Secretariat, Mr. Clement Chibayere (R.I.P.) and even with the secretary of the section. The work of the party and the Fon's Secretariat were a real school for me where I acquired a lot of skills in running a political secretariat, an administrative secretariat, running of political meetings, and saw how the Fon chaired meetings.

When I was a councillor, the Fon was chairman and I learned a lot from him when he chaired those meetings and as chairman of some committees of the council,

I was able to chair the meetings well, but little did I know that this was preparing me for some tasks awaiting me such as the Section President of the CPDM party of Mezam I, the position of the Government Delegate.

As a traditional ruler, coupled with his position as a parliamentarian in the West Cameroon House of Assembly and the National Assembly, he took Mankon to great heights giving a complete facelift in the sociocultural/traditional, economic spheres for the prosperity of the Mankon Fondom. By his training in agriculture, he encouraged Mankon people to invest in agriculture to produce enough food to ensure food self-sufficiency and to improve their finances especially in cultivating cash crops. This will empower the population to eat well, send their children to school, pay their medical bills, and construct good living homes.

The Fon set a shining example by transforming the Mankon royal palace in replacing all grass roofed bamboo houses with solid material (sun dried blocks and stones) roofed with corrugated iron sheets except for the Foh-nda (*Atsum*) which maintains its originality as the tradition demands. Mankon people are happy, well protected from any eventuality, and the population is peaceful, happy, healthy, self-confident, active, comfortable, hopeful, and now contribute positively to building a strong and prosperous nation for the legacy of the unborn generation.

He paid special attention to the development of Mankon kingdom by the construction of roads, building of culverts and bridges to facilitate communication and accessibility throughout Mankon. Drinking water for the population was top on his agenda also health facilities, the implantation of several hospitals and health centres throughout Mankon, in collaboration with the state and religious bodies (Catholic, Presbyterian, Cameroon Baptist Convention, Pentecostals), private individuals, NGOs, etc. in education, Mankon has had a boom within the last three decades in terms of population growth, shades of educational facilities ranging from nursery, primary, secondary/grammar/ technical/ commercial, high schools, higher institutions, and universities, etc. The major role of the Fon in all this was he extended a hand of friendship and offered more than

Mankon land to settle these institutions. In brief, he made the atmosphere comfortable, conducive, and friendly for all prospective investors assuring them that the door of Mankon Fondom was open to them for business ventures.

The Fon took a step further by publishing a royal act making education compulsory of school age for either sex. Defaulters who kept some children home as babysitters were severely sanctioned.

In the area of culture/tradition, the Fon revolutionized everything by encouraging, revalorizing, and modernizing the culture and tradition. The girlchild was in the centre of his activities, had rights to own property, right to succeed the parents, right to a fair share of family assets, and have equal access to opportunities among many others.

All cultural groups were restructured and made functional and registered in the palace so that order, discipline, respect for the state and its institution, respect for their parents and culture, tradition, and culture, commitment, and participation in the great task of nation building so that Mankon can be handed to posterity better than what we met.

Thanks to Fo Angwafo III, Mankon now has an Indigenous Micro Financial Institution: Micre-INSA- Micro Investment and Savings Plc.

As per the Fon's training in Agriculture, he demonstrated the value of Agriculture in Dairy and mixed farming. Watermelon for instance was first cultivated in the 1960s at Asongkah. He produced a lot of palm nuts from his palm nuts plantation for the extraction of palm oil to cover the Palace needs while the rest supported the budget of the palace.

As an educated Monarch, he put a very huge tag on literacy. Within the first fifteen years of the reign of Fo Angwafo III, SAN illiteracy in Mankon was substantially reduced.

A tribute to HRM Hon. Fon Angwafo III, S.A.N. should easily be volumes. I hope to continue. May I still highlight some information on the chairman, B.U.C. Hon. Angwafo III, S.A.N, whose quest for development had no frontiers because he wanted that Bamenda City should have special status. He and the Government Delegate of the Council decided to go international to look for sister cities in the developed world. This mission linked Bamenda through twinning with the city of Lowell in the United States in 2005. Prior to this twinning arrangement, Bamenda City had signed a similar agreement with the city of Dordrecht in the Netherlands which brought great prosperity to Bamenda with the supply of heavy equipment for city development, construction of roads and bridges, hygiene and sanitation, firefighters, and training of technical and administrative personnel for the city of Bamenda. Some of the bridges constructed included the Dordrecht Bridge, Church Centre Bridge, Tsatsa Mafor (La tita) Bridge, Alafrumbi Bridge, Alatah Bridge etc.

The Bamenda Council of Churches ran a training program financed by the city of Dordrecht for young unemployed Bamenda youths. The chairman and the Government Delegate founded and managed these programs for the well-being and good of the population of Bamenda. May I add here that this cooperation with the city of Dordrecht enabled Bamenda City to repeatedly win the most coveted prize for the cleanest town in Cameroon of seven million Francs CFA.

I had the privilege and the honour to serve the Palace as an Emissary for some assignments. I pledge my loyalty and indebtedness for this mark of trust and confidence in my humble person.

May I draw this inspiration from a French philosopher who said "le Roi Est mort, Vive le Roi" to invite the Mankon people to sing songs of praises and of Joy, to thank God for Fo Angwafo III S.A.N who has left in the annals of Mankon Fondom and beyond his indelible craws of proficiency, excellence, and patriotism.

(Tori long but time short)
What a great and honourable man of 04/04/1959!
What a noble and kind prince!
What a wonderful, patriotic, and great King,
Angwafo III, S.A.N.!
What a...!
What a...!
May this illustrious, kind-hearted, and noble prince of
Mankon enjoy mercy, empathy, and grace in the land of his ancestors.

Sanjou-Tadzong Abel Ndeh,
Nkumkwuifo, Chair emeritus, Mankon Traditional
Council, Adviser MTC

Our Father on earth never dies because he LIVES in our hearts. He is not where he has been but he is everywhere we are. With pride and determination, we will seek to emulate your shining example.

Sebiso Switdzu Tamuhlargh Angwafo

A father like none. You were not only my armour and shield, you were my confidant. I wore and adorned you and your essence with every step I took. You protected me like no other. You were my fountain and still waters, my source of inspiration and vigour, and the source of my stability. I strived to be the best I could, and I hope that I made you proud. Others knew you from the prism of a King and a political icon, but I know you as father. You guided and guarded not only mine, but the steps of your children, and all who had the privilege to know you.

Where do I start, Dad? You were a father to all, but we were never deprived of your affection and presence. Your ability to connect with persons of all ages, races and hues was uncanny. Your skill to fully engage and totally immerse yourself in that person evoked a sense of importance and significance. When you were in a discussion, you had that unique ability to make someone feel like there was no one else in the room.

Your devotion and commitment to causes you undertook was unmatched. You were one of the greatest philanthropists of your era and beyond. Education in all forms was the cornerstone of your administration. At a time when few of your contemporaries saw it necessary, you made it your mission to promote the education of girls and women. In furtherance of your educational philanthropic causes, you donated lands to missionaries, private entities, and the government for the construction of educational institutions for both boys and girls. You educated not only your biological children, but any child who possessed the ability.

Even with all your accomplishments, you were meek, humble, caring and most of all, benevolent. You entertained and fed those that had and had not. You treated everyone fairly and your wisdom was unmatched. You were the epitome of character impersonated and the values I acquired from you are innumerable but in substance, they taught me hard work, humility, and the ability to see goodness in humankind.

My most fond childhood memories with you are your unconventional ability to empower and motivate. You constantly told the children who lagged in school to follow you to the farm with their machetes and hoes, and to not remain in school just because others did. That resonated a lot with us, and made every child want to try harder. While at the farm, you sometimes sang to motivate us to work harder. I can still see you in my mind singing, "Get on board little children, get on board little children, get on board little children,

216

there is room for many and more" as we feverishly and excitedly worked. Fun memories indeed, Dad.

Humanity gravitated towards you because of your affectionate touch, aptitude, and ability to know them by name. Unassumingly, you commanded power and authority. That is evident in your operations as the keeper of our mores and custodian of our culture in the Mankon Kingdom, Cameroon politics and international travels. Your travels to the United States were not different. In the years 2002 and 2007, in your quest to see where your children and subjects had migrated to, you visited the USA. As a consummate ruler, you did not limit such visits to your children and subjects. You engaged multiple longstanding American political and educational institutions. The institutions you visited include but are not limited to; in Massachusetts, Ivy League Harvard University, the John F. Kennedy Library, the Massachusetts State House, the City of Worcester, where you addressed the city council and the City of Lowell where you established a sister city with Bamenda. In Rhode Island, you spoke at the Ivy league Brown University. In Texas, you met the Mayor of the City of Houston and in Washington DC, you visited the National Mall and the United States Capitol Building. At all these establishments, everyone gravitated towards you at first meeting because of your distinctive touch and ability to see goodness in humanity.

Father, you were a great leopard with a soft touch and heart. A source of strength to all. You_were a rare gem, exquisitely cut amongst your peers. Like a mighty baobab tree, larger than life, I was almost tempted to believe that you could defy death. Though I now lay bare, I am comforted in your intercessory powers. Your candle burns and your legend continues to live. Long live the King.

Your daughter,

Attorney Stella Bih Angwafo

Mbeh,
the 21st of May has left me speechless; where do I start!
Mbeh,
you were a caring and loving father to me.
Mbeh,
you advised I stay focused and resilient in the face of whatever life may throw at me. Moreover, never should I give in, to distractions from friends or mates. I heard, heeded and still heed to your advice

till this day. I think my blessings are due to the invaluable fatherly lessons you gave me.

Mbeh,

I love you but God loves you much more so. Rest in the eternal perfect peace of our ancestors, till our reunion to part no more.

Your Daughter,

Swiri Caroline Fobuzshi

I never knew that on May 21st, after singing and sending birthday wishes, that fateful morning, that God will call your name. I was preparing to come see you. My heart is shattered, and I wished my plans to see you were sooner. You know in life I loved you dearly and in death I do same.

It broke my heart to lose you, you did not go alone but a part of me went with you. I am comforted by the beautiful times shared with you, dad. As sad as your departure has left me, I am proud because you left me with peaceful memories. You were the best father anyone could wish for, you stood tall in making sure my needs were met and that I grew up with core values. Your teachings, wise counsel and discipline have guided and build a formidable woman. I cannot find the words to truly tell how your absence has affected me, the pain in my heart or the sadness in my eyes. If a million tears could build a stairway to heaven, then I am certain you will walk right down to us because I have tried. I know that you have worked tirelessly in your pursuit to see a better Mankon than you met, you did so gracefully and now you deserve a peaceful rest.

Am a strong woman today because you have always been a strong FATHER. Rest on Dad.

Daughter,

Swiri Ethel Angwafo

There are not enough words to describe how important you were to me and what a powerful influence you continue to be dad. Growing up you taught me how to fend for myself, face life's challenges probably because you knew you were not always going to be there. Daddy, the person I am today is all thanks to your teachings and discipline. Dad, I remember my first year in school I was always running back home crying that I wouldn't go to school but being the loving and caring but disciplined father that you are, you had to lure me into the palace and got me well beaten and made me promise to never run away from school again. I can never forget that beating as I urinated on myself and henceforth faced my education with all seriousness. You did not end there as you provided us with private teachers for follow up to ensure we succeeded in our studies. Dad you always said education was my first husband and should be taken seriously and you encouraged us to study hard by awarding prizes to those who performed well and those who failed were severely punished.

Thanks for the values you instilled in me, I am the woman I am today all thanks to you.

Not only was education your motor but agriculture was key, and you always told us "There is no food for a lazy man." You taught us farming and encouraged us to work hard as you paid us wages during summer holidays which we used for our basic school needs. This encouraged hard work because the harder you worked, the higher your wages were. I promise to follow in your footsteps.

Keeping an account of everything that I do today is all thanks to you father. With what we earn from our holiday job and with what you added we had to spend it judiciously with all the details spelt out in my account book. Father, I can go on and on, but it wouldn't end because you taught me so much. Dad, you did all you could to put me on the right path. You were my teacher, a great disciplinarian and the best dad ever. I'm grateful. You were an advocate for peace and unity, your legacy lives on, we will not fail you. Continue resting in peace.

Your daughter,

Swiri Voilet

Known as an influential political leader who shaped and paved the way for the people of Mankon. But to me as granddaughter, I saw beyond this - As I look back with great fondness, what comes to mind most vividly is my first encounter with the Fon back in 2009 (when I was 3 years old), excited and gleaming with joy my sister and I were excited to meet him.

It was his striking yet humbling presence that caught my attention, as he sat comfortably in his chair, watching my sister and I rocking back and forth on the lions inside the palace. And to this very day is the image, I remember most.

To sum up, what the Fon has left behind is not what is engraved in a stone monument but a legacy woven into the lives of generations to come, who will embark on his efforts to resolve, to address, to create, to direct, to shape, a strong foundation for the people of Mankon.

Tabehre Asanji Tawbargh I

PAPA, we regret losing a great father of your calibre to death that we can't even see. Papa with all the qualities that took you to be the custodian of the Mankon Fondom and all what you were during your whole reign Death Was Never Afraid Of You???. Death you are wicked.

Papa, we thank you immensely for the least support, guidance and advice you gave us as your children especially during the death of our Father. Just your outfit during the death celebration of our Father rang a bell in our heads till today. MBEE, you beautified our father's death celebration with that outfit, making the occasion beautiful and important in the eyes of the Mankon man. MBEE, we say thank again and again and where ever you are, resting, collaborate with our ancestors to continue *Wishing Well To The Family.* May your gentle souls leave on in peace. RIP.

Tabufor Michael Che
(Family Head)

Dad I know you were to go one day but little did I know it was so soon, one thing I stand to frown today is the fact that you have not lived to see this legacy you have given to me. What a lovely and forgiving father with a heart of gold you were. If I am to write your charisma, I will probably come out with a novel but will end here to leave the man that brought you to this planet earth to take you back to a more comfortable place in heaven. Farewell, farewell. Nice Dad to be remembered.

Your son,

Tagei Achiri Nbomnifo Angwafo III

On May 21, the strongest wind that has ever been seen for close to Six and a half decades swept across the Kingdom of Mankon and fell down the mightiest Iroko. The whole nation of Cameroon has since been in sorrow, but the "Kwifo" of the Mankon Kingdom dried our tears and sorrow by planting a new Iroko that together we shall nurture to grow as mighty as the fallen Iroko or even mightier.

Legend, since you embarked on your long journey to join our ancestors, I am sure you arrived safely and were highly welcomed. When you give an account of your stewardship to Tsemagha, Mbangnizhi, Takomatsi, Fomukong, Ndefru, and the rest in council, please let them know that you left your children behind in very difficult and trying times and we need their combined blessings more than ever before. Bless the "*ndo-ori*" so we can use it to bring peace and harmony in the kingdom. Bless the "*BU-ii Ntaw*" so we will rub it and achieve greater progress and prosperity.

On a personal Note, you are the greatest father that any son or daughter should be proud of. I can't find enough adjectives, but to sum it all you were an embodiment of wisdom and class, a great teacher. Every word that I have ever heard you speak taught someone something. A colossus and true Legend of the Mankon Kingdom and Cameroon.

You gave me everything that a Son can ever dream of having from a father. You gave me hope and meaning to life when I thought life was hopeless and meaningless. You gave me Education, married a wife for me, and today I am the proud head of a family all because of you. You did not only teach me how to fish but you actually caught fish for me as an example. My entire family will remain forever grateful to you and will dedicate our energy and service to the Kingdom.

Farewell Legend
Nkon Nikong
Welcome And Long Live Our New King

Taku Jobs

Mbeh

To me you are a great king, you are the Solomon in the Bible. I will always remember the days when I was just a child and you began to instil in me the habits of farming, rearing of animals, punctuality and cleanliness in and out of the palace. I am so grateful for all those values. Since 1986 when I completed my primary education, I have been by your side, you have been teaching me everything I need to know about social life and traditional issues of the village and other villages. With all the numerous errands I ran for you after school hours and during the holidays. I spent the better part of my youthful life with you and more of my adults years, you will not let me escape your nurturing. You took me travelling to many places in the country and around the world. The trip to the USA in the year 2008 was the most memorable for me. We spent quality time together with you giving me good advice on how to interact with people from other countries and different traditions. You can now rest in peace because you have left a peaceful Mankon behind. Farewell, my king.

Takumbeng

The Sacred Trinity!!!
Prelude.
Son of Ndefru
Seed of Fru Asa'a
Spirit of Mìŋwi-Tìŋòrə
It is of thee
And of thee
That I come to speak
Cleanse my tongue and my voice!!!
(Ancestral music chimes to a crescendo and dims to the speck that dawns to the incantation)

Rhapsody:

You came like a mistral
And standing on the top of this. **Ɨɓ azɔ̂**
You heav'd a breadth that begat a wind
That transformed this land.

You sprouted like a mushroom into a baobab
That spread the shade of evolution and development
Into the nooks and crannies of this land
Hitherto untapped by the knife of the inquisitive tapper
On this land you towered
Like **Ɨɓ atìə** in **Alaʔabikɔ̀m**
And then when the wind was strong you swayed
Then stood firm
Like the tap root of the eucalyptus that you planted in the sacred forest.

Each night you *metamcycosized* into the Lion of the grass field
And charted your fondom with the compass of ancestral precision
Holding the dividers of accuracy in your trained claws
While your whiskers ruled the same boundaries
With the Protractor of history and destiny
Like Pythagoras on steroids
Keeping all these recalcitrant Quarters-turn-villages at bay.

For six decades and counting you tamed the beast
This beast of all nations called *Politics*
You being the head beast of the troop
This beast that came with hydra heads
And tentacles of the octopus
Bearing and baring the same virus
That caught even the crab of *Ntumazah*
And the poison of his hammer and sickle
Then the elephant and the horse
Of the West and the East
Even the Conservative and the Liberal
All of these you tamed and then rode them
Like a real dragon slayer on his Unicode.

On your nightly trails
You met them each in their turn
Ahidjo the horseman
Then Biya the unicorn and other Lion man
After your saddle had been ordained
From your independence and purification
And then cast in gold
By the cloak of Kamerun
And the polish of Southern Cameroons
All of them you baited and then trapped
With this hook of King Solomon
Now dangling over them
Like the sword of Damocles…
But you did not stop there
You proceeded and gave us all
The spear of continuity
Clutched into one single bundle
Like **Mikɔŋə ŋkarə** whose tips are spiced
And laced in the tonic and sacred wine of this *elixir*

Values – our very own values
Customs and Traditions – for us to keep and hold jealously
Courage and self-assurance – for still the faint hearts among us
Effrontery and determination – for our posterity
Patience and resoluteness – for these our children who are chosen
Packed and packaged for us
In one wholesome bundle of mystery
Baptized and tradition'd *Fru Asa'a*
From the sacred shrine
Where the father and the son
Are enshrined and begotten unto us anew

From him and from this
We shall grow beyond your limits
Even your dreams and architectural designs
All because it is a new day
That you have shun unto us
In this pentecost of **Niɓ nà ɓə**
And on this land of **Máŋkùŋ Mbáŋni ɜɛ** !!!

Curtain.
(there is lightening and a thunder crescendo and then…)

Hail to his wind
Praise be the Lion
Glory to the throne
Peace to his Fondom
And eternal brightness be his camwood.
           Tambu ngang of Mákoʃwírə (for the Town crier)

HRH, my years in Mankon can never be forgotten as you made me feel at home away from home. Being your doctor will forever be counted as one of my best experiences in my career. You were not only a father to me but also a leader who instilled in me a lot of knowledge and wisdom. Your legacy lives with us and shall never be forgotten. Keep Resting till we meet again.
Your Doctor

Dr. Tanah Arnold

Your Royal Highness, I miss a husband, father, teacher and companion in you. We got married on February 25, 1965. Barely a month later my husband Ambrose Ngu whom you introduced to me as your son, told me we owe a visit to the palace. Many things crossed my mind but I eliminated them and in April we paid the planned visit.

On arrival, you were not on the throne. The Queen Mother who received us went back and in a flash you came. I was so impressed with the promptness of your arrival. We talked at length until another group came and you took leave to attend to them. When you returned we presented you with a problem of an unroofed house we built.

You asked how much will roof the house. My husband gave the amount. You said nothing but took out money from your pocket and gave us what we asked for. It was an interest-free loan. To appreciate your kindness, we paid it within six months.

You did not give an unrecorded loan only to us. You paid fees for children in primary, secondary and high schools for parents who were not financially viable. You had students too in universities in addition to your biological children.

You didn't take delight in taxing your subjects for your upkeep. Instead, you engaged in full scale agriculture by keeping a poultry, pigs and fish. You owned hectares of palm nuts and guavas. You worked in your plantation. You went an extra mile by lending a helping hand to children of the royal family. In charity you adopted some children and educated them.

As a father who cares for his children, you joined politics in order to put favourable laws in place. You started as an independent parliamentarian and ended up with the post of first vice president of the Cameroon People's Democratic Movement (CPDM).

You chaired the Bamenda Urban Council for two terms.

You gave your personal land to government, missions and individuals to build schools in Mankon.

Your programme was always crowded but you organised it in a stress-free manner. Your assignment board was hung at a very strategic point in the palace, which you saw while going in or coming out. This reminded you of all assignments and meetings for the day. You showed a mastery of managing time by never ever attending any meeting or occasion late. You were nicknamed a "Time Bomb" by many.

My relationship with you saw your son Professor Francis Nyamnjoh marrying my daughter, Dr. Henrietta Mambo. We lived an amicable life as a family because you were with me in good and bad times. Your delegation led by you to my late husband's death celebration showed a deep intimacy between our families.

In religion, you were not left behind. You supported your wives and children to belong to churches of their choice. This open-door policy made you a member of all churches. Jesus showed his gladness by personally coming to the palace and taking you on the last day.

Rest in peace, in the bosom of He who visited you.

Mrs. Theresia Ngu

The lion and king of Mankon, the greatest Fon I have ever known. He was most courageous and resourceful to us and the entire North West. My father, the Sarki, calls him the light of BANDE. He named me Anye and gave me all the love and care a loving father could offer his son. I still feel him with me each day. The Fondom gates were wide open to me at any time of the day. Oh, my king, the indelible mark you caved in my heart shall remain and I and the Hausa People, will never forget you. I miss you, the lion of Mankon.

The Sarki's Office

My father, you were a source of inspiration to your children and the people of Mankon and beyond. You did a lot of reforms and look everyone before you with problem as a solution provider.

I remember when you sent me to Pamol as small as I was, to be trained as a nursery attendant in palms. It is true that you are "missing", but your works and spirit will stay forever.

Mbeh, I was ready at all times and offered unflinching service as a son and also pray that God should grant you a peaceful and eternal rest.

Son,

Tse Fonguh

My heart bleeds and is completely shattered, I have lost a legend, an icon with the heart of gold!!!. My father, you were just a selfless human being. I cannot believe that I am writing this about you. You taught me how to be self-reliant and that hard work pays. As you will always say,' life is in the living and not in procrastination'. You opened your doors to passers-by, destitute and strangers and made sure every child you met excelled in school whether boy or girl.

226

Your generosity was contagious and immeasurable and you never frowned even at those ungrateful people that you raised. You always ask the rhetorical question to me 'Ndatare do you know that one day you will not find me here? It is today I can understand and provide an answer. Here am I without you. Unbelievable but real!!!

Sleep tight and watch over us just like you did while here on earth.
Adieu Daddy
Son,

Tseghama Ndatare Angwafo III

Fo Angwafo III used these words whenever we are given some work to do. As children, we will want to use force and which will not permit us to do the work properly. "You see the ants are always busy and also as many as they are the work is always easy", remember his majesty, Fo Angwafo III used to be an agriculturalist and I have profited much from him and the entire Mankon people.

In 1992 during the political crises in Cameroon, I was in Bambili and your majesty used to send the car to pick us up after closing for holidays and because of the crises the driver didn't come to take me home so I had to trek on foot from Bambili to Mankon palace this made me come home two days after only with my report card and after meeting your highness, you asked why I came so late and after telling you how I managed to come home, you were so amazed that you told me you are my army keep on. This is one thing I can't forget because today your prophecy came true and everywhere I go for training I can't suffer.

Your Highness, you did what you were supposed to do, and I pray and know that you are with your ancestors, may you and our forefathers continue to look on us and that your wisdom be upon us all so that we as your children of Mankon be united and keep the flag of this great kingdom flying as high as possible.

My mentor, my hero.

Tseofo Angwafo III

What shall I say? Papa "big" as you are! Important as you are! I didn't believe one day you will be no more. Physically you are no more but spiritually you are always there.

Our late father, Fo Ndefru III, gave me, your junior brother to you to care for. In 1955 you sent me to class one in Basel Mission

227

School Ntingkag Mankon. In 1958 you took me to stay with you and attend N.A school Befang in standard VI. You sent me to PTTC Batibo from 1967-72 where I obtained Teacher's Grade I. Thank you papa for your paternal care.

What have you not done, everything humanly possible?

You went to Arochuku Ibadan Nigeria by canoe where you obtained a diploma in Agricultural Engineering. Upon return, you worked briefly in Bambui. You opened many Agric farms and experimental farms in Befang, Menchum Valley and all over Wum division.

You inherited your father's throne in 1959 till 2022. You worked so hard that Mankon people unanimously authorized you enter into politics in 1962 barely 3 years on the throne. You raised Mankon into a First Class Fondom. You have taught Mankon modern Agricultural technics e.g., farming across the slope and the use of organic manure and forbidding the burning of "Ankara". etc.

As a shrewd politician you were voted into the West Cameroon House of Chiefs, West Cameroon House of Assembly as an independent candidate. You were voted into the National House of Assembly and retired from active politics in 1988.

Papa where is Auckland? Far into the Pacific ocean, yet you went there for the good of this beloved country. Can anyone help me to mention the untold works of HRM? You were taken ill on and off, attending health facilities in S. Africa, Yaounde and Mankon until this fateful day 21/05/2022.

You have given this country to us on a golden plate. You have left this in PEACE. You wish this Nation to live in PEACE and LOVE as you were a Fon of PEACE and LOVE welcoming people of all races in Mankon Land.

Papa, live in eternal peace and if nobody reciprocates your generosity, Almighty God will. Remain Blessed in your eternal kingdom.

Your Eldest son,

Tsi Ghamoti Angwafo

Saturday, May 21, 2022, late that afternoon was the day the hero, and leader of contemporary time made his just come wish a reality. The surprise prophesy became a surprise to itself which the world and Mankon Marvelled at his sense of wisdom (the king Solomon of our time). Your admiration for aesthetics, epistemology and the ecosystem was a success. Words are limited to describe many things but I'm happy God made you the "on move mover" or the just judge within the circle of the nation, families and communities. Mbeh, you said to me "Tsi education is the key to your world of tomorrow, honesty and integrity, be a diligent man." I will miss hearing these words of yours but I am so grateful for the impact it has on me.

I join the host of angels and our ancestors for a safe trip home, like Shakespeare "We are all actors in this world, when your script is finished you live the scene" Socrates says in the Republic "only God alone knows" and just like apostle Paul in the Bible, you kept the faith in you as per our last discussion was in, signs looks and simile in April.

Your boy(nephew),

Tsi Julius Ndefru
(I.T. king, strategist and love builder)

Dad,

"Nimo " you always called me with a smile on your face whenever we had a conversation. Oh dad! You have left a space that can never be filled in my life. My dearest father, You have been such an inspiration to me from the day I was born. Growing up you always taught me hard work, love and compassion. During my hardest moments and when I faced several challenges you urged me to keep working and trusting the process. You made me understand the struggles of life and for that I am grateful. You were a definition of a true leader and a father. Watching you handle the entire Mankon community and still handle your family with so much love and care is one thing you will always be remembered for.

Even on your last days daddy you told us all to live in love and harmony which speaks volumes of the lovely man you were. Thank you for instilling great values in me and I promise to continue to put everything you taught me into practice. Who will call me "nimo" again? I sleep and get echoes of you calling me "nimo " but I can't see you. You once told me a day will come when I won't see you again and when that day comes I should be strong. I try every day to stay strong for you. Farewell my darling father until we meet again.

Daughter,

Mrs. Tuma Agnes Angwafo

As grandpa usually said, "a day would come when I will close my eyes and you will continue from where I ended". That day has come, and it is a hard pill to swallow.

Today I celebrate the great man you are, living with the great moments we shared, remembering the virtues of forgiveness, hard work and obedience amongst others you taught me.

Grandpa would always remind me I am named after him, and I have the obligation to keep working hard and not relent in my efforts because the Fon doesn't rest. You would take me on tours at "ntah-fo" where we will inspect your fish pond, your piggery, farms and harvest fruits while teaching me to be a better man in words and deeds.

Your constant support in my upbringing has left an irreplaceable spot in my heart for you. I will forever miss the selfless grandpa I have, who spent almost all of his life serving his community and family.

I know you are out there watching over me grandpa, thank you for all the sacrifices, love and concern you showered me with. I wish I could hear you call me Anye Angwa once more…

Your grandson and namesake,

Tuma Anye Angwafor

I developed consanguinity in Fo S.A.N. Angwafo III of Mankon during my school days at the University of Yaounde from 1990. I carried out research, working closely with the Fon for sixteen years to write a biographical synthesis of the Fon which was published and launched in the Bamenda Congress hall in 2008. Summarily, the following few words are not even descriptive enough of the missing Fo S.A.N Angwafo III of Mankon:

And the lord God said to the Mankon people I will give you a king,
I the Lord will give you a king.
A righteous king,
A wise and peaceful king.
And it came to pass in the Mankon Fondom.
And the promise of God came to pass in this land.
For 1925 the 21st day of May, a prince was born.
For in 1959 the 4th day of April,
The prince Solomon AnyeGhamoti Ndefru was crowned,
Fo Angwafo the third of Mankon Fondom.
And the people clapped,

And sang and sang and praised the Lord.
The people were right to rejoice,
For the Fondom has grown in leaps and bounds,
With the leadership of Fo Angwafo III,
A farmer and a teacher,
A lover of culture, a developer and a politician.
Fo Angwafor the third, the wise,
A lover of peace, we praise the Lord.
Glory be to God for all his love,
And life you lived in this sinful world.

I pray God to grant Fo S.A.N. Angwafo III a place in his bosom,
And equally grant wisdom and greater achievement to our new
Fon, Fo Angwafo IV.

Wankah Wilfred Nde
(The national President of MA.TU.
and the DDSE of Mezam)

He was a great man who came into our lives through the
matrimony of his son, Tamuhlargh, and our daughter, Dr. Alenda.
We shall forever remember him for his fatherly love for us.

Farewell Great Man, the Fon.

Mrs. Priscilla and Mr. Benedict Agendia of Bamenda

Part 8

Cameroon and the World at Large

Years ago, I was in Kameroen for a project in Binshua. Through a contact through daughter Aliah, I had the honour to be received by Fon Angwafo in Bamesa. I had the opportunity to have a pleasant conversation with this imposing wise man who told me a lot about the traditional customs in the region. He was the same age as my father, and I saw similarities in their character and personality, so that visit stayed with me forever. I cherish the photo next to him in traditional clothes.

Anne Mie Descheemaeker (Belgium)

Remembering HRH Angwafor III

His Royal Highness Angwafor III
Fon of Mankon, he was and we knew.
His presence was made known or announced by echoes of:
The biggest bamboo of the raffia bush
The egg of the Cardinal bird
The baby that baths from the mortar
The sun that rises in the east and sets in the west
These are but a few of the litany of titles reserved for nobility and royalty

You were one of them blessed with longevity!
You may be lost in the physical, but you are found in the spiritual.
Memories of you and your deeds are fresh
My mother of blessed memory was raised on a piece of land
Whose title bears your signature.

His royal Highness M ST Galabe II (1927-2021)
Traditional natural ruler Gah of Baligham
My grandfather, HRH Ngongeh III of Awing was your brother
You often visited the Awing Palace
Each visit was marked with remarkable kindness to my dad.
With a child's mind I observed with admiration
Mu Quifor, Son of the Quifor,

Your generosity has left an imprint that will forever endure.
You have defined longevity in so many aspects
In a moving world readaptation is the price of longevity, to sustain you have to evolve
You once said stress, tension and worries should be avoided,
But embrace gratitude as a virtue
Longevity and generosity, the hallmarks of your legacy.

A royal gift from God to mankind,
You demonstrated less envy, materialism and self-centredness, a king with self-esteem you were

It seems like yesterday, but it's been years
When you came to Chicago to visit families and friends

I was privileged to serve you, inherited royal blessings from royal hands
The warmth of those hands I still feel, your fatherly voice still echoing.

The past is felt in the present, the lost is not lost
Say hello to Ngongeh III of Awing, Galabe Gah of Baligham, Asa'ah of Awing
Our other ancestors, do not forget.
Tell them what you have seen and left behind.
In your reunion conversations remind them of our coming soon.
Discuss our longings and prayers
May we experience peace in our land!
May eternal peace be your rest.

Ayafor Florence Neba

Fon Angwafo III of Mankon(Centre), Fon Ngongeh III of Awing (Right) and
my father Pa Jacob Asaah Ayafor (left)

When I started my work with the Atanga Peace Project and decided to educate our traditional leaders to become peace ambassadors, a lot of people said that they will never do it. My father encouraged me to have faith in them. He was right. I was very humbled when after my presentation at the Bamenda Congress Hall in 2009, the traditional leaders all signed up and gave me their contact numbers. One of the first numbers I called after returning to the USA was HRH Fon Angwafo III. I trembled as it rang, expecting a Nchinda to answer. I almost dropped to the floor with humility when the person at the other end was none other than HRH. He was full of complement about the work I was doing to promote our culture and promote peace in our communities. He asked if I could bring more of that education to them the traditional leaders. Even though I was not sponsored and was using my own resources, I could not say no. I asked him if he will participate in remote learning through pre-recorded programmes that I will send for the leaders to gather at a set venue and learn. This was 2009 before Covid19 and zoom. He said YES and so it began. They will gather at St. Frederic (former PCC) and Michael Mubang will facilitate a class that I had prepared by video and PowerPoint. They completed the program and were awarded Atanga Peace Project certificates signed by my father Pa Joseph Iban Atanga (late Pa Highland). He and many others including the Fons of Akum, Mbatu, Chomba, Bawock to name a few, became the first peace ambassadors. In spite of the challenges, I had to do all I could no matter the personal cost because he said YES. I also believe that because a Paramount Fon of his statue believed in the program, it made it easier for others to join. We will continue to work because of their dedication and commitment to learn.

Dr. Bernadette Atanga

It is with a very heavy heart that I write this tribute in memory of his Highness, Fo Solomon AnyeGhamoti Angwafo III.

His father, Fo Ndefru was friendly to Papa Martin Atang, the founder of Catholic Mission Mankon in Bamenda. The Fon usually stopped over for talks with Papa Martin Atang before being carried to climb the Ayaba hill to get to the District Officer's office. It is worth noting that all Government offices were located in up Station at that time.

Papa Martin Atang's home was thrown into mourning when Fo Ndefru disappeared. Papa Martin instructed us -the children- to go to Alamankong to cry Fo Ndefru's disappearance and witness the stoning and installation of Fo Angwafor III as the new traditional custodian of the culture and values of Mankon people.

Fo Angwafo III was a very smart and knowledgeable person. This was confirmed by a group of Pan African Institute for Development-Buea students whom I arranged to visit His Royal Highness in his Palace in 1987 during Zone Studies, an integral component of the students study in Buea. Fo Angwafo III demonstrated that he was up-to-date with state-of-the-art information about world issues, current events, and current information about the African countries the students came from.

There is no doubt that we have lost an icon of a very family-oriented and a peaceful person. May his gentle Soul rest in perfect peace... Amen.

Dr. Christopher Atang
Houston Texas USA

Memories of Values

I consider myself blessed, because privileged and honoured to have known and interacted with the 20th monarch of Mankon Kingdom, His Majesty Fo'o Solomon AnyeGhamoti Ndefru Angwafo III.

By the grace of God, I met His Majesty on different occasions in my native Bambalang, in his own palace at Mankon, as well as in Ndop, other parts of Bamenda, Yaounde and elsewhere. Each time, I was struck by the sheer stout, gorgeous and imposing stature that augurs well for his royal status.

Serenity, underpinned by culturally based noble humility with an infectious spontaneous smile was the hallmark of Fo'o Angwafo III. Perchance, a blend of this with his chosen Christian name Solomon, imbued him with such rare wisdom that is comparable only to that of his Biblical equal, King Solomon.

His Majesty Fo'o Angwafo III was not only a loving father of all people he met; he was also generously caring. He made sure I ate and drank well whenever I came to Mankon palace, alone or accompanied. And guess what? Whether I came with a bag or not, I would always leave with a package from him for my household!

The emblematic Mankon Fo'o was surely an icon to many, even if some envied him. Our father who disappeared recently leaves in my mind the image of the epitome of a good leader: hardworking, self-reliant, tolerant, patient, respectful and respected, God-fearing, and grateful to everybody who contributed anything, however little, to enable him selflessly work for God by peacefully serving mankind in their pursuit of happiness and self-fulfilment! The venerated King Angwafo III kindly shared these values and more with me! The greatest one is GRATITUDE!

Indeed, the Legacy of Fo'o S.A.N. Angwafo III Lives on, and will live on! May God bless the King!

Muunteuhgeuhnteuh (Ephraim Banda Ghogomu)
Special Counsel to Mbaw Yakum Throne

Gone, but not forgotten: A tribute to Fon Angwafo III

What a magnificent rock of wise, calm, strong and empathetic leadership Fon Angwafo III has been over the decades!

I learned about The Mankon paramount ruler's death through social media on May 21st, 2022 before receiving a confirmation from family members. An outpouring of grief, shock and uncertainty took over citizens expressing their grief online. I could not believe one of the world's longest-reigning monarch who was often seen as a pillar of stability in our beloved country was gone.

Many posted images depicting themselves in a position of reverence, in a show of the respect they had towards the missing king. I posted a private photo depicting a close relationship I was privileged to have with the twentieth king of Mankon whose modernity was firmly grounded in traditions. I was also amongst the many who joined celebrations to mark the 50 years into his reign in 2009, reflecting the prominent and influential status of the Royal Family of Mankon in Cameroon.

The story of his life *"Royalty and Politics"* published in 2009, is a unique analytical and insightful reflection into his reign. The tendency of the king to side with the government in power caused some Cameroonian to question his impartiality. However, his influence was still viewed as pivotal when dealing with negotiation and reconciliation. The king's devotion to the welfare of all his people inspired greater admiration.

I was privileged to be close to the missing monarch and the royal family. I was fortunate enough to witness some incredible interactions with members of the royal family, and had the opportunity to be part of the dynamic lives of some of them and shared with each other our life stories and contrasting backgrounds. My family as a whole will treasure the wonderful moments spent together for the many years to come.

Fon Angwafo III, the great monarch is gone but will never be forgotten. He will be remembered as a warm and caring person, a great politician, a diplomat, with an ability to reach out to ordinary people. He has been one vital and valued constant in an ever-changing world, representing security and stability for our country, during the ups and downs of the last six decades. There is no doubt that at his departure he leaves the Mankon's monarchy in Cameroon far stronger than it was at his accession.

Francois-Xavier MBOPI-KEOU
Full Professor and Chair
Department of Microbiology, Parasitology,
Haematology, Immunology & Infectious Diseases,
Faculty of Medicine & Biomedical Sciences,
University of Yaounde I

His Royal Highness Fon Angwafo III:
Baobabs never really die if their roots are not destroyed
Life has many phases.

Death is only a transitory phase from earth into the world beyond. HRH has travelled...

Every once in a while someone comes along in life whose actions are so inspiring and thought-provoking that make us ask ourselves great introspective questions about who we are and what the real purpose of life is. That person motivates us to learn more, to grow more and to be more.

HRH Fon Angwafo III was one such person - a man larger than life, a man whose mistakes were lessons in themselves, a man who embodied so many facets of leadership.

During my service at the US Embassy in Yaoundé, I was honoured to be part of a team that paid several visits to the Mankon Fondom as part of our Cultural Diplomacy outreach programs. During one of such visits, I was privy to an exclusive one-on-one with the Fon. In the course of our conversation, I was able to peek into the mind of this great landmark in the history of the North West Region.

239

Our bonding moment came when HRH made me understand that he was instrumental in my late father's educational pursuits; and that henceforth, I would become a special daughter of the palace. During our conversation HRH came across as one with unique strategic insight and relentless passion for his Fondom and kinship. His imposing stature bestowed on him an almost invincible personality which I think gave him the ability to seem unperturbed, regardless of the seemingly ominous circumstances in the nation. He had such strength of character-quietly enthusiastic, overtly determined but cautiously optimistic.

Our minds touched, our thoughts clicked, and HRH conferred on me a cloak of nobility from the Mankon Palace (*See photo*). I will always carry with me that touch of his wisdom, humility in service and quiet strength.

In his words: "*a forest does not make noise when it grows but its presence is always noticeable. Always let your presence speak for itself,*" he concluded.

HRH's journey on this earth will not soon be forgotten.

As Patriarch and legend, he left wisdom-prints, leadership-prints and heart-prints in the lives of so, so many...and I am honoured to be counted among the many.

HRH Fon Angwafo III: You were Royalty, Honourable, Your Excellency, Mentor, Leader, Legacy shaper, and Father - all at once.

Your legacy will forever be etched in the history of Cameroon.

Thank you for your service to humanity. Thank you for engraining the tenets of our beautiful traditions and customs.

Thank you for being such a blessing to this nation.

Travel on Patriarch.

Travel on Statesman.

Travel on Father.

Travel on...Travel on...Travel on...

Yaah/ Mafor Gladys Shang Viban
Then Cultural Affairs Specialist US Embassy Yaounde

Photo Caption - from left to right -Mathew Smith (Deputy Chief of Missions), HRH and Yaah Gladys Viban)

To All Mankon

Never has the saying, "This is the end of an era", been more apt!!

I am in my late 50s, and as a Bamenda boy have never known any other Fon of Mankon than Fo Angwafor III RIP. The term

"Bamenda boy" may have annoyed the missing Fon - but I believe he came to realise Bamenda as his nemesis reality.

Fo Angwafor III has towered over most other traditional leaders of his era in his 63 years on the throne with a canny combination of political dexterity (e.g., he has stayed in his Palace all through the Southern Cameroons crisis unlike most other Fons), largely good judgement and sheer gravitas. Liked him or loathed him, he has been a material and consequential traditional leader of Southern Cameroons. He will be long remembered.

In my time in SaHeCo, we fondly referred to HRM as "Ngia Nde"! And we meant it fondly indeed.

He oversaw Mankon during the very complex and unstoppable challenges of urbanisation (Mankon becoming largely Bamenda against his utmost protestations) and against a cancerous party political interference into traditional leadership. This latter, he navigated better than most even though he was very senior in party politics.

His longevity also both provided stability to Mankon and a strong semblance of "rien ne change" despite "tout change au tour de nous"

He will indeed be a hard act to follow.

Fo Angwafor III – rest in peace

Hycinth Sama Nwana
SHESAN
Surrey UK

I am Jato Richard Tonga.

A Journalist at Radio hot cocoa in Bamenda

One of the Private Radios Our Beloved Father Fon Angwafo III of Mankon used to love so much.

I just wish to recount some moments I had with the Fon as a Journalist with the radio.

When Rumours first circulated on the disappearance of the Fon, I reached out to do an interview with him at the palace when one of his daughters then student of PSS Bafut informed me the Father was in. After eating Achu served out of the Palace's hospitality, the Fon came to the reception room.

The Fon asked: "'Hot cocoa' how is hot cocoa radio, hot?"

I said, "Yes, Your Highness." He told me, "You have come and I know why. You have seen me. Seeing is believing. Go and tell the world. Thanks, my son."

That was it.

Permit me to salute the people of Mankon.

The hospitality of the Mankon people is that which I have never seen before in my life. Fon Angwafo III, May Peace reign upon the King. Long live the King.

King Solomon, Fon of Mankon. I am blessed to be that Journalist the Fon would attend to even when the Fon would receive no other person. The Fon had a soft spot for me.

The Fon would advise me on the importance of journalism to build and not destroy.

The King would go so slow in an interview at all moments when I or other colleagues would go for an interview.

The Fon loved the press and would be very careful in his choice of words to the media.

The Fon will invite me at times to meet him on his farm for interviews to see his realities.

In all this, Fon Angwafo remained very humble and forgiving to the media or media person who touched His integrity.

His kindness to me was like chain. Even out of the Palace at any given official or private activities, the Fon would call me Hot cocoa, your transport.

I never saw the Fon at any given moment and left empty-handed.

The Palace of Mankon is my home today, everyone accepts me in the palace as the Fon gave me very important attention all the time.

True, I will miss Him.

Thanks to God the King is back.

Jato Richard Tonga
Journalist

Par ce biais, je tiens à vous présenter toutes mes sincères condoléances pour le repos éternel de Papa. Puisse l'Eternel Tout Puissant l'accueillir paisiblement dans ses parvis !

Une bibliothèque qui s'en va après avoir rempli sa mission ici-bas, un grand baobab qui tombe mais qui fort heureusement laisse des racines fortement ancrées sur le sol pour assurer une relève digne de ce nom.

Celui qui part après avoir rempli ses nombreuses missions n'est plus à plaindre car il repose désormais dans la plénitude. Il passe le relais aux autres qui auront désormais la lourde tâche d'assurer la relève et la continuité des sentiers ouverts.

Prendre le témoin n'est jamais chose aisée, c'est la raison pour laquelle je saisis cette occasion pour vous redire ce dont vous savez sans doute mieux que quiconque : c'est à la fois une forte et lourde responsabilité mais aussi beaucoup de bénédictions !

Puisse l'Éternel, Dieu Tout Puissant continuer à veiller sur vous, vous fortifier et vous combler de Sa Sagesse à tous égards !

Mmamouko et toute la famille de Belgique

I Shall Forever Remember King Angwafor III's Giant Smiles

As a cop reporter in Bamenda, I met His Majesty multiple times in Bamenda, mainly at the Town Hall run by the CPDM party. But my first close encounter for a press chat was after his palatial residence near the former Roxi Cinema hall was burnt down by rioters. I was expecting to meet an angry king. Instead, I met a calm father of all children. He was unhappy with the excesses of the opposition but had no harsh words for those he clearly knew were behind the arson.

Fo Angwafor III like his Chomba colleague of blessed memory always called me Joe! Both men were always vocally happy with my journalism of balance, accuracy and fairness. They would encourage me not to depart from reporting the truth. They always answered my phone calls.

I saw Fo many more times during his political outings than anytime else. Party event organisers always kept his interventions last. And like the Biblical King Solomon, Fon Angwafor III would dish out a dose of wisdom. His message always sank well into the minds of party comrades who often jammed the Congress Hall. Laughter and thunderous applause would erupt during his speeches. Clear evidence that he was spilling out humour and wise sayings.

Then, I took an appointment for an intimate interview with the monarch. I arrived on time on the fixed day. He allowed me to come very close to him for proper recording, even if palace notables clearly did not like it. The former Government delegate to the Bamenda City Council, Ndeh Sanjou-Tadzong was amongst those who sat through the interview. They heard me asking taboo questions that no Mankon person would dare mention in public. But the king was at ease. He would not put a figure to the number of wives or children he has. Our lively conversation transformed into an elaborate interview public in the maiden edition of Summit Magazine. Titled King

Solomon the wise, the front pager sold well during its launching in Bamenda.

Fon Angwafor had a sharp memory. He could vividly narrate how he started his working life in my village, Aghem. It seemed his mind held an archive of the events that led up to the Foumban conference and how John Ngu Foncha was not transparent with his leadership and dealings with President Ahidjo.

Fo Angwafor was a very likeable person. His vocabulary was rich with proverbs, wise sayings and humour. He was a teacher in my conversations with him. But he was also an excellent listener. He would not miss a moment to tell the world how important farming is to the life of his people and the nation. Tolerance, peaceful cohabitation, education, development and progress are the issues Fon Angwafor would not miss to harp on in our press chats.

At one time, we discussed compiling a conversational autobiography for him. It is not his fault that there was no follow-up. The monarch was often just referred to as Fon Angwafor in conversations. I remember him as a Big man. A big king. His big shoes. The picture of his giant body on the day he was enthroned, sixty-three years ago, is as fresh in my mind as the first time I saw the picture. Of course, I shall forever remember his big smile and his white, solid teeth.

Randy Joe Sa'ah
BBC Correspondent, Cameroon

Part 9

Historical Perspectives and Outlooks

The day The World knew me because of You!
The Royal Transcendence!

The time is 5:45 pm and it is a typical winter evening in Minnesota. The plane has landed and the Mankon community has defied the biting cold and dressed in their traditional regalia and adorning the arrival section of the Minneapolis St. Paul (MSP) Airport. The Colours and the out-of-place dressing is causing quite a stir and a stare. The community is mobilized and they have turned out in their numbers – almost two hundred and still arriving. I have just arrived from the two-hour wintry drive from Rochester Minnesota where I am a Public Defender by day. All logistics are in place and the Protocol is in place.

Suddenly, the normal rush and bustle of the Airport comes to a standstill. There is a magic and majestic calm that descends on all. All is still and quiet as if responding to the magic and majesty of the moment. The Airport is still. The world seems to have come to a halt. The fragility of the moment seems to be a premonition for transcendence and transformation. It seems the world will change. It seems the world has changed. And then, there is a methodic and holy glide of a wheelchair at the top of the almost fifty-metre rolling steps from the upper level of the walk way unto the ground arrival port that has been converted into a Mankon traditional plaza. The wheelchair is rotated one hundred and eighty degrees so that it is facing the direction from which the Asian Wheelchair Driver lady is coming from. She adjusts quickly on the rolling stairs and fits harmoniously unto the belt that starts gliding seamlessly towards the ululating "Mighty Wave" in Minnesota.

For one fleeting moment, it feels like Pope John Paul II being magically glided from his window balcony in St. Peter's Square unto the waiting sea of pilgrims from all over the world. The glide of fifty metres is halted in time and space and the whole wide world reflects eternally for the World Wide Web to behold the spiritual Father of *Ala'nkyi* , cross oceans and mountains on his maiden evangelical journey wherein the core values, customs, traditions, face and person of the Mankon *id, ego* and *superego* would be in full display.

On the rolling stairs, at the MSP Airport, charioted on a wheelchair by an Asian Lady (airport attendant), Minnesota became the mirror in which the world would behold the harbinger of Peace, Truth, Authenticity and Nativism. MSP, like Minnesota became the microcosm of the Macrocosm. Minnesota became Mankon and Mankon became the World. You were the Chariot of our Gods. You were the rear mirror of our past and the crystal ball of our future and posterity. You were flesh among us. The world saw You and You made the world to see us – all of us who, hitherto, just struggled to blend in and pass for *them* too. But today, we were different because You came and through You the world saw us. Today we are a Child, a Woman and a Man. Today WE ARE because YOU ARE. That is why the Chariot must alight and we behold you.

Ululations break out from the prompts of our Mothers. Yes, they too were here. In the cold they had stood. From the cold they had come in their tropical regalia (*toghe* before the world seized it), to behold You – the ONE. You, the Bridge without guard rails! You, the Lion of the Pride! You the ruler and the rider of the Clouds! Not even the Minnesota cold could deter them. The yawps were thunderous. The squeals were thrilling. The yells were sustained and coordinated. The joy was complete. The ecstasy was orgasmic. The celebration was peaked. And the reverence was total, unabated and unabashed. And the world stood still and noticed. The Fon was not only in United States but in Minnesota.

The wheelchair driver was taken aback but her consternation had no place and notice in the nirvana that You were and that You had brought and caused. Before I could calm her fears, her better instincts of admiration, adoration and adulation kicked in and she exploded into one hilarious bolt and jolt of brown ebullience. She wanted to ask and learn but nobody was there to give her notice and attention because the Tusk of the Elephant was busily proclaiming the presence of the Tiger in this jurisdiction. *Takumbeng*, the Prince, and *Nkwenti*, the Queen Mother, had now managed to navigate the rolling stairs and were now placed behind Your Majesty as custom and history ordain. Nimo Mambo Nkwab, of Makushuri from Ntofi, was the first to "shoot the elephant". "Mighty Wave" then followed. And You called all of us by name beginning with "*ngway Ndzoya*" (my own mother) to "Buy one take two", through "*maeyongbweri*" down to "*Aza Tabah*", you enunciated our genealogies and our follies, all in greetings. Even so, the uninitiated stood and marvelled and will wait for their own occasion wherein their rites of passage would be granted. These, you did and again Minnesota was marvelled and, above all, Minnesota watched, adored and imbibed it. Then Minnesota knew us – just because You had come. Just because You were here with us – in Minnesota. For two hours at the Airport, the spirit of Mankon flew to all corners of the World – just because of You.

The Convoys took us Home – I mean to the Palace and You graced us for a week – a whole lifetime. A week that went down and diluted irrecoverably and irredeemably, all the historical and spiritual waters, fountains and springs of Mankon – Your Fondom, our Heritage and our Legacy. Mankon, your Essence and our Nature. Mankon, the promise of our Posterity and the source of our Prosperity. Mankon, Your Mighty Wave and our eternal lineage.

Your Palace was in Minnesota for one whole week. During which You performed one spiritual function or the other. During which You attended one function or the other. During which You were *res ipsa loquitur* for the world. When my own mother, Nimo Mambo Nkwab (now with you), finished the ritual of 'washing the palace' (greeting), prostrate on Minnesotan soil, it was the greatest sparkle and the shiniest radiance that I ever beheld on her face – just because You were here and with us!

Every minute of every hour counted for an achievement. It is therefore unthinkable that I, or anybody for that matter, should be expected to recount, relay, relate or reproduce your actions, activities and achievements in one forum or in one mere lifespan or lifetime. If one was forced to limit Your achievements only to One a year, we will be detailing Sixty-Three (63) gigantic achievements. If we narrowed the years to months, we will be talking of Seven Hundred and Fifty-Six (756) Months of *ginormous* achievements. If we streamlined them to weeks, we will be challenging ourselves to Three Thousand And Twenty-Four (3,024) Weeks of gargantuan achievements. What if we tried winding down to days, we would have to contain with explicating Twenty-One Thousand One Hundred and Sixty-Eight (21,168) Days of towering achievements. And then to think that in Your reign you clocked Five Hundred and Eight Thousand and Thirty-Two (508,032) Hours of rocket achievements for Mankon – Your Fondom, is of epic proportions. These are numbers and even in numbers You are innumerable!

That is why the world will forever see You in numbers and more. That is why Mankon will forever see you in shapes, forms, places, faces and places. That is why the Royal family will forever see You in

249

Phases, stages, wages and pages. And I will forever see You in Spirit and in Soul. Then our Ancestors will see You in Whole and with the Pole – the Bamboo of *Kwifor* and the staff of Power, to hold and to give. Now that you have given, we must take in communion and in union with Your Son.

For all these reasons and because of You we are Known and I am Seen. Because of You Mankon is bigger and must *germinate*. Because of You the world has moved forward and is now moving faster and faster.

Because of You we are!

Because You came WE even now ARE!

Fo Angwafo III comes to Minnesota.

Tambu Ngang

The Biography of Fo S.A.N Angwafo III of Mankon
Early Life of The Crown Prince

Mankon is the largest of the Fondoms that make up Bamenda City. The years 1925 and 1959 are of special importance in the History of Mankon. On May 21st, 1925, the crown Prince AnyeGhamoti Ndefru was born in the Mankon Palace and in 1959 he succeeded his father. His father, Fo Ndefru III was born around 1881, enthroned as Fon of Mankon in 1919 and disappeared in 1959. His mother, Mafo Theresia Mankah was born around 1900 in Mankon and she was the daughter of Akenji-Ndemasiri and Switdzu both of Munkyi. She died on April 17th, 1994.

Prince AnyeGhamoti had only a direct brother who unfortunately died at the early age of twelve. He, however, had many siblings with whom he grew up in the Palace. He was well schooled by his mother in the culture, the life and lore, and history the Mankon people. She made sure that the tradition, customs and etiquettes of the Palace were inculcated into her son. His father Fo Ndefru III also played a primordial role in this traditional Education. From the age of five, the Prince was trained on how to serve the father as a page. As testified by an eyewitness, the Prince used to accompany his father on most of the Fon's official outings or for some special meetings in the Palace. At birth the crown Prince was named AnyeGhamoti Ndefru and when he ascended the throne in 1959 he was called Fo Solomon AnyeGhamoti Ndefru Angwafo III. The Prince learnt and spoke fluently Mankon, Mungaka, Bafut, English, Pidgin and Fulani

Languages. He was the first Fon of Mankon to acquire a Western Education.

Educational Career

AnyeGhamoti Ndefru started formal education in Government School Bamenda Station from 1934 to 1936 and Catholic Mission School Big Mankon from 1937-1938. Between 1939 and 1940 he was out of school because his father wanted him to help him in the Palace. In 1941, he resumed Education at the Basel Mission Boys School Nsem – Bafut where he passed the Common Entrance Examination into standard five. From Bafut he went to the Basel Mission School Mbengwi in 1943 and spent only one week there because of a poorly interpreted notion of discipline, whereby the senior pupils maltreated the junior ones as testified by his schoolmate, Ade Peter Achoa. He opted to go back to Government School Bamenda Station where he completed Standard Six in 1944. At this school, he was elected as school head boy. He was withdrawn from school for some time by his father to assist him in the contract business of supplying food to the Bamenda prison and on the basis of lack of money to pay fees. His high sense of duty, outstanding intellect and demonstrated leadership qualities led the headmaster of Government School Bamenda Station, Mr. Adekuke Adeku, a Nigerian, to threaten suing Fo Ndefru III if he did not send the Prince to Secondary School. After a little trepidation in the Royal Court, AnyeGhamoti Ndefru wrote the Entrance Examination into Aggrey Memorial College in Nigeria and passed.

In 1946, he enrolled in Aggrey Memorial College, Arochuku in Eastern Nigeria. Shortly after his enrolment, his father could not pay the school fees, principally because the contract of supplying food to the Bamenda Prison through which he raised money had been abruptly terminated. As a resourceful and ambitious student, the Prince took to farming on arable land around the college to finance his education. He was elected janitor of the school experimental farm and the school library. Academically, he performed brilliantly well in the college and took four instead of the customary five years to obtain the Cambridge School Certificate and a certificate in Agriculture in 1950.

In 1950, he came back to Cameroon and with the Diploma in agriculture, he gained employment as an Agricultural Assistant in the then Government Agricultural Experimental farm in Bambui between 1950 and 1951. While in Bambui, he wrote the Government

Civil Service Examination to be confirmed as an established Staff and succeeded.

In August 1951, he was admitted into the Higher School of Agricultural Techniques (Moor Plantation) in Ibadan, Nigeria and graduated in 1953 with an Agricultural Assistant Grade III Diploma. The Prince also read elements of Social Sciences such as Anthropology, Sociology and Political Science. He came back to Cameroon, Mankon, in 1954 and in 1959 he was enthroned as Fo S.A.N Angwafo III of Mankon.

Civil Service Career

Solomon AnyeGhamoti Ndefru was employed by the Nigerian Civil Service and later was transferred to the then Bamenda Province. He worked in Wum Division which is present day Menchum and Boyo Divisions. He opened experimental farms in Befang where he nursed oil palm seeds, coffee, cocoa and coconut seedlings and distributed to farmers to plan.

He established feeder experimental farms in Naikom, Esimbi, Weh, Esu in Wum and Abuh, Njinikom, Bello and Meli in Kom. By diligent and painstaking application to his work and the resulting efficiency, he was promoted to an Agricultural Assistant Grade II in August 1956 and in September 1958 to an Agricultural Assistant Grade I. Incidentally, his Civil Service career was brief as he had to resign from his base in Befang in 1959 following his accession to the helm of the Mankon Fondom.

His Social Life

In social life the Prince had a very brief period of bachelorhood. He got married to his wife, Emilia Nanga-Maatsi. On becoming the Fon of Mankon in 1959, he became a polygamist and had many children. The number of wives and children is, like the stars in the heavens, unknown.

Fo Angwafo III was a baptized Christian in the Presbyterian Church in Cameroon but as the Fon of Mankon, the spiritual leader and guide of Mankon he recognized all Christian denominations and granted religious freedom of worship to his subjects.

Fo Angwafo III As Traditional Ruler

Fo Angwafo III was the twentieth Fon of the Mankon dynasty. His reign spanned 1959-2022 during which Mankon grew in leaps and bounds. He revealed great qualities of leadership and a high sense of responsibility in holding several posts such as school head boy, janitor of the college experimental farm and library and treasurer very early during his school days. His contributions to development as the

Fon of Mankon certainly had its roots in his school days and his upbringing in the palace.

In 1961, he introduced the practice of appointing executives in each of the traditional Institutions and insisted on the need to preserve minutes of meetings for posterity.

He promoted the learning and writing of the Mankon Language and the formation of cultural associations for the development of Mankon. He revamped the Mankon Cultural and Development Association (MA.CU.D.A), and formed the Mankon Youths Cultural and Development Union (MA.YO.CU.D.U.) in 1992. Still in Cultural renaissance, he encouraged the revival of the Mankon bottle dance in 1984.

In 1988, he enacted the Royal Acts I and II which regulated and guided the process of land ownership in Mankon because of pressure on land leading to many land disputes.

He promoted Education by granting land for the construction of public, confessional and lay private schools and colleges in Mankon. Land was also granted for the construction of health facilities like the Ntingkag District hospital, Alabukam, Ntahkah, Alamandum and Ngomgham health centres.

In the early 1990s, the Fon streamlined funeral celebrations that used to be very expensive and time-consuming by reducing their duration from seven to three days.

Fo Angwafo In Local Government

The Fon also participated in local government. Between 1964-1968 the Fon was the President of the Mankon Urban Town Council responsible for local administration of lower Ngemba made up of Mankon, Chomba, Mbatu, Nsongwa, Ndzah, Mundum I and II and Upper Ngemba made up of Awing, Baligham, Ndzong, Santa Mbei, Pinyin, Baforchu, Baba II, Alatening and Akum.

Between 1968-1977, he was the chairman of the Mankon Urban Town Council which was renamed Mankon Area Council in 1968. Between November 1977-1996 he remained the chairman when the status of the council was raised from Rural to Urban Council when Bamendankwe and Nkwen amalgamated with Mankon and it became known as the Bamenda Urban Council (BUC) with special status whereby the Head of State appointed Government Delegates to the Council such as Jomia Pefok in 1977, Sanjou Tadzong Abel Ndeh 1992 etc.

Fo Angwafo III: The Farmer

Fo Angwafo III will always be remembered for his contributions in the promotion of modern agriculture in Mankon. He launched a war against bush burning and the farming of Ankarah in Mankon even though these practices have not been completely eradicated.

In 1964, he embarked on the planting of eucalyptus and cypress at Akfungbe which was emulated by many Mankon people. It was the same scenario when he opened coffee farms and palm oil plantation, around the palace, Asongkah, Alabukam and Alamadum in 1975. He produced palm oil for the Royal family upkeep and for Commercial purpose.

In 1974, he initiated the Asongkah Green Revolution Effort group. It was a Cooperative enterprise aimed at contributing to Cameroon's Socio-economic development through the private sector in agriculture. The project started as a self-help food sufficiency group and gradually upgraded into a Cooperative Society. He also formed other self-help farmers groups such as Nte-Afon Young Farmers Group and the Dynamic Group Farm. The Fon's interest in farming demonstrated to the public that as a traditional ruler, he could also be a successful farmer. The Fon's agricultural activity was a radical departure from certain bad traditional norms practised in Mankon in the past.

In Mankon food items and palm wine were usually collected as tributes from people in the prominent markets such as Mutefo, Mbangoh, Ntsualam, Muwachu and taken to the palace but this traditional practice, *"Ashebbe"* was abrogated by Fo Angwafo III upon his enthronement. He made the royal family independent of the public for basic necessities in life like food and palm wine.

Through farming he was able to raise money to sponsor many children in school. It should be noted that education was one of his priorities. He created an adult literacy centre in the palace to educate his wives. His agricultural involvement marked an era of cultural and economic evolution in Mankon as the royal family no longer depended on the Mankon people for food and palm wine. On the contrary, the Fon and the Royal family repeatedly fed the populace during many socio-cultural events.

Political Career

Upon enthronement in 1959 Fo S.A.N Angwafo III would have been in confinement for six months in the palace to be imbued amongst others with Royal etiquette. Circumstances however forced him in to a premature exit from the palace. He had to attend the preparatory conference held in Mamfe from 10-11 August 1959 to plan for the February 11, 1961 plebiscite in British Southern Cameroons. His political profile was most illuminating and remarkable.

On July 25th, 1959 after three months of confinement he began his political career by participating in political discussions on the alternatives of the plebiscite question in British Southern Cameroons. On August 9, 1959, he travelled to Mamfe to attend the preparatory conference to discuss the question of the plebiscite.

In 1960, he was elected to Southern Cameroon's House of Chiefs and in 1961 he was the treasurer in Southern Cameroon House of Chiefs while the president was the Fon of Bafut and the Fon of Bali was the vice president.

On October 1, 1961 with the two federated states in Cameroon, the Southern Cameroon House of Chiefs (SCHC) was renamed the West Cameroon House of Chiefs (WCHC).

In 1962, he contested and won elections into the West Cameroon House of Assembly (WCHA) 1962 -1966, won the second mandate 1967-1973 on the CNU ticket, 1973-1983 and 1983-1988 on the Cameroon's Peoples Democratic Movement when he retired as parliamentarian.

Between 1966-1969 Fo Angwafo III was adviser during Fon Galega of Bali who was president of Mezam section of the party that was formed in 1966.

In 1969-1981 Fo Angwafo III took over from Fon Galega as president of Mezam CNU party and as deputy speaker in the (WCHA).

In 1983, when President Paul Biya visited Bamenda, Fo Angwafo III performed one of his duties as president of Mezam section by reading a welcome speech in the Bamenda Conference Hall. He served in the Foreign Affairs and Constitutional Laws committees of the National Assembly. He was appointed as the alternative Judge to the court of impeachment between 1983-1985.

In 1988 he retired from parliament and active politics after serving the nation as parliamentarian for 27 years (1961-1988).

Fo Angwafo III appealed to the Cameroon head of state to construct the Bamenda Congress Hall following the government plan to hold party congresses in major towns in Cameroon. The Fon's intercession with the Head of State let to the construction of Bamenda Congress Hall, completed in 1985.

The Fon provided land for the relocation of the Mankon Motor Park on the site where the Bamenda congress is constructed to Ntarikun Park. The present Ntarikun market finally took over the park and the park was again relocated to Muwachu-Mile Eight Mankon.

In 1990, he was elected as the first national vice-president of the Cameroon People's Democratic Movement, a post he held until his disappearance in May 2022.

On November 7, 1995 Fo Angwafo III accompanied the Cameroon head of state on a Commonwealth of Nations, Heads of Government Submit, held in Auckland, New Zealand, after Cameroon was admitted in to the Commonwealth of Nations as the 52nd member on November 1, 1995.

Medal Award

On March 13, 1973 Fo Angwafo III received a medal award from the head of state as Officer of Cameroon Agricultural Order of Merit.

On 20th May 2000, he received another award, The Commander of Agricultural Order of Merit.

He was decorated with a medal of Grand Officer of the National Order of Valour by the Cameroon head of state.

On Saturday of August 2, 2006 at 2pm, Fo Angwafo III won and was awarded a converted noble, prestigious, honour and award as the Africa Man of the Year 2006 by the American Biographical Institute (ABI)

Fo S.A.N. Angwafo III until his disappearance in May 2022 lived a very healthy life. He was generally known as the "the wise King", "King Solomon". He was full of wisdom and humour and until his demise; he had good sense of focus, coherence in ideas and excellent vision. With age came corporeal challenges with going about. Fo Angwafo III, the philosopher king and teacher was very generous with counsel. Fo S.A.N Angwafo III of Mankon was disappeared in late May 2022 leaving behind the royal family, the entire Mankon people and the Cameroonians as a whole to mourn Him.

Wankah Wilfred Nde

Ask me of one celebrated leader who could proportionately combine traditional administration, national political engagement and local socio-economic development for his people with sagacity and alacrity, I will instantly name the iconic figure, Solomon AnyeGhamoti Angwafor III, 20th monarch of the Fondom of

Mankon. Though his transition to the world beyond came after close to a centenarian (97years) lifespan, the people of Mankon, like the North West Region and the rest of Cameroon were wrapped in great lamentation when the hero got "missing". As diverse as newspapers interests are in Cameroon, news of his passing for some moments became crucial headlines on every tabloid. Certainly, Angwafor's fine stewardship made Mankon popular and enabled it to rise to the status of a paramount chiefdom following the Chieftaincy Reorganization Law in West Cameroon in 1966 and the 1977 Chieftaincy Reclassification Decree in the United Republic of Cameroon. Born in 1925 and enthroned in 1959, he was a traditional ruler par excellence who happened to have exited as adviser to the Fons in the North West Regional House of Chiefs. He had an imposing physiognomy, appealing charisma and profound sense of discernment which largely won him great admiration from his subjects, peers and other high standing public authorities.

As an agricultural engineer trained in Nigeria in 1953, he promoted development in that sector and in education. He rendered his services to his subjects and educated them on the need to invest in sustainable agri-business oriented farming. As an agricultural engineer, he did not only restrict the desire to spur agricultural development to the confines of the Mankon Fondom, but readily provided wise counsels to several traditional rulers to emulate the example in their Fondoms. Permit me quickly mention that I share these testimonies not only from an academic perspective but as a grandson to one of the lead traditional rulers, the Fon of Bum in the Bamenda Grassfields that the Great enterprising monarch of Mankon left penetrating legacies in terms of value-added agricultural transformation.

An offshoot of Fon Angwafor's primary acquaintance with the Fon of Bum was to trade ideas on the importance of planting palms to extract and even market vegetable oil. He even recommended and directed on the type of high-yielding and adaptable 'American' cloned palms that could meet the edaphic specificities of Lakabum, the seat of the Bum Fondom and its immediate environs. The palm smallholder scheme around the Lakabum Palace today, although aged and yearning for regeneration, are credited to his initiative. The entire royal family, queens, princes, princesses and royal retainers of Lakabum have all lived and enjoyed this transfer of scientific knowledge that brought the most essential domestic vegetable oil assets closest to all and sundry.

257

His philanthropic acts abound as he sponsored not only his biological children but also children whose parents he might not have known. Angwafor's principle was; malice towards none, but charity for all. By any reckoning, Fon Angwafor III was a unique and magnificent man. His children and wives can well reflect on his love and care for them.

The Fon's entry into active politics in Southern/West Cameroon gave him the possibility to contribute to his desire of reunification just two years after he was enthroned. That Ahidjo and Biya found him as a capable ally is indisputable as he played significant roles in the Cameroon National Union (CNU) and in the Cameroon Peoples Democratic Movement (CPDM), until his demise in May 2022. President Ahidjo saw in him a very discreet and beneficent politician. The hero whose life overlapped two major Republican leaderships, was the last major participant of the Foumban Reunification conference. A conference whose outcome would later shape immensely his political choices and those of his people.

The wealth of political ideas he incarnated and his progressive desire to see Cameroon a prosperous, socially friendly and economically viable country made him not only to facilitate the birth of the CPDM in Bamenda in 1985 but to wholeheartedly embrace President Biya's New Deal Government vision which emphasised communal liberalism and its attendant governance tenets of rigour and moralisation. As the first Vice National President of the party, he sustained this ideal amidst the pressure of change and hostility that accompanied the multiparty system and doubts on the collective agenda of the CPDM party to save the country from the excruciating effects of the economic crisis that gently began in the mid-1980s and exacerbated by the early years of the 1990s.

However, his well-intentioned acts, Fon Angwafor III of Mankon became victim of the 1990s political violence when multi-party politics resurfaced. During that period, he suffered property damage in his facilities especially those at Fons Street Bamenda. As if that was not enough, he was regarded as a persona non-grata by his detractors. Moreover, in the context of the Anglophone crisis of 2016, Fon Angwafor was castigated and given all sort of tags for siding with the Biya regime on the one hand and for supporting separatist tendencies on the other hand. Even with such controversial branding, the bona fide traditional ruler maintained his serenity and tenaciously glued to his conviction that peace, national unity and territorial integrity was the right course to be pursued by all Cameroonians.

Contrary to his traditional peers who took umbrage behind threats and insecurity to seek for refuge out of their ancestral lands within the context of the socio-political crisis in the North west and South West Regions, Solomon the Great and Brave chose to stay amidst life's uncertainties. In the words of Prof. Victor Julius Ngoh, he stayed back preferring to be killed among/with his people, if so necessary. From the way he led his life, the wisdom he possessed and, the tribulations he faced, we find no better example than that of King Solomon of the Bible to liken him with. He was certainly born a king that is perhaps why he was subsequently called Solomon, a premonition somewhat for the moment he was going to wield the dregs of authority in Mankon.

Fon Angwafor III was also an astute diplomat especially in traditional diplomacy. He knew how to select his friends and render the relationships long-lasting even when they shared incongruent political views. One of his historic friends and colleagues as earlier mentioned was my grandfather, Fon John Yai Kwanga of Bum, enthroned in 1954. Fon Yai who was an adviser to the Kamerun National Congress(KNC) and later Cameroon People's National Convention(CPNC) party led by Dr. E.M.L. Endeley that militated for the end of British titular rule over the Southern Cameroons within the Nigerian framework. This position was interestingly at variance with Fon Angwafor's which was more in line with the Kamerun National Democratic Party(KNDP) stance animated by Dr. J.N. Foncha, that preferred independence by reunification with Cameroon. Even when the Fondom of Bum was relegated to a Second Class Fondom in 1966 by the KNDP Government and replaced by Mankon as a First Class Fondom, the Fon of Mankon still maintained good-natured social relations with the Fon of Bum. The encounter between the two potentates, rather than being strained by political differences ended up in a nuptial contract when Fon Yai made a royal betrothal of one of his daughters, Florence Fondoh, to Fon Angwafor III. This union established in the early 1970s became the social fabric that consolidated interminable ties between Bum and Mankon. Thanks to this connection, one of Cameroon's most prolific scholars, Professor Francis Beng Nyamnjoh had the opportunity to be educated by Fon Angwafor III and to occupy a privileged position as one of the adopted sons of the Mankon royal stead. This fraternal relationship was not only restricted to a few but extended to the entire Bum community in Bamenda. Bum is one of the groups that were provided settlement in the heart of Old Town (Abakwa, Ntambag) and which Fon Angwafor faithfully ensured that the people were accorded all the love and hospitality of the Mankon people. Whenever Fon Yai was in Bum Quarters at Old Town, Fon Angwafor usually sent palace emissaries with wine and food to keep him comfortable in the course of his sojourn.

It was in line with this memorable nexus, that I was happy to be one of the rare persons who led a powerful Bum delegation to visit the Fon on April 24, 2022, shortly before his transition to glory in May after being informed of his ailing health. The close to one-hour encounter with him was quite revealing and the pictures taken to share the last moments shall remain the best testimonies for posterity to mark the special social ties lacing Mankon and Bum maintained by Fon Angwafor III. Fate gave us the opportunity to savour the last words of wisdom from 'Solomon the Wise'. The Bum family, notably myself, Rev. Father Anthony, Regina Teh Yai, Bangsi, Goodwill Chia Kwanga, Celine Yai, Frederick Khena, Cyprian Bangsi, Pauline Yai and an invited friend Dr. Raphael Achou Etta who trouped around the Fon would never forget the episodic smiles that expressed to those who could discern meaning, a life well spent on earth.

When Fon Angwafor III of Mankon took his position in the royal sepulchre and, when his successor was to be enthroned, the twin celebration in his homestead was a motley of men, women, the young and the old, united in grief but in joy for a fulfilled life.

Here lies a monarch whose love for village and nation was unwavering and who in spite of all odds left inauspicious legacies for posterity to explore and exploit. I am quite sure that the Lions don't die. They only rest as their legacies live on. Adieu and eternal good rest, King Solomon!

Nixon Kahjum Takor, PhD
Faculty of Arts
Department of History and Archaeology
The University of Bamenda

The Benevolent Monarch, S. A. N. Angwafo III:
Reminiscences and the Unfinished Royal Business; What do the Mankon People Want?

1.1 Introduction

I saw Fon Angwafo as a child. I saw Fon Angwafo as a teenager. I saw Fon Angwafo as an adult and I saw Fon Angwafo as a university don. I became so used to the fact that I owned the Fon and we owned the Fon that I forgot he was a mortal. I was blind to the fact that he was gradually fading into the ancestral realm. My distance from home as an academic nomad and a member of the Mankon diaspora blinded me from the reality that the clock was ticking for the father of the Mankon people until I was taken unawares by his demise. This situation is terrible for me as a historian and the voice of the oracle because I cannot perform the way I am supposed to perform. I have been truly caught off guard in the diaspora by these developments. I am therefore confronted with this challenge of struggling to tell the Mankon people, my children and grandchildren and posterity who Fon Angwafo III was and what he meant for the Mankon people, what he meant to me and what he meant for posterity. As Kwifor has already announced so colourfully and so poetically, the *Nukwi nifo* Festival is at the corner. It is our 'thing'. It is a once-in-the-lifetime event of a Fo. But what happens after the great festival of the Nukwi nifo? What should the agenda for the new order look like? What I try to capture in this eulogy for Angwafo III in the form of royal policy is not new at all. I am simply struggling as a historian to tell my story while establishing continuity with the past informed by my long interaction with the Mankon royalty. My writing is more of a personal account and from my multiple interactions with the Fon. This will enable me to state some of the unfinished royal agenda that has to be attended to which includes (the name of streets in urban Mankon, the positioning of Mankon elite in the national political landscape in which they are largely absent, and the case for German reparations for the Mankon people who suffered severely in the hands of the Germans during the colonial period.

Let me, at least, afford a preliminary synopsis of the Kingdom of Mankon. I would not allude to the Fon's curriculum vitae, or the well-deserved encomiums poured on him by others. I will do something different by highlighting the unfinished agenda of the business of the Mankon Fondom.

1.2 The Mankon Fondom (kingdom), its Fons

Mankon (historically spelled Mankong) is a geo-historic polity constituting a large part of Bamenda in the North-West Region of Cameroon. The Mankon fondom is bounded in the North by Bafut, East by Bamendankwe and Nkwen, West by Ngyembu, Meta and Bali and South by Mbatu and Nsongwa fondoms. Mankon is situated about 1000 metres above sea level with an estimated surface area of 315 square kilometres and a population of about 400.000 inhabitants. It is strategically located at the crossroads of the Bamenda Grassland which comprises the North West region and every Grasslander (*graffi people*) must traverse Mankon before heading to their final destination. Mankon shines as a prominent first-class Fondom (Kingdom) in North West Region of Cameroon owing to the political weight of Fon Angwafo III who doubled as Monarch and the first Vice President of the ruling Cameroon People Democratic Party (CPDM) and because it is the heart of Mankon City Council. Mankon is the most cosmopolitan city in the North West region and has attracted scholarly exploration by several high-profile Royals, Statesmen and scholars including, but not limited to, Fo Angwafo, Musongong, Luke Ntse, Che, Christopher Chi, Nyamnjoh, Francis B, Nyamnjoh, Henrietta, Awasom, Nicodemus Fru, Warnier, Jean-Pierre , Thaddeus Anye Achu, etc (*see references*).

May it be emphasized that the Mankon Fondom represents one of the oldest monarchies in the Grassfields of the North West Region that established itself under Fo Ndemagha I and all Mankon Fons emanate from this dynastic line. It was not easy for the Mankon people to occupy such a strategic geographical area because it is at the crossroads of the Grassland and was perennially exposed to marauding invaders struggling to displace them from their fertile land. For the Mankon people to have settled and maintained their current site for more since circa 11th century shows that they were inveterate warriors. They had to defeat numerous incoming warrior groups that unsuccessfully struggled to displace them.

The Mankon society is essentially patrilineal and the crowned Fon is usually a designated son of the deceased king who must have been "born on leopard skin", meaning that he must have been born after the Fon ascended the throne. J-P Warnier (1993) points out that "the symbolism of kingship is multifaceted and redundant. The king is not only seen as a container. He is also a leopard, a successor descended from a prince originating in a prestigious and distant country, the son of a native farmer, a wife-giver and a wife-taker for all, a metaphorical father, and a 'good devil'. Fon Angwafo III is a descendant of the royal dynasty that can be traced to the founder of the kingdom, Ndemagha I, a courageous fighter and the bravest of the brave. The list below displays the well-known Mankon royal genealogy.

(i) Ndemagha I (Founder of the Mankon Kingdom)
2) Ndemagha II

3) Ndemagha III
4) Takomatsi I
5) Ndemagha IV
6) Takomatsi II
7) Ndemagha V
8) Tangwanu
9) Ndemagha VI(Mbangnizhi)
10) Tseymagha I
11) Ndemagha VII
12) Tseymagha II
13) Ndefru I
14) Ndemagha VIII
15) Ndefru II
16) Angwafo I
17) Fomukong (1799-1866)
18) Angwafo II (1866-1919)
19) Ndefru III (1919-1959)
20) Angwafo III (1959-2022).

1.2 Growing Up and Associating with the Palace

I am a historian, by inclination and training, and I was properly acknowledged on page 70 of the King's widely read biography titled: Angwafo, Fo. *Royalty and politics: The story of my life*. African Books Collective, 2009. I was acknowledged among others owing to my periodic interaction with the Fon over the years and the quality of the depth of discussions of historical matters we had. The Fon showed a lot of enthusiasm in such discussions and always demonstrated his encyclopaedic knowledge of our history.

My encounters with Fon Angwafo III were initially on a family basis or in the context of the Mankon Student's Association (MASA). My mother, Mrs. Awasom nee Regina Ngum Ndefru grew up in the Mankon palace under the parentage of Mafor Theresa Mankah Ndefru who was responsible for my mother's education up to standard VI. My mother's father, that is, my maternal grandfather, was the junior brother of the Queen Mother of Mankon, Mafor Theresa Manka Ndefru, who treated my mother as her first daughter. My mother's bride price was paid directly to Fon Angwafo III. I was told I should go and meet the Fon to show me 'my piece of land' in Mankon and my thinking is that Mafor Mankah was the brainchild of the idea. My father and mothers insisted that my fourth daughter who is 26 years today should be given the name Mankah Mafor and

I did so graciously and with alacrity. Because of this maternal connection, my intimacy with the royal family was perennial and tight. Let me quickly add that the Fon was the Father of all Mankon people, and he was a good listener to all. I am therefore not trying to suggest in any way that I was favoured or I was his favourite. I am simply telling my own story with royalty.

When I was in Primary 4 in 1967, I was sent to spend the 'third term holidays' with Queen Mother, Mafor Mankah Ndefru. Although she was the mother of the Fon, her house was quite modest. I slept in her room on a bamboo bed, and I ate our traditional stable food, which is achu, fresh groundnuts and maize. She arranged for me to meet the Fon on the third day of my stay with her, and that was my first time setting eyes on him. Gifts from the Fon included a bag which contained exercise books and readers.

I periodically visited the Fon again when I was a teenager in the context of the annual Mankon Students Association meetings that traditionally took place during the Third Term Holidays. The Fon's address to students was always followed by the much-awaited entertainment. In his address to us, the Fon often emphasized the aspect of our culture and tradition and warned that we will be totally derailed if we failed to master the Mankon language which was the vehicle of our indigenous philosophy and knowledge systems. The Fon underscored what the erudite Professor Francis Nyamnjoh describes as "Modernising Traditions and Traditionalising Modernity in Africa." Fon Angwafo III was essentially a pragmatic progressive who endeavoured to combine the two spheres of tradition and modernity.

My relationship with the Fon changed when I graduated from the University of Yaoundé as a professional historian who had done a lot of archival work and was able to reveal many things about our past as a true modern oracle. Historians are good storytellers, but they insist that history must be the true account of the past. History must be evidence-based. Most of what I report was obtained directly from the Fon in Yaoundé at the Ntoh Fo (the King's palace) located within the precincts of the National Assembly or in other parts of Cameroon when he was on tour to see and encourage his people. Fon Angwafo III had a house permanently reserved for him by his bosom friend, S.T. Muna, President of the National Assembly of Cameroon from 1973 to 1988, within the precincts of the National Assembly. Each time parliament was in session, I seized the opportunity to visit the Fon and I had long chats with him, something he loved very much. I did not conduct a formal structured interview with the Fon because that would have broken the flow of our conversation. I had the capacity to absorb and engage the Fon because of my detailed knowledge about Mankon and his father's very poor relationship with the British colonial administration for no fault of his.

1.3 The Colonial Context of Street Naming in Mankon by the Immigrant Hausa Muslims, the Beginning of the Mankon Identity Crisis and the British hatred of Fon Ndefru III

Urban Mankon developed into a commercial hub under the immigrant Hausa traders who settled in the area after they were expelled from the Bamenda Station by the German colonial administration because of racial residential segregation. The Germans could not stand the noise of the Hausa imam calling the faithful to prayer and the noise turned them off. The Hausa were expelled from the Bamenda Station and Fon Ndefru III gave them land to settle in Urban Mankon. The Hausa strangers proceeded to name their settlement Abakwa and placed it under a Hausa Chief called the Sarikin Hausawa. All incoming strangers who settled in urban Mankon to do business also started calling the settlement Abakwa and they popularized this alien name. Names are very important, and the place of names reflects a people's identity and ownership of a place. If, as Mankon people, we allow urban Mankon to be called by a Hausa name, we are definitely in an identity crisis.

There is no doubt about the fact that the name of a place tells us the identity and landlord of the place. After the exit of the Germans from Cameroon following their defeat in World War I, the British came to believe that Abakpa Bamenda belonged to the Sarikin Hausawa and was a separate entity from Ndefru III's Mankon because urban Mankon was called Abakwa. The British colonial administration therefore established a direct relationship with the Sarikin Hausawa and dealt directly with him in administration and taxation matters. This practice was illegal and illegitimate because the landlord of Abakwa-Mankon was Fon Ndefru III and not the Sarikin Hausawa who was a stranger. The British excluded Ndefru III from the urban governance of Mankon because of a wrong name imposed on the urban centre by the Hausa immigrants and incoming settlers. The problem between Fon Ndefru III and the British arose from confusion over the nomenclature of urban Mankon. The British

265

erroneously believed Abakwa belonged to the Hausa people when it was the sphere of the Mankon people.

I told the Fon that his father was a victim of the wrong name that was given to urban Mankon by the Hausa and other settlers. The White man came to believe that Abakwa belonged to the Hausa strangers and not the indigenous Mankon people. The British administration saw two Mankons, the rural part of Mankon belonging to Ndefru III and Abakwa belonging to the Sarakin Hausawa. This confusion emanated clearly from wrong naming because we allowed strangers to name our town for us. I presented a hand-designed map with street names by Ndeh Ntumazah, a prominent Mankon elite, who was very concerned about the matter because of the shabby treatment given to Fo Ndefru III by the British colonial administration. My father, Stephen Anye Awasom, who was a member of the Mankon Urban Council in 1954 under the reforms of the Local Government in British Africa, told me about the politics of street naming in Mankon and advised that I was better placed to discuss it with the Fon since I had archival knowledge of the matter, and it concerned the Fon's father and Mankon. I did just that like a storyteller with the aim of pulling the Fon deeply into the matter.

History tells us that Fon Ndefru III consistently rejected the name of urban Mankon given by the Hausa as Abakwa Town from the commencement of British colonial administration. This wrong name resulted in the Sarikin Hausa, being recognized as the Native Authority of Urban Mankon. The British colonial administration officially gazetted the Sarikin Hausawa as the Native Authority of Abakwa Town. In other words, the colonial authorities named the Sarikin Hausa Chief of Abakwa which is Urban Mankon.

"What is in a name?", people often ask this question. There is the politics of ownership in a name. The Sarakin Hausawa was gazetted the Native Authority of Abakwa Town in the place of Ndefru III, the legitimate landlord of Mankon, because urban Mankon was wrongly named Abakwa by the Hausa settlers. The gazetting of the Sarikin Hausa as the Native Authority of Abakwa had financial implications. He received 10% rebate for all the taxes collected from Urban Mankon and pocketed the money. Fon Ndefru III did not receive a mite. He was totally marginalized because he was not seen by the British as the legitimate landlord of urban Mankon. The naming of the streets of urban Mankon is a political act that generates political and economic dividends and the Mankon elite must understand this fact from our history.

Ndefru III was infuriated by this marginalization in the land of his ancestors and by the continuous loss of revenue. He wrote a succession of petitions to the colonial administration praying them to correct the error by recognizing him as the legitimate landlord of Mankon. He stated categorically that the Sarikin Hausa was his tenant and not his suzerain. The British argued that the Sarikin Hausa was resident in cosmopolitan Abakwa and was an efficient tax collector. They saw no need to replace him with Fon Ndefru III who was about 10 miles away from urban Mankon. The British threatened several times to destitute Ndefru III if he attempted to disrupt the administration of Abakwa town. The Hausa settlers Ndefru III magnanimously gave land to them to settle had now become autonomous of the Fon and were no longer paying homage to him because of the British. This thorny issue of Ndefru III-Sarakin Hausa conflict was resolved in 1954 under the new Local Government reforms that were introduced The Mankon Urban Council was established with Fon. Ndefru III as its chairman and this enabled him to regain his authority after over 30 years of exclusion from the management of the urban sector of his fief.

After the demise of Fon Ndefru III in 1959, signposts were erected all over the urban Mankon with Mankon indigenous street names. These signposts were periodically vandalized by 'strangers' and some relaxation with the issue of street names set in. I had several discussions with the Bamenda Urban Council Delegate, Abel Ndeh Tadzong, and he promised to give me the relevant files to make an authoritative write-up for the exercise to resume in earnest. In the meantime, he struggled to rename streets in urban Mankon, and this attracted a torrent of criticisms from Boh Herbert and other CRTV journalists, and this helped to polarize public opinion on the matter.

1.4 The Naming of the Streets of Urban Mankon as an Unfinished Agenda

The issue of the naming of streets in Mankon is still topical and is an unfinished business although it has been submerged by the ongoing political unrest. In 1983, I raised the issue of the naming of streets in urban Mankon that touched the Fon very much and his countenance changed. What are the implications of this incomplete naming of streets in urban Mankon? Mankon has not won in the politics of street naming in urban Mankon. The obvious implication is that the Mankon elite are not even known as the landlords of urban Mankon which is the heart of politics in the North West region. The

Mankon elite have been permanently submerged and eclipsed in the political realm in favour of others who pass for Mankonians under the name 'Bamenda'. Our identity as Mankonians has been diluted because **we are nameless**. The issue of street naming in urban Mankon is critical for the recognition of the real geographical stretch of Mankon and its indigenous people. The recognition of the Mankon elite and their positioning in national politics is a task that must be achieved, and we must be bold to name streets in the lands we inherited from our ancestors, and nobody should dare stop us from achieving such a goal. This is a game of identity politics. NO retreat, NO surrender. This must be an important agenda for consideration in the post- Nukwi nifo festival which is in the offing.

1.5 How Fon Angwafo III averted the impending use of Napalm on Mankon to eliminate alleged UPC Guerrillas Hiding in forests and bushes in Mankon

The Mankon elite have arguably criticized the Fon for not doing enough to project them politically beyond his nuclear family although this is the collective endeavour of the Mankon elite and not just the Fon. Fon Angwafo did more than just positioning people in the political realm. When Dr J.N. Foncha died on 10 April 1999, the Fon told me that politics becomes very dirty and dangerous when you are blackmailed, and you do not have the opportunity to defend yourself. You must be very lucky if you can tell your own side of the story to those in high office. The Fon was lucky to have had the opportunity to tell President Ahmadou Ahidjo his own side of the story after he was thoroughly blackmailed by J.N. Foncha concerning the UPC militants in Mankon, some of whom had settled in Old Town Mankon since the colonial period owing to French colonial misrule.

Now, why had Foncha to do such a terrible thing against the Fon and the Mankon people? First, the Fon was a convincing political figure and rising star who could potentially challenge Foncha's prominence. Second, Foncha nursed a personal grievance against the Fon. Foncha had solicited the Fon's membership of the KNDP party in the aftermath of reunification and independence, but the Fon turned it down because he preferred then to be neutral in party politics. He was the Fon of Mankon people of different political persuasions in West Cameroon including Nde Ntumazah's One Kamerun, (OK) party, a close associate of the radical UPC party in East Cameroon. As the Fon put, "I am the Fon of all Mankon people, and I did not want to divide my people". Foncha was unhappy that the Fon refused to join his party and started looking for means to destroy him and the Mankon people.

Foncha attempted to blackmail Angwafo III to Ahidjo by alleging that the Mankon people were overwhelmingly pro-UPC and supporters of Nde Ntumazah's OK. Foncha warned Ahidjo against the Fon of Mankon and the Mankon people on the allegation that the Mankon people were pro-UPC and were harbouring the UPC guerrilla fighters in forests and bushes. These guerrillas were engaged in cross-border raids into East Cameroon. Credence was given to this allegation because there were many Bamileke refugees in Mankon town and some were engaged in anti-Ahidjo politics.

Few know about the Fon's selfless efforts in rescuing the Mankon people from extermination by the totalitarian Ahmadou Ahidjo regime in the 1961/1962 turbulent years of Cameroon history fanned by the UPC nationalists. Nde Ntumazah, a Mankon citizen almost caused Ahidjo to rain brimstone and fire on Mankon from the air because of his association and collaboration with the UPC. Ntumazah's One Kamerun political party, was an affiliate of the Union des Populations du Cameroun (UPC) political party, engaged in a guerrilla war aimed at overthrowing the Ahidjo regime. Ahidjo was such a brutal dictator that his opponents were served with death. Ahidjo contacted the French military to evaluate the security situation in Mankon and they contemplated using napalm on the bushes and forests in Mankon. Napalm is an incendiary device used in firebombing campaigns. Napalm burns at temperatures ranging from 800 to 1,200 °C. It was allegedly widely deployed from the air against the Bamileke insurgents during the colonial war of independence. Ahidjo carried out his investigation about the allegations Foncha made against the Fon and realized that Mankon was not harbouring UPC insurgents and there were no guerrilla fighters in Mankon. The Fon still met Ahidjo to give him all the assurances that his people were not subversives. The Fon's diplomacy saved Mankon from Ahidjo's vengeance. The Fon deserves credit for this benevolent statesmanship.

1.6 The Mankon Kingdom and the Quest for German Reparation and Germans Arts Restitution

I want us to speak to our past and our relationship with Germany which Fon Angwafo III struggled to make meaning of. There is a lot that must be said about Germano-Mankon relations that needs to be highlighted as a platform for policy formulation. The Fons of

Mankon since the time of Angwafo II have shared a hate-love relationship with the Germans. We could build on that relationship for the benefit of Mankon now and in the future.

Mankon's first encounter with Europeans was with the Germans at the tail end of the 19th century. That encounter was not a happy one because we paid in blood and tears and untold destruction and arson. Mankon Kwifor today can legitimately sue for reparations from the Germans for the unprovoked aggression against the peace-loving Mankon people. By asking for reparations from the German government, we are not setting any precedent at all. Chancellor Angela Merkel's government agreed to pay Namibia €1.1bn (£940m) over historical genocide in the Agency Report of 28 May 2021. It was the first time that Germany recognised it had committed genocide in Namibia during its colonial occupation in a gesture of reconciliation. Germany should also recognize that it conducted genocide in Mankon in the 19th century. We fought the German invaders in the last decades of the 19th century and early 20th century for our survival and we paid very heavy casualties.

What caused the war between the Germans and the Mankon people which came to be known in history as the Mankon wars? The peace-loving Mankon people had no desire to attack the Germans, but they were provoked into doing so. In 1889 Eugen Zintgraff, a German explorer, penetrated the highlands of Bali in the Bamenda Grasslands where he established the Baliburg station. Zintgraff signed a treaty of friendship with Fon Galega I, paramount ruler of Bali, and raised him to the rank of paramount Chief of the Bamenda Grasslands to the consternation of the neighbouring Kingdoms which were not friendly with the Balis. The German-Bali alliance meant that Fon Galega of Bali had to ensure the regular flow of labour from the hinterlands to the German coastal plantations, a task that was to meet with opposition from the other peoples of the Bamenda Grasslands. Mankon was targeted for labour supply and the provision of food for the German entourage. The Mankon *laleh*, the official spy of the Mankon state, briefed Fon Angwafo II of all the machinations of the Germans and their Bali allies and he immediately started preparing for war.

Eugen Zintgraff first approached the Fon of Mankon through two envoys ostensibly with the intention of opening trade with Mankon, but *laleh* opined that the Germans were slave raiders and had to be resisted. *Laleh* was not far from the truth because the real intention of the Germans was to enlist Mankon as a labour supplier to the German coastal plantations. Fon Angwafo II did not trust the Germans and had Zintgraff's emissaries murdered. The Germans were furious and imposed reparations of 10 ivories and two oxen and the Mankon people refused. Zintgraff decided to attack Mankon on 30 January 1891 in the first Battle of Mankon.

German colonial forces, allied with the Bali people, were led by Eugen Zintgraff and severely outnumbered the Mankon. But *Laleh* did a beautiful job by revealing to the Mankon warriors the positions of the Bali-German troops. Under the leadership of King Angwafo II, the spear- and machete-toting Mankon warriors inflicted a heavy blow on the Bali-German forces armed with guns and cannons. Four Germans military officers namely Lt. von Spangenberg, Huwe, Thiede and Nebber lost their lives while over 180 Balitruppe (Bali soldiers) died in battle The brave Mankon people lost 1,500 warriors (E.M. Chilver, 1966:27) who died struggling to save their people from modern slavery.

The crushing and humiliating defeat of the Germans by Mankonians and their Bafut ally in early 1891 compelled Zintgraff to give up the colonial service and return to Europe. He was just overwhelmed by the witticism of the traditional Mankon military that had so successfully stood up against a well-trained and equipped modern military force.

Laleh warned the Mankon royalty not to sleep on their laurels because the Germans would soon be coming for them in a revenge attack. In a bid to appease the Germans, Fon Angwafo II sent a peaceful delegation to the Germans and compensation in ivory and labour on 9 December 1891. But *Laleh* revealed that the Germans were preparing to attack Mankon again. Without any waste of time, Mankon made a surprised attack on the German patrol under Pavels in the night of 10th December 1891. The Germans answered with full force killing 200 Mankon warriors but they did not surrender and simply changed tactics by buying for time and re-arming.

The third Mankon War against the Germans took place in 1901. The Germans were better prepared and took on Mankon full scale with their sophisticated weapons. This war left in its wake unprecedented genocide as Germany almost depleted Mankon of its entire population and set almost all houses on fire. Mankon capitulated after a protracted but painful resistance. What a brave people the Mankon people were! In recognition of the extraordinary bravery of the Mankon people, the Germans offered the Fon of

Mankon a traditional German military wear which Mankon Fons proudly put on during the Fon's annual dance.

Whatever the excesses of the Germans for which we are holding them accountable today, they recognized merit and the military ingenuity of the Mankon people. I hope a special monument would be built to commemorate the Mankon fighters of the 19th century against imperialism. We need another monument to celebrate the professionalism of the *Laleh* royal spies in communicating vital information that we exploited to teach the German lessons in military warfare in Africa.

Picture of Fo Mankong in German military regalia

Kwifor can make a case for German reparations because apart of the casualties of the colonial war which we suffered in the hands of the Germans; they also looted our precious Art objects. Our looted rare arts objects are pregnant with meaning for they are bearers of the memory of our past. German is currently very involved in the restitution of stolen African arts during the colonial period and Mankon stands to benefit from this apologetic gesture. Kwifor will hopefully pursue this restitution matter with the German government in this current favourable climate marked by Germany's willingness to return to Africa priceless artefacts that were stolen during the colonial era. Colonialists looted thousands of artworks from the continent. Following auctions, some of the African art ended up in museums and private collections across Europe. Many African Kingdoms are currently benefiting from this German gesture of the restitution of African stolen works of art. Why not Mankon?

The Mankon Royal Museum has enough space to accommodate our stolen works of art. Mankon Palace also hosts a unique and venerated age-old traditional architecture, ATSUM, a large sacred palace temple that is a curiosity for scholars and the young generation of Mankon people. Restituted Mankon art would further internationalise tourism in Mankon.

1.7 Conclusion

Fon Angwafo III was unequivocally a great, benevolent King who had his Mankon people at heart and would go to any length to shield them from political extermination. My training as a historian and my wealth of knowledge in detailed issues about history, especially the history of the Mankon royalty and its marginalization of the British colonial administration made me an indispensable client of the Fon, who was also an encyclopaedia of knowledge. There is no doubt about the fact that the Mankon elite have not benefited from their landlord position of the gigantic Fondom of Mankon. The identity of Mankon was first eclipsed and diluted by the Hausa immigrants who occupied urban Mankon and named it Abakwa. The beneficiary of Abakwa was not the Fon of Mankon but a pure stranger-the Hausa Muslims. The British refused to rectify this situation on grounds that the Sarikin Hausa was an efficient administrator of urban Mankon. The Mankon elite have not asserted their identity as the proud owners of Mankon; they have not put a Mankon stamp on all parts of urban and even rural Mankon. The naming of streets is a crucial exercise that is a task that must be done if the Mankon people have to be recognized. Because of our very central position, we paid the price of colonial wars against the Germans. Mankon initially resisted and defeated the Germano-Bali alliance in two great wars but they lost in the third and last war in 1901.

The Germano-Mankon war resulted in pure genocide as almost the entire Kingdom was wiped out from the face of the earth. The issue of reparations for the Mankon people is urgent. Furthermore, the question of the restitution of art objects by German must be given fresh thinking. Germany must be held accountable today the same way they have conceded to some of their erstwhile dependencies and called for accountability for the crimes Germany committed against humanity.

References

Angwafo, Fo. *Royalty and politics: The story of my life*. Bamenda: Langaa, 2009.

Anye, Thaddeus, A Social and Economic History of the Fondom of Mankon, 1990.

Awasom, Nicodemus Fru. "Hausa Traders, Residential Segregation and the Quest for Security in 20th Century Colonial." *Security, crime and segregation in West African cities since the 19th century* (2003): 287.

Awasom, Nicodemus Fru, "The vicissitudes of twentieth-century Mankon fons in Cameroon's changing social order." In: *The Dynamics of Power and the Rule of Law: Essays on Africa and Beyond, in Honour of Emile Adriaan B van Rouveroyvan Nieuwaal* (Leiden: African Studies Centre, 2003): 101-120.

Che, Christopher Chi. *Kingdom of Mankon: Aspects of History, Language, Culture, Flora and Fauna*. Bamenda: Langaa, 2010.

Che, C. C. "A concise and analytical history of Mankon kingdom: About 1197-2012." *Bamenda: Agwecams Printer* (2013).

Chilver, Elizabeth Millicent, and Phyllis Mary Kaberry. *Traditional Bamenda: The pre-colonial history and ethnography of the Bamenda Grassfields*. Vol. 1. Ministry of Primary Education and Social Welfare, 1967.

Chilver, E. M., & Kaberry, P. M. (1970). Chronology of the Bamenda Grassfields. *The Journal of African History*, *11*(2), 249-257.

Chilver, Elizabeth M. *Zintgraff's Explorations in Bamenda, Adamawa and the Benue Lands 1889ó1892*. Bamenda: Langaa, 2010.

Musongong, Luke Ntse, Royal Enthronement in the Ngemba Fondoms from Precolonial times to 1989, ENS, YAOUNDE, 1996

Musongong, Luke Ntse , *The Rise and Fall of Mankon Confederacy, Bamenda-Cameroon, C.1800-1827*. Lambert Academic Publishing, 2017.

Musongong, Luke Ntse, *Evolution and Challenge of Governance of the Mankon Kingdom*, Lambert, 2017.

Ndenge, Alphonsus Fongang. "The Kingdom of Mankon (Ala'Mankon)." *Mankon. Arts, Heritage and Culture from the Mankon-Kingdom (Western Cameroon)* (2005): 27-40.

Notué, Jean Paul, and Bianca Triaca. "The treasure of the Mankon Kingdom." *Cultural Objects from the Royal Palace. Le trésor du royaume de Mankon. Les objets culturels du palais royal. Mbalmayo: Institut de formation artistique* (2000).

Notué, Jean-Paul, and Bianca Triaca. *Mankon: Arts, Heritages and Culture from the Mankon Kingdom.* 5Continents, 2005.

Njinuwo, E. (2015). Communicating the Meanings of Objects in Community Museums in Anglophone Cameroon-Case Study: Mankon Community Museum.

Nyamnjoh, Francis B. *Modernising Traditions and Traditionalising Modernity in Africa: chieftaincy and democracy in Cameroon and Botswana.* Langaa RPCIG, 2015.

Nyamnjoh, Francis B. "'Our Traditions Are Modern, Our Modernities Traditional': Chieftaincy and Democracy in Contemporary Cameroon and Botswana." *Modern Africa: Politics, History and Society* 2.2 (2014): 13-62.

Nyamnjoh, Henrietta, and Michael Rowlands. "Do you eat Achu here? Nurturing as a way of life in a Cameroon diaspora." *Critical African Studies* 5.3 (2013): 140-152.

Pemunta, Ngambouk Vitalis, and Ngwa Donald Anye. "Modern State Law: Regulating Tradition or Protecting the Environment in the Mankon Kingdom of Northwest Cameroon?." *Endemic Species.* IntechOpen, 2019.

Swiri, R. A. (1998). *Lexical expansion in the Mankon Language* (Doctoral dissertation, Universite de Yaoundé Yaoundé).

Warnier, Jean-Pierre. *The pot-king: The body and technologies of power.* Brill, 2007.

Warnier, J-P. "Chapter Three. The skin-citizens." *The Pot-King.* Brill, 2007. 63-81.

Warnier, Jean-Pierre. "Territorialization and the politics of autochthony." *Cultures and Globalization: Heritage, Memory and Identity* 4 (2011): 95.

Emeritus Professor Nicodemus Fru Awasom
University of Ghana, Legon-Accra

To His Royal Highness, S.A.N. Angwafo III, the Fon of Mankon

We are deeply saddened to hear that His Royal Highness, S.A.N. Angwafo III, The Fon of Mankon, this royal personage, this first-class Fon, this farmer, this versatile personage, this distinguished Cameroonian, this politician, this custodian of Mankon tradition, has passed away.

My thoughts and deep condolences are with the Royal Family: His Highness, John Fru Angwafo, who will be enthroned with an official Royal name, the Queen Mothers, the Princes, and Princesses.

His Royal Highness, S.A.N: Angwafo III, was born in May 1925, in the Mankon palace where he grew up, dwelt in, and was nurtured in the full glare of the limelight of Royal history and practice. Though then only a youthful thirty-and-four years of age, he was already well-groomed in the tradition of strength and courage to bear the burdens or the kingly crosses and tap the pleasures of governance.

Sixty-three years ago, S.A.N. Angwafo III, for the first time, sat on the royal ceremonial chair. This royal personage served as the Fon of Mankon, one of the ancient kingdoms in the Grassfields of Southern Cameroons known for its long tradition of culture, since his enthronement in 1959 and held this role until he got missing on Saturday 21.05.2022.

For his political aspiration, he believed that the new vision and views that will carry Cameroon into the 21st century must be pragmatically grounded in educating the masses to achieve critical democracy. Consequently, in July 1960, he won election into the then Southern Cameroon's House of Chiefs, having fulfilled the conditions laid down for such elections by the commissioner of Southern Cameroons J.O. Field; and the first session, presided over by J.O. Field himself, met in September 1960, with twenty-one members present.

Gradually and positively, by December 1961, he had won election into the West Cameroon House of Assembly as the first independent candidate and ex-member of the Southern Cameroon's House of Chiefs. Indeed, since the inception of the Cameroon National Union party in 1966, he was elected president of C.N.U. Ngemba subsection 1985-1988.

At various times, between 1972–1988, he was elected to the National Assembly, and he played important roles on two committees: the Constitutional Laws Committee and the Foreign

Affairs Committee. Regardless of political challenges, his passion for unity and service through politics, had propelled him to the first vice national chairman of the C.P.D.M. party, since 1990 till date.

His Royal Highness Angwafo III also had ramifications in the Native Authority and Council Administration. For at different times, between 1961 and 1996, he was Chairman, Ngemba Council, Chairman, Mankon Urban Town Council, Chairman, Mankon Rural Council, and the Chairman, Bamenda Urban Council. In these roles, his mesmerizing ideas, his quick thought, and his impeccably thought-out contributions to development bore the sharp indices of the mind of a healthy administrator.

By the end of his chairmanship, the following urban projects were realized: construction of the Mankon Municipal Stadium, 1961–1962; construction of the Mankon Main Market, 1962–1965; and the construction of the Mankon Urban Town Council administrative building, 1964–1968.

"Health for all by the year 2000 A.D." was a recent world-wide axiom. S.A.N. Angwafo III, like his father, had begun to tread that path for helpless humanity over five decades ago when he donated land generously for the establishment of hospitals and health centres.

Still around health, he influenced the rehabilitation of the Scandinavian pipe-borne Water which spasmodically passed into limbo; however, its demise was sudden.

Another remarkable goal of His Royal Highness, since 1960, was promoting education for Mankon and the State. To this end, he consolidated many existing schools, and donated land for the establishment of new schools.

S.A.N. Angwafo III was a friend of the Church, or Christian Religious Organisations, and the Muslims since 1959. Besides promoting education, he provided land generously for the building of Churches; above all, he cooperated with the Christian Missions in the spread of Christianity in Mankonland; hence, Mankon is the seat of many Christian missions.

Two Roman Catholic Church Pontiffs were very pleased indeed, to hear that Angwafo III, like Ndefru III, was friendly and generous enough to the Catholic Church. So, he was awarded two Papal medals of congratulations: the first, by late Pope Blessed John XXIII; and the second, by late Pope John Paul II.

With the expanding population, he reorganized Mankonland into seventy-six administrative councils or villages and, with the full support of "butabatse" or clan heads, initially appointed councillors to administer them. Today the seven-man councils are constituted by open, free and fair elections by the Mankon subjects themselves.

Territorially, he has, over the past decades, maintained good relationships with the nine Fondoms that have boundaries with Mankonland. In view of his leadership qualities, inter-fondom disputes were always amicably resolved.

In the first quinquennium of the Fon's accession to the throne, he began teaching the new methods of agriculture practically. He then set three model farms. The first, which was located at Azomamukan, the present site of the Bamenda airport, was divided into paddocks and farming plots. On the livestock farms, cattle, sheep and poultry were raised; on the farming plots, maize and plantains were produced: and the orchard produced guava and pawpaw.

Another flourishing farm was established at Asongkah. The farm, like that of Azomamukan, was divided into three plots, viz, the orchard, poultry, and a palm oil plantation.

His Royal Highness influence was further manifested in the structure of the knoll farm, adjacent the palace, where animals were raised since 1980. The raising of sheep and poultry was part of the scenic splendours of the knoll and breath-taking settings of the farm and its palace-connecting lane; indeed, an environment where soul and spirit develop in peace and contemplative serenity.

His Royal Highness, therefore, has been inundated with farming honours: On March 13. 1969 he was awarded the Officer of Cameroon Agricultural Order of Merit by the then Head of State, His Excellency, Ahmadou Ahidjo; On April 20. 2000, he was again awarded the Commander of Agricultural Order of Merit by the Head of State, His Excellency, Paul Biya, for valuable contributions to agricultural development in Cameroon.

Leadership demands the power of vision, your Highnesses, who influence the society, to pay the price for the future. Whatever be the community, someone must decide; there must be a kind, thoughtful, tolerant, but firm authority to govern and to guide; else there is chaos.

Thaddeus A. Achu PhD, UNICAL

Knowledge, books, education… What for?

"I believe in education" wrote Fo Mankon (*Royalty*: 63)[1]. No doubt. Considering his uncompromising will to attend school in his

---

[1] Henceforth I will refer to *Royalty and Politics. The Story of my Life*, by Fo Angwafo III S.A.N. of Mankon, Langaa RPCIG, 2009 as "*Royalty*".

childhood and youth, his eleven days trek to Nigeria to access secondary education, his will to acquire a university degree in agriculture at Ibadan, his respect for scholars, the number of learning institutions he opened up in Mankon, his will to have his children go as high as they could, his interest in books and publications, there is little doubt about it.

Education… What for? Who am I, as a scholar, to raise such an almost derogatory question? How comes I dare sit here at my desk, pondering over fifty years of writing and publishing books and articles with the encouragement of the Fon and yet doubt the usefulness of it all? Who has initiated the process and for what reasons? Why has the Fon seated me on a chair as a researcher, with *ndor* around my neck and a name to honour? What has happened in the course of so many encounters that I, a White academic, have been turned into something else, very different, a kind of hybrid, never to return to my original European-ness? Knowledge, research, books, education, what for?

In his biography *Royalty and Politics*, the Fon gives many clues. Knowledge is an alternative to violence and armed fighting. It helps understand and discuss with other people. It is a key to any meaningful achievement. It is a means to acquire professional qualifications. It helps in going beyond the narrow circle of the local community and have access to the world at large. Yes indeed. Who can object to that?

Yet Angwafo is cautious. Education is worth nothing unless one has the will and does not sit idly waiting for Father Christmas to bring money and employment just because one has a degree: "I believe in education. I believe in fighting for opportunities. (…) Education must not become an end in itself. We must always ask ourselves what a degree enables us to realize. The value of the degree will tell the job he has done with it, but he needs to be able to go ahead, seek or create the job. A degree must be actively productive to be relevant. In itself, the degree is nothing. Only by producing something does the degree become a meaningful achievement" (*Royalty*: 63).

Thus, knowledge and education are far from being self-evident for the Fon. They are only part of his truth. There is something else: the drive to be actively productive. Without it, knowledge and education are worth nothing. If that something had not been there right from the start, *Sangto'* would not be sitting at his desk, pondering over fifty years in the shadow of the Mankon palace. Let us go back to those seminal years, between 1959 – Angwafo's succession to the throne of Mankon – and 1962, his accession to national politics. For the young successor to Ndefru, it is a time of intense questioning, discussing, shifting of orientation and purpose, a time of curiosity as well – a will, a drive to understand and do something relevant to what Angwafo understood of the situation. Understand what exactly? I should think, just everything, starting with agricultural science and going all the way to what has happened in history that has led to the colonial encounter, its arbitrariness, yet its deep inscription in the African and the European past. During those years, there does not seem to be any limit to Angwafo's curiosity and drive to learn and understand. "Until you die, you never stop being educated" he wrote in 2009 (*Royalty*: 64). Indeed, but especially in those crucial years of rapid change. And learning implies discussing with other people.

First of all, discussing with close associates. In 1959, for this modern-minded young man, about to earn a degree in agricultural engineering, with a foot firmly set in the civil service, with promises of being a high-ranking executive, assuming the succession of an unpromising chiefdom probably doomed to wane and wither under the scorching wind of change and state-building, it was a most un-auspicious prospect. Angwafo could not leave it at that. He had to discuss. He did. But in the discussion, the elders of Mankon, his *Maafo*, the women of the palace argued and won the case. Then it was a matter of discussing with the British administration, politicians like Foncha, with other chiefs about the issues of self-government, representation, leadership, democracy, law, empowerment, local customs. One had to analyse the words, the notions, their contents, their implications. One had to find equivalents in English, in Mankon, in Pidgin. One had to debate and learn from one another (*Royalty*: 67). Among those others, there were foreign scholars, and, above all, two of them, Paul Gebauer and Sally Chilver. Let's have a look at those *Mekare*.

Paul Gebauer was born in Germany in 1900. He fought a few months in the army of the Kaiser in 1918, then moved with his parents to the United States, became a member of the German/American Baptist church and tried a number of jobs while being more and more attracted to the ministry. After his training as a pastor, and having acquired the American nationality, he was assigned to Cameroon in 1931, where he founded the Baptist Mission and Convention, first among the Kaka, then in Nkwen. He participated in WW II as an Army chaplain, this time under the

American flag. His approach to Mission work was quite original for the time:

"We shall not take our culture to them, for they have one of their own. We shall not burden them with our American civilization, because theirs is one of their own. We shall not go to them on behalf of the cotton trade or tailoring profession of Fifth Avenue fashion shops but rather to encourage them to remain "Africans of the Africans" as to their styles and customs. We shall not offer another religion to them, for they are sick at heart about the many which they already have. We shall not discard their practical system of education, but we shall perpetuate and perfect it suitable to their peculiar needs. We shall not laugh at their art and crafts but encourage them to carry on and to perfect the expression of their appreciation of the beautiful[2]."

This was a new approach at the time, and rather opposed to current trends in colonial policy, including of the missionary variety, intent on bringing "civilization" to the Africans. As such it led to some misunderstandings. All too keen to respect local customs, Paul Gebauer stripped his Christianity of many of its parochial Western trappings to such an extent that the Kaka resented it and accused him of only transmitting a second-rate religion just good for colonized people, and duly alleviated of much of its supernatural potency, just to make sure that Africans would not have access to the genuine stuff. You can't win, can you?

This was not the kind of misunderstanding that would dawn on the Fon's mind. When he met Gebauer, a strong encounter took place between the smart European missionary and the inquisitive African ruler. The Fon writes about him (not named, but easily identifiable): "What really moved me were the Baptists! I made the approach to the Baptists. I was drawn to them because in 1960, they had a Baptist missionary here who was a very good and influential man. He used to visit me – we talked politics, talked sociology, talked anthropology, and he could go to South Africa, and bring me books. I have most of my library from him, and he had quite a big influence in the region, especially in the Nkambe area. I enjoyed his approach to religion – he helped, he kept speaking. He was here in Nkwen and built many schools there. I had to approach him for a primary school, and he built the school at Musang." (*Royalty*: 48).

---

[2] Quoted from Allan Effa, « The Legacy of Paul and Clara Gebauer", *International Bulletin of Missionary Research*, Vol. 30, No.2, pp. 92-96.

Angwafo met with other intellectuals. Each and every time, he applied his ingenuity to get the most of the encounter: "I was more or less a leader in the House of Chiefs, followed by the Fon of Bafut... In addition to the studies I had done in school and college, I benefited much from anthropologists, historians and other scholars and researchers who came by to study the various aspects of Mankon traditions, customs and society. Discussions and conversations with them were most enriching. Some gave me a few books and so on. In those days I was still a young man and I was still interested in reading" (*Royalty*: 22). However, he carries on by saying: "My education and exposure to ideas brought a lot of hatred for me." We shall return to this important point.

Did he have Sally Chilver in mind when he mentioned "anthropologists, historians and other scholars" in the context of the seminal years 1959-1962? This is most probable since the British historian visited Mankon precisely at that time. There is no written record of their meeting, but both the Fon and Sally Chilver mentioned it more than once, so impressed they were by each other. I know for sure that they agreed to bring a researcher in Mankon to document the history of the kingdom. It happened to fall on me and that's where I fit into this narrative. Let us have a look at the brilliant character who was Sally Chilver, and at what happened following her encounter with Angwafo.

Elizabeth Chilver was born in 1914 in Constantinople where her father served in the British Civil Service. She obtained an MA in Oxford, started working as a journalist in 1937, became a temporary civil servant during WW II, resumed her work as a journalist for the *Daily Mail* in 1945-1947 and then became the Secretary of the Colonial Social Sciences Research Council (CSSRC) for a duration of ten years. She also sat on the Economic Research Committee of the Colonial Office.

It was in such a capacity that she made the acquaintance of Phyllis Kaberry, a woman-anthropologist who had been recruited by the Colonial Office and sent to Nso' in the Cameroon Grassfields to study the role of women in agriculture, which seemed to be the key to modernization. She published her findings under the title *Women of the Grassfields* (1952, reprinted by Routledge in 2004), an influential book that contributed to pave the way for women studies in anthropology.

Kaberry and Chilver were British women-academics nursed by Oxbridge radicalism, critical of everything colonial, sympathetic to

African civilizations. Chilver reckons that the period of ten years during which she served at the CSSRC was "an extraordinary open-minded one on the side of the Colonial Office"[3]. The researchers were not interested in political decisions. Why? "I think the answer lies far more in the nature of the academic animal, than in the nature of the colonial bureaucracy. The academic animal is a contemplative and critical animal, with a passion for issues to which critical acumen can be effectively applied. It is not fundamentally interested in the Middlegarth of political decision." Accordingly, the CSSRC had very little impact on decolonization policies. Yet it offered a lot of opportunities for academic animals to roam at large, and this is what Chilver did when she was attracted to the Grassfields by Phyllis Kaberry. They toured the Bamenda Province repeatedly between 1958 and 1963, much of the time together. They had in mind the production of a regional survey in the style of the International African Institute. It was published in 1968 in Buea under the title *Traditional Bamenda*.[4] The two of them had been most impressed by the enormous social and cultural diversity of that area. They thought it should be a priority in the anthropological and historical investigation about Africa. At the same time, writes Chilver, "there was a slightly new emphasis in the direction of research: the recovery of local rather than imperial history"[5].

It was for the purpose of such historical research that Sally called at the Mankon palace. The date is not known for sure. It was around 1961, in the context of access to independence. Knowing Sally quite well, I am sure that, when she met the Fon, she spoke her mind, with humour and sort of tongue in cheek regarding the current situation in the British colonial empire. As a historian attuned to current research in Africa, she certainly aimed straight at the issues of the day – unification with Eastern Cameroon formerly under French mandate, law, the style of administration, representation, self-government – put however in historical perspective, that is, the regional dynamics of the last two centuries, the Chamba and Fulani raids, their impact on the local situation in the Grassfields, the coastal

---

[3] E. M. Chilver, "The Secretaryship of the Colonial Social Science Research Council: a Reminiscence", *Anthropological Forum*, Vol. IV, n° 2, 1971, p. 108.

[4] E. M. Chilver, and P. M. Kaberry, *Traditional Bamenda, the Pre-Colonial History and Ethnography of the Bamenda Grassfields*, Buea: Ministry of primary Education and Social Welfare, and West Cameroon Antiquities Commission, 1968.

[5] E. M. Chilver, « The secretaryship… », *op. cit.*, 1971, p. 106.

slave trade, the German colonial conquest, the British and French mandates.

Sally Chilver summarized her findings on Mankon in *Traditional Bamenda* (1968: 56-60). Being fluent in German, she subsequently worked on German colonial publications, especially at the library of the Royal Geographical Institute in Britain, putting the history of the Grassfields in the broader context of the German conquest and its preliminaries in the coastal areas.

We can only guess at the contents of the lively discussions between Angwafo and Sally Chilver. But no doubt, the Fon had her in mind when, in the context of the years 1959-1962 he writes: "I benefited much from anthropologists, historians and other scholars and researchers who came by to study various aspects of Mankon traditions, customs and society. Discussions and conversations with them were most enriching" (*Royalty*: 22). The rest of the story shows that he considered Sally as a dependable and trustworthy person, not moved by self-interest but by the urge to develop knowledge, understanding, and adding up one more page to the analysis of African history in the course of colonization and decolonization. He asked her to come again and push forward her enquiries just as Phyllis had done in Nso', and Gebauer among the Kaka. Angwafo knew that Mankon people had to do the job but that they would not have the qualified persons before some time. Change was taking place fast. Elders were joining their dead ancestors. One had to do something without delaying any further.

Sally declined the invitation having many other commitments on her agenda. Then the Fon told her to send someone else – whoever, even a student. Sally was a researcher, not a university teacher. She did not have any student at hand. But she made a note of it.

Mind you, being educated, patronizing foreign academic animals, sharing connections in global networks, "thinking things through in a cold headed manner" (*Royalty*: 40) did not deserve only compliance and respect. Far from it: "my education and exposure to ideas brought a lot of hatred for me" (*Royalty*: 22, just after mentioning the discussions with anthropologists and historians). Why? Because the Fon was accused of trusting every available resource for his own benefit and aggrandizement: a seat in the House of Chiefs, and on top of that, an elected position as a representative to the National Assembly, combined with international connections and recognition. And, more than everything, because he had two qualifications: one in the tradition, the other one in the formal educational system, whereas party leaders and other fons had only one of the two: "Political party leaders – the KNDP particularly – were so frightened I was well educated both in the modern sense of schooling and also in the ways and interests of the land of Mankon" (*Royalty*: 23). His profile was unique, and, in that sense, dangerous for the other leaders in the political competition.

Neither was the situation altogether easy on the side of academic animals. Sally Chilver and Phyllis Kaberry had a feeling of urgency. In 1963 they published a two pages manifesto in the journal *Abbia*, published in Yaoundé, in favour of "Historical research in Bamenda Division", stating that the task exceeded their means, that it had to be undertaken by local researchers, that it was purely scientific and educational and had nothing to do with party politics:

> "It is a matter of urgency to recover everything that can be known about the traditional constitutions of the Bamenda Chiefdoms from old men who remember how these systems worked, and who may themselves have played a part in Chiefdom government. This conviction is based upon the belief that the modern world has something to learn from the experience of the past, and that a sense of Cameroonian nationality must be based upon the sympathetic understanding of the Cameroonian contribution to the world stock of social and political ideas"[6] (p. 117).

They set the rules to be observed and added up a 14 pages questionnaire as "Notes and Queries" in historical/anthropological research. This article came probably too early to elicit any adequate response. Yet the information was being circulated in British and American academic circles. Igor Kopytoff, a Professor of anthropology at the University of Pennsylvania met Sally Chilver and started doing research in Wum. Sally passed the word that the Fon of Mankon would welcome a researcher in his kingdom. I was a student of Igor. I presented to him a research project on Ivory Coast (it was by no means a good one). He turned it down and instead directed me to Mankon.

I called at the palace in May 1971 for a first contact, some ten years after Sally Chilver had talked with the Fon. On my side, the prospects were unpromising. Unlike Kaberry and Chilver who were seasoned and experienced researchers with an intimate knowledge of

---

[6] P. M. Kaberry and E. M. Chilver, "Historical Research in Bamenda Division", *Abbia*, n°4, Dec. 1963, pp. 117-133.

the African continent, I didn't have the slightest qualification in that respect. I had everything to learn. But the Fon welcomed me and facilitated my contacts with the Mankon people. I spent two months in Cameroon, with a couple of weeks in Yaoundé and the rest in Mankon. My brief was very vague as regards what the Fon expected from me. What he had said to Sally Chilver, relayed to me by Igor Kopytoff, was that he welcomed historical and anthropological research. That was all!

Jacqueline Leroy, a linguist and my partner at the time, came along with me to Mankon in June 1972 for a two years fieldwork. It soon became apparent to me that there were quite different expectations as regards the kind of narrative I was expected to produce. The history of Mankon was far from being a fairy tale. There had been severe conflicts in the past, within the kingdom and with neighbouring polities, aggravated by the German conquest and, as from 1916, the British mandate. Was I expected to record the various versions and points of view, including of course that of the palace? Was I expected to reflect only the version of the royal clan, given it was the Fon who, so to speak, had recruited me, or else again to investigate the cases and arbitrate between the different points of view?

Such investigations were not likely to produce the kind of anthropological dissertation that was expected from me by my supervisor and the graduate college of the University of Pennsylvania for the completion of my Ph.D. I had to conform to a strictly Western discourse on an African society in accordance with the academic criteria of the "scientific" approach developed since the 18th c. by European and American scholars. The misunderstanding was potentially damaging for the work I was expected to do.

Yet the Fon gave me a free rein. For one thing, he had sucked the milk of the Western *Alma Mater* at Ibadan where he had assimilated the conventions of academic scholarship. Furthermore, he had enjoyed discussing and trading notes with Paul Gebauer and Sally Chilver. He knew I had to address those issues and find a way out of the conundrum. But I have another tip that is clearly suggested by the narrative recorded in *Royalty and Politics*, that is, right from the start and even before his refusal to assume the succession of his father, Angwafo was convinced that politics is all about conflicts and conflicts management, and sometimes failure to resolve the conflicts. As soon as he was caught to succeed his father, he assumed all the conflicts and addressed them head-on: with the notables, with *Maafo*, with the women of the palace to whom he yielded, with Foncha and the KNDP, with other Fons, with those who criticized his various political decisions.

One can look at politics in different ways, roughly as an attempt to construct an ideal city in conformity with some sort of utopia. Or else, one can look at politics as interconnected social spaces and institutions on which different expectations and interests converge and compete with each other. For a long time, social scientists, in line with part of the public opinion, conceived of society as an integrated community of people. A healthy society was seen as an entirely pacified group of people, devoid of conflicts and divergent interests, in line with the organicist metaphor that was popular at the time. This view has been abandoned in the 1930s and most social scientists consider that human beings have different vested interests in life, sometimes conflicting, sometimes converging and being aggregated in collective action. Members of the same society share a number of cultural traits but have different points of view on their past and their desirable future. There are personal hatred and there are privileged friendships. There are competing interests. All in all, a healthy society is one in which conflicts may proliferate but find various means to be handled, managed, and in the end cause change. This is certainly the way Angwafo saw politics, as the handling of many different interests potentially conflicting, sometimes even violently, but also likely to produce collective action and change. This is what history is all about.

This is one more reason to cultivate knowledge, research, books and education. How can you expect to arbitrate conflicts and reduce the level of violence unless you acquire a good understanding of the various parties to the conflict and of all the relevant data, and therefore keep in close touch with them? Take for example the tension between traditions and modernization as it was perceived in the 1960s: whereas modern elites have studied and learned government from the Europeans, writes the Fon, "if the government were to know the difference and study or research the traditional laws and customs of the various kingdoms, they should find that there is nothing bad in this institution and we would have made more progress" (*Royalty*: 36). Conflicts often arise from mutual ignorance. And again: "the real challenge is thinking things through in a cold headed manner, to ensure that we do not throw the baby of tradition out with the bath water in our desperate haste to embrace modern systems of power. We should study our traditional institutions side-by-side with the imported system we are trying to implement" (*Royalty:* 40).

This is a clear rejoinder to what Kaberry and Chilver had written in *Abbia*: the study of local history and customs is essential to nation building. But this is also true the other way round: there is no way to understand what colonization did to African *and* to European people unless one acquires a clear understanding of what has happened *on both sides* in the course of history. If this is the case, then local people have to meet strangers and welcome their own brand of knowledge with all its contents. This is why Angwafo, and his father before him, had an active policy of "encouraging strangers to settle in Mankon" (*Royalty*: 25, and see the whole page on the presence of assimilated strangers in Mankon). A message and a philosophy that contemporary Europe finds it hard to swallow, forgetting the fact that not a single human being, not a single society is self-sufficient, complete and replete with its own truth and belongings. All of them are incomplete and need to complement others and be complemented in an endless process.

Consequently, I think the Fon was above any concern regarding the way I conducted my research provided I did not trigger any unwanted reaction among the people with whom I worked. Anyway, I was not really interested in old conflicts that escaped any reasonable investigation, but rather in the institutions of the descent groups (*atse*, sg.), the successions to the position of heads of descent groups, the genealogies, the rituals performed to "throw the heads" of dead elders, the associations, etc. Early in my investigations, it occurred to me that the production of foodstuffs and small livestock, crafts, household economy, together with regional specialization and trading, were key issues in the history of Mankon and neighbouring kingdoms. These topics were highly significant yet unproblematic.

I find it surprising that, after two years of fieldwork the Fon gave me the title of *Sangto'*. I had not yet produced any text, nor my PhD dissertation, or any report, let alone any publication. The Fon had nothing in hand that could stand an evaluation. It was a gesture that turned Jacqueline Leroy and myself into a couple of assimilated strangers, with an encouragement to come again, keep producing knowledge, bring it as a tribute to the palace and share it with the people. This is what we did in subsequent years, and eventually all along our academic careers. In appreciation of our work, the Fon wrote: "I am particularly thankful to Jean-Pierre Warnier, a French anthropologist and historian who has written extensively on various aspects of Mankon since the 1970s, and who has always sent copies of his writings to the palace, where he is known as *Sangto'* – the palace Courtyard – a title I gave in 1974 in recognition of his achievements for Mankon. My acknowledgement also goes to *Mafo Sangto'*, Jacqueline Leroy, his wife at the time, for her two detailed books and a number of articles on the Mankon language" (*Royalty*: 69) – a generous appreciation since this process is two way: if we have brought our share to the kingdom, it is also because, to begin with, we have received a lot from the people of Mankon and their Fon.

It is only years after Angwafo had given me the title of *Sangto'* that I understood the logic of it all. The Fon is the container of the Mankon country – *Ala'a*. He is the gateway of anything that may come to it. His function is to let in any resource to be assimilated as a kind of good food and to expel from it all the bad people and substances that may have come across its envelope. Angwafo saw it as part of his job to attract within Mankon a White historian and anthropologist and a White linguist as potential resources worthy of being assimilated because they would bring along some amount of knowledge, together with cross-cultural contacts. This was an immense privilege. Vice-versa, we benefitted most from our presence in Mankon in terms of education and knowledge. A fantastic access to cultural and social worlds so far unknown to us. It was an encounter on both sides, each one bringing his stock in trade, like spare parts, to the other party.

My first written account was my PhD dissertation. I sent it to the palace. Whilst it was appreciated as a contribution to the recording of Mankon institutions, it caused a certain disappointment because it was in line with university requirements and not with the local expectations concerning the narrative of Mankon history. Just one example: the list and genealogy of the Fons extends far back in the past and includes at least twenty names. Of those, I listed only the last eight ones. This was not to say that the dynasty was a recent and short one. Not at all. According to Western conventions in the social sciences, I concentrated my attention on those Fons for whom there was a convergence of information so strong as to provide a firm ground for a historical reconstruction, that is, a grave, the foundation of one or several descent groups within the royal clan, a connection with datable events such as the Chamba raids at the beginning of the 19th century, etc. It was a knowledge, but a knowledge of some sort: that of the academic animal.

Academic knowledge then, but what for? It is far from being self-evident. Yet the Fon was adamant. He wanted that sort of knowledge in addition to many other sorts: that of the local healers – *ngwon ngang* – that of the medical doctor like some of his sons, that of the agricultural engineer but also that of the local farmer – mostly women. But why should historical and linguistic knowledge complying with Western scholarly criteria be valued? Such a question may be turned on its head: not *what sort* of knowledge, but *who are the people* to share in it? As years went by, the circles of people to share it got larger. At first, the palace, some Mankon people and the anthropologist got to share a knowledge that was 100% local. But other people in the NW Province took part in it, together with colleagues at the University of Yaoundé, in Europe and America, to the point when a "Grassfields Working Group" was founded, met several times in different places and nurtured many publications in Cameroon such as the *Elements for a History of the Western Grassfields* by Nkwi & Warnier[7], and elsewhere.

At this point, it becomes clear that knowledge is indeed a two-way process, an exchange, a discussion between two or more persons or groups who communicate, share in the same contents, trade and complement each other. The important point here is that some Westerners (not all of them by far), instead of ignoring and sometimes despising African civilizations, learned to discover that they were in need of them and to appreciate them. The members of the Grassfields Working Group, most of them University lecturers, translated their knowledge in publications, teaching programs, museum exhibits, catalogues, conferences, documentary films. They paved the way for a different understanding of the African continent. They played a crucial role in the illustration and preservation of African heritage and to the conflict-ridden movement of restitution and recognition. The Mankon Museum is yet another tool in the cultural dialogue taking place between the West and the rest. This would not have been possible unless communities like Mankon and their ruler had not welcomed several strangers, for them to get to know the local traditions and practice.

Angwafo was convinced that, in the "global village" people had to know each other and talk to each other. Given the number of conflicts – sometimes violent – that plague our planet, one may wonder if knowledge has even the slightest impact to prevent or solve

---

[7] P. N. Nkwi and J.-P. Warnier, *Elements for a History of the Western Grassfields*, Yaoundé, Université de Yaoundé, printed by SOPECAM, 1982.

them. One may even think that it may make things even worse. Was it not the Fon himself who said that his education, his scholarly connections and his qualifications attracted a lot of hatred against him? Yet he wouldn't budge: knowledge is valuable as such and must be encouraged. To wit, the fact that one of the priorities of dictators and authoritarian regimes consists in establishing a total control on research in history, the social sciences, school curricula and the media.

May I stress something that the Fon does not seem to have expressed in so many words but that he certainly had in mind: when Paul Gebauer and Sally Chilver called in Mankon and met him. They were attracted to him by their own drive to learn: a *libido sciendi* would say the Western erudite. After the merchant and the military, they were a different kind of Westerner, eager to know about African civilizations. For what purpose? To steal African culture for their own benefit and aggrandizement or out of sheer curiosity for other kinds of human beings? As far as I am concerned, there is no doubt that I built my whole academic career, all the way to being a Professor of anthropology at the University Paris-Descartes on my field research in Mankon and the NW Region. My debt in that respect is enormous. Some people in the Grassfields think that academics made pots of money with their books. This has never been and will never be the case since most scholarly publications cost far more to their authors than they bring in terms of royalties. But still, I owe my career to such an interest that conflicts with other ones – mostly economic and strategic.

In my own case, it started with a long-term and difficult apprenticeship of everything Mankon. Although I am convinced I did no more than scratch the surface, this detour by another civilization than mine turned me into a different kind of human being. I have learned to discover that I needed the complement brought by other civilizations. I began to see things quite differently from the way my fellow citizens see them, who have not had that kind of experience. Oftentimes I wish I could send them on a three months internship in Mankon to create a cultural shock and change their minds. Angwafo and Mankon have imparted to me an entirely different kind of knowledge that I share with the minority of those – scholars and amateurs – who have acquired a sense of Africa. For this, I'll be ever grateful to the Fon who was convinced that knowledge, education, books are needed and even essential because every human being, every civilization, is incomplete and is engaged in a never ending process of being happily complemented by others, if sometimes at the cost of tensions and conflicts.

Emeritus Professor Jean-Pierre Warnier (*Sangto*)
Université Paris-Descartes, Sorbonne,
Paris, France

HRH Fo Angwafo III SAN: Journey of Self-Reliance

HRH Fo S.A.N. Angwafo III was found on April 4, 1959 and disappeared on May 21, 2022 after 63 years and 48 days on the throne of the Mankon people. Unique among traditional rulers in Cameroon, his reign spanned a period of profound and, sometimes, tumultuous political, social, educational, and cultural developments and almost magical scientific discoveries and technological innovations in the world. And again, unique among fons, chiefs, and lamidos in Cameroon, he was not only the most durable and keen observer of these transformations in Cameroon but also willingly or unwillingly, wittingly or unwittingly an active participant in and architect of their trajectories.

Concomitant with his role in the transformations in the fabric of Cameroon's politics, economics, society, and education during his reign was his presiding over the sometimes unavoidable and disruptive changes occurring in Mankon itself and her people as Mankon was transformed through urbanization from a village into a major multi-ethnic and multicultural cosmopolitan city. HRH Fo S.A.N. Angwafo III, therefore, was also a keen observer, sometimes perhaps neither as an architect nor as a participant, of the profound metamorphosis in the traditions and culture of Mankon resulting from urbanization. But as king, he was condemned to address them. To navigate through these challenges, HRH Fo S.A.N. Angwafo III needed a character forged by the tempest of events and experiences preceding his mounting the throne of Mankon.

That he was born between two "world" wars and grew up during harsh global and especially personal economic conditions moulded the personality of HRH Fo S.A.N. Angwafo III into several characteristics, amongst which, in my opinion, self-reliance was the overriding one. The autobiography of our father, *Royalty and Politics: The Story of My Life*, contains so many events that serve as ample illustrations of self-reliance that it should have been subtitled *Journey of Self-Reliance*. In fact, this autobiography challenges its readers to be self-reliant. Unlike other (auto)biographies in which pictures contain captions connecting them to narrated events, the autobiography of HRH eschews this approach. In a book of 141 pages, exactly one-half (pages 1 to 70) contains the narrative in text while the other half (pages 71 to 141) is a pictorial narrative without captions for the pictures. Intended or not, the reader is being challenged to rely on his/her analytical and synthetic abilities to connect the pictures to the events in the verbal part of the book while deducing any unwritten part of the story.

His various roles (shepherd, judge, warlord, priest and seer, and centre of the ruler class) as the king of Mankon and first-class *Fo* in the North-West and in his roles as member of the West Cameroon House of Chiefs, West Cameroon parliamentarian, and First Vice-President of the Cameroon People Democratic Party, HRH always embodied the principle and practice of self-reliance as can be clearly glimpsed from his autobiography.

On a personal level, this self-reliant tendency of HRH Fo S.A.N. Angwafo III defined my relationship with HRH for more than three decades. When my brother and I were admitted into Cameroon Protestant College (CPC), Bali our father, who was a palm wine trader, took us to Fo Angwafo III in the hope that HRH will provide some financial assistance from the Mankon State Union. In his reply, the Fo pushed our father to be self-reliant by advising him to use his raffia palm bush as collateral for a loan to send us to CPC. Our father followed this advice and was able to pay our fees for only the first term in CPC during which my brother and I wrote and passed the government scholarship examination which guaranteed our education in CPC for five years. However, in my mind as a child who was intimately acquainted with the meagre financial resources of his father, I saw the advice of the Fo as an intentional attempt to halt my education. On that spot in the palace on that day, I vowed never to have anything to do with the Fo and the palace. Only later did I realize that Fo had issued an unquestionable royal instruction to our father to rely on his own resources to assure the attendance of Fo's children at CPC. Without this royal instruction, our education could have ground to a halt because we may never have gone to CPC for that first term and would have, consequently, never obtained the government scholarship to continue our education. Paradoxically, HRH Fo S.A.N. Angwafo III knew my decision but, as a good father, he subtly dragged me into his inner circle. It was a very indelible personal lesson about self-reliance.

Even in the designation of the next King of Mankon, HRH Fo S.A.N. Angwafo III selected a self-reliant prince, a technician. In choosing the name of our missing father for himself, HRH Fo Angwafo IV loudly announces his intention to continue the practice of self-reliance for his people. However, self-reliance requires self-confidence built on a solid foundation of respect for our traditions and culture. My hope is that HRH Fo Angwafo IV will lead a renaissance of respect and hunger for our traditions and culture. Central to this revival is teaching of the **core values** of Mankon people and a codification of our **folklore**, which serve as a medium for the transmission of our culture and traditions. Were this to occur, HRH Fo Angwafo IV would have led his people to always Think Mankon, Act Mankon, Promote Mankon.

Dr. Ndeh Ntomambang Ningo
Saint Monica University Higher Institute, Buea
and University of Buea

"Times were hard, but there was no giving up"
A Tribute in his own words to Fo S. A. N Angwafo III of Mankon, Foremost Cultivator of the Soil, Mind and Soul 1925-2022 (Birth 1925, *Atsum* 1959 – *Alankyi* 2022)

Fo Mankon has disappeared!!!
Fo Mankon is missing!!!
Long live Fo Mankon!!!!

This isn't a moment for tears. It is a moment for celebration; celebration of the eternity of life in which death is merely a transition to other modes of being and living.

Fo Solomon AnyeGhamoti Angwafo III has left *Atsum* to join his ancestors at *Alankyi* with a message to share on the state of things in Mankon and the world he leaves behind.

He started his journey of reunion with his ancestors on May 21, 2022, the same day he was born 97 years ago, and from the same place he was born. Named AnyeGhamoti at birth and marriage, he adopted Solomon along the way. He was enthroned and titled Fo Angwafo III on April 4, 1959, following the passing of his father, Fo Ndefru III. His mother was Theresa Mankah, the daughter of Akenji-Ndemasiri and Switdzu, both from Munkyi (Asongkah), one of the quarters of Mankon. His brother having passed away at the age of 12, he became the only surviving son of his mother.

Fo Angwafo III demonstrated a lifelong commitment to cultivation. To him, living was not just about tilling the soil for sustenance, it was also about tending the mind and the soul. He valued agriculture and culture. In both fields, he would like to be remembered as an innovator who facilitated productive conversations between change and continuity, tradition and modernity, Mankon and elsewhere. Be it in agriculture or culture or education, he has always argued:

> "To me, education is the key to any meaningful achievement. I have known this since the day I first set foot in school. I have encouraged my children to get as much of it as possible, and have prioritized it despite the many other challenges demanding a share of our meagre resources. Although education necessarily comes with new values, I believe that a thorough grounding in our own ways best prepares us to adapt the values we adopt through education." (p. 52)

His childhood was royal in name only. He had to toil and sweat for almost everything. As the only child to his mother and without an uncle to support him in a palace where the practice was to outsource certain parental responsibilities to maternal uncles and aunties, Fo Angwafo III learnt to fend for himself from a very tender age. In *Royalty and Politics: The Story of My Life*, he recollects:

> "My mother had an only brother who was not financially able to help her or even to extend the help to me. And so, imagine that in such a large family, though our father was interested in education, the number of wives, the number of children, the number of extended family overpowered him and so he couldn't support our school. One of his principles to us his children was for our uncles to support our schooling. I had no uncle to go to." (p. 1)

He may have been lucky to have been allowed by his father to go to school – something not common for princes in his day –, but paying his fees and maintenance while at school was a challenge. However, he was not someone who yielded easily to obstacles: because "I had no viable uncles to help me, I turned to helping myself." (p. 4)

He elaborates on what he did to mitigate the challenges. To provide for himself at school, he "used to keep a tomato garden and to grow cabbages as well" (p. 11) In addition:

"I had to go to the Fon's farm to fetch firewood to sell at Ntambag. We also caught fish, mud fish, with hooks to sell to civil servants, the elites, the rich people in town, and with the money thus earned, I was able to buy a few things to maintain myself in school. Sometimes we had to draw water for the settlers at Ntambag, to make a little cash to buy pencil and exercise books. And so we lived on like that." (p. 4)

His financial problems were only compounded when he travelled to Nigeria for further education. As he recounts, "Although my father had given me his blessings to enrol at the Aggrey Memorial College, he could not pay my fees because his contract with the government to supply food to prisoners was abruptly terminated." (p. 9)

Once again, his creative ingenuity around gardening and farming came to his rescue:

"I was very popular there, and was appointed the Janitor of the college experimental farm and library, which meant that I stayed in the dormitory. During holidays, I couldn't go home. There was no transport money again, and there was the Nigerian Railway strike. The small money sent to me from home was missing. I explained my situation to the Vice Principal, so the yams I grew all went back to the school when I harvested, and from this I earned a little money to keep going. Times were hard, but there was no giving up." (p. 9)

"The hard work and determination paid off. I took four instead of the statutory five years to obtain the Cambridge School Certificate and a certificate in Agriculture. On graduation, I received a testimonial from the principal and proprietor of the college, Mr Alvan Ikoku, dated 31 December 1950 that read:

"'This is to certify that Solomon Ndefru was a student here from 1946 to 1950. He passed secondary class five in 1949 and studied a further year (1950) in class six. He was elected College prefect in 1950 by both staff and students and has revealed great qualities of leadership and responsibility in bearing what is regarded as the highest honour of the school. Solomon is loyal without losing his right of criticism, sensible and honest. His courtesy and sense of humour make him a great winner

through. I expect great things of him in the wider life beyond the College campus.'"
(p. 9)

The college principal's great expectations of Solomon in the wider life beyond came to pass abundantly. The Fon's achievements, even his critics would agree, have been phenomenal. He has succeeded as a pacesetter in agriculture. As a father and leader of Mankon, he has taught by example, insisting on traditionalizing modernity and modernizing tradition in a careful and delicately balanced articulation of change and continuity.

As a traditional leader, he succeeded more than most in challenging party politics to recognize and represent chieftaincy as integral to democracy and statecraft in which chiefs or kings are not merely relegated to the whims and caprices of elite politicians acting under the canopy of political parties. He demonstrated that it is possible to straddle both the hereditary and elected offices with fascinating ambiguity that challenges scholars to rethink conventional categories and concepts. This is what he means when he affirms that, "As far as I can remember, our traditions have always been modern, our modernities traditional." (p.70)

The place of traditional authority in a modern state

As the most educated Fon in the region when he inherited the throne from his father, Fo Angwafo III became the first chief/king to be elected MP in 1961 in a keenly contested multiparty election in which he ran as an independent. He ignored calls for his resignation as either MP or chief by those who thought it was improper for a chief (whose position is ascribed or by might) to hold an elected office (achieved or by right). From his defiance it was clear that he did not subscribe to the dichotomy between ascription and achievement, might and right, traditional and modern. Upon the reunification of the English and French Cameroons in 1961, he was arm-twitted into party politics in 1966 following Ahidjo's swallowing all parties to birth a single party: Cameroon National Union (CNU). He stayed on as MP until his retirement from active politics in 1988. However, the launching of the SDF in Mankon and the dramatic resignation from the ruling CDPM in 1990 of John Ngu Foncha brought Fo Angwafo III back to the centre of local and national politics. He was appointed to replace Foncha as the national vice-president of the CDPM. Fo Angwafo III has been described as "a shining example of a pragmatist" and a man of many faces who skilfully married two different political cultures. He failed to see why chiefs and kings should be treated as apolitical animals or placed above party politics, when they are citizens just like anyone else. He has repeatedly defended himself in interviews with the press and with researchers, by asking: "How can you deprive a citizen of involvement in politics simply because he holds a traditional title of fon?"

This is a central theme in *Royalty and Politics*, as the following excerpts show:

"Some people say being a Fon and participating in politics are incompatible roles. They are entitled to their opinion, but I see things differently. I have a different understanding of my role as Fo Mankon and my role as a politician. I think a politician is one who rules people and Fo Mankon is the one who guides and keeps the traditions and customs of the Mankon people as a ruler. So, as far as politics is concerned, whether I am a politician or not, the sphere of activities include politics – all in one." (p. 29)

"I cannot see how the Fo is supposed to rule if he is forbidden active participation in politics. The Fo of Mankon was a ruler before partisan politics, and being Fo has always been a political office. I can't see how a good political arrangement could succeed in any set up where the Fo is excluded." (p. 40)

"I don't see what the Fo is supposed to do and what not to do. I feel that the Fo as a leader, as a legislator – traditional one – can continue to do that. It is up to government to clearly define the powers of the Fo, be these active or residual, but without ambiguity, so the Fo could continue with the business of administration. The struggle to abolish this and introduce that, based more on the sentiments of the moment than on any clear long term strategic plan, has done more harm than provided solutions to the burning question of the place of traditional authority in a modern state." (p. 40)

"The easiest thing, I believe, is to rush into condemning our traditional systems of government. The real challenge is thinking things through in as cold headed manner, to ensure that we do not throw the baby of tradition out with the bathwater, in our desperate haste to embrace modern systems of power. We should study our traditional institutions side-by-side with the imported system we are trying to implement. We should see what is good in it, retain it, and support it to grow" (p. 40)

Dancing to the tunes of changing times

"We have stayed relevant largely by taking things into our hands to mobilize and organize ourselves around matters of common interest to us Fons." (pp. 40-41)

"To maintain ourselves as embodiments of the particular cultural communities we head, we have had to dance to the tunes of changing times, constantly having to negotiate our positions within the contradictions between state and our communities on the one hand, and in relation to competing expectations within the communities on the other. Was it not Chinua Achebe, the Nigerian novelist whose books are well oiled by Igbo proverbs, who made a bird say, 'since men have learnt to shoot without missing, I have learnt to fly without perching'? Changing times for me and my colleagues have meant the ability to evaluate constantly and negotiate various innovations on the landscape of our politics and societies. We cannot afford to perch or rest on our laurels, lest we are swept away by the tides of change." (p. 41)

"It strikes me as hypocritical for more and more of the same people, who are so highly critical of Fons in modern politics, not to be satisfied with their achievements within the modern sector and bureaucratic state power. Increasingly, they come to us Fons seeking traditional titles of notability, with some ready to fight and kill for these titles. If chieftaincy was that incompatible with modern politics and bureaucratic state power, why then should they so desperately need recognition through traditional titles?" (p. 41)

"As more and more Fons and chiefs elsewhere have discovered their game, we have sought to beat them at it through mobilisation and organisation to defend our common interests. We don't always succeed, given the ability of the modern political elite to manipulate and divide in order to rule, but the fact that we can count some successes at all is a good sign that united we can indeed conquer. It was precisely to draw attention to ourselves as a group of leaders, with an important role to play in modern Cameroon, that we decided to honour President Paul Biya with the title of 'Fon of Fons' when he took over as head of state from Ahidjo in 1982. If the ritual meant that the President could benefit from our support as fellow Fons, it was also a message to him that he must do all in his powers to make us actively relevant to modern political processes." (p. 41)

"The benefits to Mankon of my active participation in politics have not only been increased political recognition and representation, but also greater socio-economic development. The developments are there for all to see, from the number of schools to medical services through businesses, pipe borne water projects and road infrastructure. There is the Congress Hall, the Airport, the motor parks, the Mankon Main Market, the Urban Council, the Mankon Museum, and many other development initiatives as testimony of my active involvement in politics in the interest of Mankon. It might not be as much as we would wish, but I have, since my childhood days, learnt to dream with my feet firmly on the ground. A bird at hand is worth two in the bush, was something I learnt as a school boy." (p. 32)

Attracting opportunities for Mankon

Angwafo III's prescience and nose for opportunities with Mankon in mind is equally evidenced in his attitude towards Christianity and the churches as vectors of a type of modernity that had come with encounters with Europe. The attitude was and remains one of generosity to all the churches. "Not only have we welcomed the various missions to set up schools and build churches, we have embraced all of them within the community and even in the palace." (p. 48) His thinking is well incapsulated in the following paragraph from *Royalty and Politics*:

"As a child growing up in the palace, we were exposed to all the religions, because there was not a Christian denomination that did not visit my father, talking to him, seeking to convert him and so on. But it was the Catholics who really wanted to have a second school in addition to Sasse, up here. I seized that opportunity. I didn't specially want a Catholic school. All I wanted was a secondary school near enough to accommodate the Mankon children…. Nigeria was too far away. I had had the experience of schooling in Nigeria and didn't see any Mankon man who could pay transport and keep his children far away in Nigeria. Throughout my stay in Nigeria, I didn't see anything, any Bamenda man there. So, I knew it would be very good if I had a secondary school, so poor parents could afford to send their children to school. I thus saw the approach by the Catholics to open a college as an opportunity for me to attract the school to my own land. I didn't propose the idea. Same for the Basel Mission!" (p. 48)

"Not only have I allowed my wives and children to go to the churches of their choice and attend mission and government schools indiscriminately, I have even allowed my children to wed in church." (p. 48)

"As I'm saying, since1960 I have all these struggles worrying me and God has still preserved my life. I'm sure that after my death, those who compile my balance sheet shall note that I never wavered from my agriculture. That I had had the advantage of going to parliament, making laws, debating laws, understanding the law and being able to sift what traditionally is wrong, and applying my decisions with the knowledge of the law." (p. 45)

As chiefs and kings become more literate, they are going to see the wisdom in his insistence on representation and participation beyond tokenism. Already, many are following in his footsteps. Pertaining to agency, certain chiefs, mostly those that have gone to school, have succeeded more than others in negotiating conviviality between modern and customary bases of power, and between the interests of the state and those of their chiefdoms. The talents, abilities, education, networks, connections and creativity of individual chiefs and kings determine who succeeds with whom, where, how and with what effects. Some have become part of the new elite at the centre of national and regional power. Through their individual capacities or via networks and various associations, these chiefs and kings stake claims on national power and resources for their region, chiefdoms or kingdoms over and above the pursuit of a common good for all.

The influence of the women of the palace

Judging from how he defended chieftaincy and the right to active participation by chiefs or kings in politics, one might be led to think that becoming Fo Mankon was something he had always aspired to in his youth. Nothing could be further from the truth. He hated being made Fon and vigorously resisted until he was eventually convinced otherwise by the women of the palace during the interregnum. In *Royalty and Politics*, he insists he never had any ambition of becoming Fon. He describes being made Fo Mankon "the greatest surprise in my life" (p. 15), adding:

"Although my mother had, in my upbringing, taken time to school me in the ways and values of the land, and had made sure that the traditions, customs and etiquette of the palace were well internalized by me, I didn't want to be Fo Mankon." (p. 16)

He thought he didn't have what it took to be Fon, something he believed his brothers had more of:

"I was also ignorant of what the whole thing was about. I believed my brothers were more qualified and was ready to concede the title to any of my junior brothers who was interested. I was promising to pay half of my salary or part salary to help which ever brother would take the throne. Had any of my brothers shown interest, I would certainly have done all to pass onto him the challenge of stepping into our father's shoes." (p. 16)

Just like his principal at college, the kingmakers of Mankon had seen leadership in him and would not yield to his attempts to wiggle himself out of the calling. So, when the women of the palace urged him to stop resisting and embrace his destiny, he finally succumbed:

"So I told myself, 'let me take up courage and see whether I can do this thing.' At thirty-four years of age, I was confirmed Fo Mankon." (p. 17)

This made of him the 20th Fo Mankon.

Continuing a tradition of welcoming and integrating strangers

A legacy of his, inherited from his father and enhanced, and which he would like his successor to continue, is the solidarity Mankon as a kingdom has shown strangers. This is a theme abundantly explored in *Royalty and Politics*. He is proud of the kingdom's "open door policy of encouraging strangers to settle in Mankon, initiated since the reign of Fon Angwafo II, my grandfather" (p. 25)

"It was this open door policy and the influx of Hausas from Nigeria that attracted people from various origins, who engaged themselves mainly in commerce, construction and manufacturing." (p. 25)

"Francophone Cameroonians, mostly Bamileke, who came seeking refuge or opportunity, were easily accommodated by my father, especially following the partition of Cameroon after World War I. Even when an attempt was made to repatriate the Francophones who had sought refuge in his Kingdom, Ndefru III objected, arguing that he was entitled, as a Fon, to offer protection to these people. The fact that the rest of Mankon was still largely inhabited by Mankon people earning their living mostly from farming, hunting and fishing by no means meant that Fo Mankon should be indifferent to strangers." (p. 26)

Thanks to the hospitality and solidarity shown towards strangers, "Ntambag became the eye and ear of Mankon in the modern urban world, meant to link the rural and the urban in continuous dialogue and interdependence." (p. 26)

Handing the baton to the next Generation

"The best recognition I can hope for in appreciation for the efforts I have made to promote education in Mankon, is for the young and upcoming generations to borrow from the example of all these anthropologists and historians and ensure that our culture and experiences are well documented. For, it is only in documenting and preserving our past that we are best able to organise the present in the interest of the future." (p.70)

"The Mankon Museum is testimony to the fact that the best way of consolidating our traditions is to make them modern, and that our modernity only makes sense to the extent that it is firmly grounded in our traditions. In many ways I feel my life encapsulates this negotiation and reconciliation of continuity and change. I am what my father was not, but I clearly couldn't have been without what my father was. I have contributed my modest best in giving Mankon a sense of direction and meaning within our everchanging and ever familiar landscape. It is up to our young and upcoming generations to take the baton and excel in honour of Mankon, Cameroon and Africa." (p.70)

Fo S. A. N Angwafo III spent his entire life as a pacesetter. He has moved from *Atsum* to *Alankyi*. He will continue to be present even in his apparent absence, and we will continue to learn from him in forging the way forward.

Fo S. A. N Angwafo III leaves us in the well-cultivated hands of Fo Fru-Asah Angwafo IV, who has a message of consolidation and solidarity for us all:

"The load is huge, but with you people around me, we shall rise to the top. Our father, the Rock, did everything and we just need to complement where there were some shortfalls."

Francis B. Nyamnjoh
Professor of Anthropology
University of Cape Town

Part 10

His Royal Majesty Fo Fru-Asah Angwafo IV: An influential Leader who educates

His Royal Majesty Fo Fru-Asah Angwafo IV is the new Fon of Mankon. He is the 21st leader of this prominent, First-Class Fondom in the Bamenda metropolitan area of the North-West Region of Cameroon. He was presented to the Mankon public on June 7th, 2022 in a colourful event that showcased the best of Mankon tradition and culture. The event took place in the presence of thousands of Mankon people, many of whom bearing smartphones and related gadgets, determined to record every single moment of the unfolding, to share with absent relatives, friends and the diaspora on Facebook, WhatsApp, Twitter, Instagram, TikTok, YouTube and kindred platforms, as well as to preserve as an archive for future generations and remembrance. The event enthralled many across the length and breadth of Cameroon and beyond. Social media were abuzz with posts of photos and videos and commentaries. The conventional media were present as well, and the coverage elaborate and comprehensive. The Fo of Mankon who had disappeared in the person of Angwafo III had resurfaced as Angwafo IV. Mankon had lost and found its leader.

HRH Fo Fru-Asah Angwafo IV was born at Ntaw Mankon on 12 December 1972. According to recorded history, he is the 21st Fon of Mankon since the founding of the Fondom with Fo Ndemagha I. His presentation to the public on June 7th 2022 marked his official ascension to the Mankon Royal throne. In name, cultivation and commitment to stewardship at the service of the Mankon Kingdom, its diaspora and its guests, Fo Angwafo IV has signalled his intention to follow in the footsteps of his beloved father, Fo Angwafo III, who went missing on May 21st 2022, and who willed him as the successor. Change in continuity, consolidation and solidarity are his emphasis.

Fo Angwafo IV is the youngest son and one of the seven children of Nimo-ntaw Beltha Lumnwi, the twin and eldest daughter of the Ndiforbanyong family of Ntaghien in Mankon, who passed away on March 22, 2018. He is married to Nimo Alieh Emmaculate Akombo Angwafo who is also a teacher, daughter of Mr. Joseph Chi Akombo and Mrs. Marsah Grace from Mukwebu quarter in Mankon. They have several children both biological and adopted.

Educational life

Education for princes and princesses at Ntaw Mankon started long before primary school. Even toddlers were expected to start the day with brooms, learning to keep the palace clean. The tasks increased with age, to include farming, gardening and other tending duties the Fon and Nimo-ntaws felt fit to assign the children. In this way, formal schooling was just an extension of what the princes and princesses had been initiated to from birth.

In tune with this tradition, HRH Fo Fru-Asah Angwafo IV grew up in the Mankon palace, helping his parents with farm work, like most kids, while attending Government Primary School Ntingkag in the 1980s.He later attended the Government Technical College and High School Bamenda, to graduate with a Certificat D'Aptitute Professionelle (CAP), PROBATOIRE and GCE Advanced Level technical in Accounting specialty. He attended the Government Technical Teachers Training College (ENSET) of the University of Douala and graduated with a Diplome de Professeur de l'Enseignement Technique du Première Grade (DIPET I). He enjoyed teaching technical education, taught for about a decade to gain experience, got married and started his family, and returned to the same University for further education to obtain the Diplome de Professeur de l'Enseignement Technique du Deuxième Grade (DIPET II).

Professional life

HRH Fo Angwafo IV is a highly qualified and very dedicated educationist. He believes an educated person can better interpret their environment, develop their society, but also better manage their life, thanks to the knowledge they acquired in school and from the wisdoms of traditions passed down from one generation to another. Simply put, it is much harder to manipulate an educated, well-informed person than someone who lacks education or culture. Acquiring new knowledge helps people to critically approach any information, because such people primarily rely on facts when they pass judgments about anything. Thus, better education helps people to better understand social conflicts and the needs of others. He has therefore dedicated his life to teaching other children as well his own. Education and cultivation are enriched by experience through travel and encounters with other people and other places. He has been fortunate, as a teacher, to serve in various Government Technical Colleges in Ndu, Oku, Alabukam-Mankon and Fundong from 2002 to 2011. It is the experience gathered working in these various places that he mobilized when, in 2012 he was appointed pioneer principal of Government Technical College Ntankah in Mankon where he constructed the new establishment and served for five years. He constructed 8 classrooms and provided drinking water to school and community through the Parents Teachers Association (PTA). In 2017 he was transferred to Government Technical College Nkeung, Nkwen still as Principal, a position he currently holds before his enthronement as the 21st traditional ruler of Mankon.

It comes as no surprise to anyone who knew Angwafo III to hear that, Angwafo IV, besides being a dedicated school administrator, is also an avid farmer and gardener. While teaching, in collaboration with his wife, he ran poultry business and continued to breed animals such as goats and pigs, a passion he learnt from his predecessor Fo Angwafo III, who was a trained agricultural technician and practicing farmer. Since February 2021, the new Mankon Fon is also the current President of the Board of Directors of Rainbow Cooperative Credit Unions, an umbrella organization for credit unions whose head office is in Bamenda, North-West region. He was scheduled to travel to Scotland UK for the world council of credit unions, a microfinance conference in July 2022, but he will no longer travel because of his new responsibilities.

Fo Angwafo IV speaks Mankon, English, French and Pidgin fluently.

308

Fo S.A.N Angwafo III in Photos:
From the Golden Jubilee in December 2009

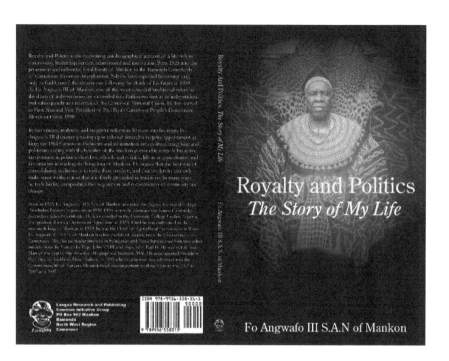

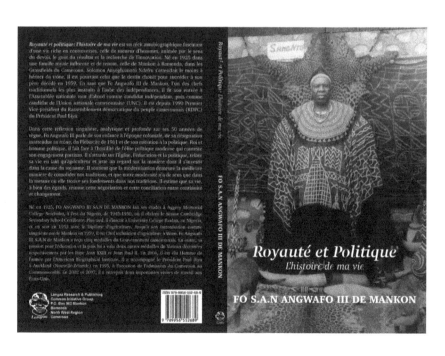

CPSIA information can be obtained
at www.ICGtesting.com
Printed in the USA
BVHW090056231122
652558BV00008B/43